Small
Business
USA

Small Business USA

The Role of Small Companies in
Sparking America's Economic
Transformation

STEVEN SOLOMON

CROWN PUBLISHERS, INC.

New York

The author wishes to acknowledge permission to reprint selections from
Joseph Schumpeter, *Capitalism, Socialism, and Democracy,* Copyright 1942,
1947 by Joseph Schumpeter, Copyright 1950 by Harper and Row Publishers,
Copyright © 1976 by George Allen and Unwin Publishers Ltd.

Published by Crown Publishers, Inc.,
225 Park Avenue South, New York, New York 10003
and represented in Canada by
the Canadian MANDA Group

CROWN is a trademark of Crown Publishers, Inc.

Manufactured in the United States of America

Library of Congress Cataloging-in-Publication Data

Solomon, Steven.
  Small business USA.

  Includes index.
  1. Small business—United States. I. Title
HD2346.U5S74 1986   33   6' 42' 0973   86-4547
ISBN 0-517-56240-5

10 9 8 7 6 5 4 3 2 1

First Edition

To my father,
who, by doing, helped show the way.

Contents

Small Business USA

1

The "Invisible Hand" of Small Business in the Economy

Throughout this twentieth century, U.S. economic power has been typified by the great industrial corporation. Small business, on the rare occasions it has been seriously considered as an economic force at all, has been viewed as a sympathetic but anachronistic leftover from a simpler economic era. Yet, to everyone's amazement, since the mid-1970s, in America's worst economic decade since the Great Depression, the small businessman—the shopkeeper, the restaurateur, the regional advertising agency, the travel agent, the suburban construction contractor, the surplus goods wholesaler, the two-man-pit coal miner, the component supplier, as well as the computer software engineer—has had a strikingly visible impact on the transformation of the American economic landscape.

Small business' role, though overlooked, has, in fact, *always* been important. It was the dominant agent of the long period of U.S. economic development in the nineteenth century. It has driven the historic rise of the service sector, which marks a new phase of capitalism's evolution. It has never ceased generating business innovations. Throughout U.S. history, it has motivated Americans as an economic ideal and has been the vehicle by

1

which millions have reached for, and some have attained, the American dream. Above all, it is an enormously powerful economic force. It represents about two-fifths of current U.S. gross national product and provides employment for half the private sector work force. The small business share of GNP amounts to about $1.3 trillion. If considered alone, that would rank it among the top four nations on earth, after the United States as a whole, the Soviet Union, and about on a par with Japan.[1]

But it does not stand alone. This is why its economic importance has been overlooked until now. Big business, augmented by government and labor unions, has always been the most visible and powerful engine of prosperity. Small business' contributions were harder to evaluate because they were often complementary and widely scattered among individually inconsequential companies. When aggregate measures were tallied, small business' share of economic output, confirming everyone's expectations, was found to be declining steadily.

As a result, frequent assessments of small business have been, in effect, eulogies of its demise. In the era of the Robber Barons, J. D. Rockefeller, founder of the great Standard Oil Trust, pronounced, "The day of combination is here to stay. Individualism has gone, never to return."[2] Writing three generations later in *The New Industrial State*, during the age of go-go finance and frenzied conglomerate mergers, John Kenneth Galbraith took mordant and accurate account of small business' position in the economic order: "By all but the pathologically romantic, it is now recognized that this is not the age of the small man."[3]

Yet these eulogies were premature. Notwithstanding its declining share of economic output, small business has demonstrated amazing persistence. Not only has it survived eras of industrial concentration and oligopoly, it has also occasionally touched off entrepreneurial booms which have briefly driven the economy.

Most unexpected has been its wholly unforeseen role since the oil price shock of 1973. During more than a decade of stagnant living standards, high unemployment, soaring inflation, and rising budget and trade deficits, small business' engines have kept on visibly producing wealth while the triumvirate of big industry, government and labor was unable to continue the prosperity it had produced since the turn of the century.

While technological upheaval, foreign competition, and economic volatility disrupted the predictable environment large corporations need to maximize secure and growing profits, small business created millions of new jobs, hatched new industries based on technologies that are at the core of future U.S. economic competitiveness, and helped spark a fresh outburst of entrepreneurship which is reawakening the "animal spirits" of free market capitalism just when the American economy most needs it.

The world economy is undergoing a new industrial revolution. Small business has been one of America's hidden productive assets, an unexpectedly powerful catalyst in the transition from the mass-production smokestack age to the dawning era of a deeply interlinked global economy driven by knowledge technologies.

Some see small business' unexpected performance as the birth of a new heydey for small business. Others think it is a fluke. Most simply don't know what to make of it.

The central thesis of this book is that the aggregate small business economy is—and has always been—a powerful complementary fourth force to big business, government, and labor in the modern economy. Furthermore, its economic functions are essential to the well-being of the American form of capitalism. It has three chief economic virtues: (1) It facilitates change; (2) It ballasts the economy; (3) It is, in reality, the main business support of the values of the free market social-economic environment in which all U.S. economic activity takes place.

As a fourth force, small business supplies a vital charge for the economic restructuring necessary to produce desperately needed growth in productivity, which ultimately translates into higher living standards. Also, as gravel laid beneath railroad ties helps absorb the shock of thundering trains, it minimizes the vulnerability of the major industrial corporations to potentially catastrophic disruptions in unstable times and makes them more efficient in healthier periods. It is the employer of last resort in the private economy. Although it competes with big business, small business is an essentially *distinct* entity with diverse characteristics. While big business helps provide planning and caution, small enterprise provides a window through which the elemental free market forces—creative and chaotic—of Adam Smith's "invisible hand" help guide economic fortunes.

Small business in the aggregate performs many of its most salutary functions indirectly—and often involuntarily: It bears the brunt of economic downturns and periods of uncertainty, performs many of the least rewarding but necessary tasks in the U.S. economy, and absorbs much of the fall-out from the economy's highest risk activities. These functions drive small business toward its characteristic low profitability and high mortality profile. But they also provide cushions in the economic environment that protect the profitability and well being of the giant corporations that manage the basic industrial superstructure from which America's wealth largely emanates.

Small businessmen perform many of these roles because the superior economic power of big business drives them toward doing so. This underlines another essential feature of the aggregate small business economy. Although it is a complementary force in the economy, it operates from an uncomfortable position of inequality. Its dispersed power makes it subservient to the power of big business, which routinely commands the highest profit zones of the economy.

Although there are many activities where small businesses are the most efficient producers of a goods or a service, and occasional instances where they produce innovations in cutting-edge industries, small business generally must work with the economy's least desirable economic resources at its least promising opportunities.

During America's long periods of prosperity, small business' economic contributions were overlooked simply because other, more easily identifiable factors loomed as all important. It was not until the last decade, when capitalism began experiencing disruptions associated in part with a historical new industrial revolution, that the importance of the small businessman's roles stood out on the economic landscape.

The Economic Transition

It has become increasingly evident that America and other industrial nations are entering a new, postindustrial economic era marked by interlinked global markets and the information technologies of the computer, telecommunications, bioengineering, and new materials. It is a transformation akin in import— and in economic disruptiveness—to the reallocation of assets that occurred in the last twenty years of the nineteenth century when entrepreneurs and financiers seized upon the new technologies of electricity, the internal combustion engine, and industrial chemicals to create the modern industrial corporation, which catalyzed America's transformation from an agricultural to a modern industrial economy.

This economic transition is restructuring fundamental business economics and long-standing business strategies. Business organizations today must be restructured to adapt more efficiently to the speeded-up pace of technological and market change. In rapidly evolving industries profitability increasingly depends on a very quick return of initial investments before technology or market conditions render a product obsolete. In practice, this requires the rapid penetration of home markets to act as a springboard for global marketing. It also demands that business managers reduce or eliminate their commitments in these industries to expensive single-purpose machinery that turns out large quantities of standardized products with returns on investment anticipated over many years. Instead, managers and workers must learn how to manipulate new reprogrammable computer-aided manufacturing technologies with the capability of rapidly altering the goods being produced.

More than new technologies alone are bringing an end to the old era. The increasingly specialized tastes of affluent consumers are causing many mass markets to splinter into smaller market segments.

Blessed for so long with a huge internal domestic market, U.S. corporations in the past rarely needed to worry about foreign markets. But today many traditional domestic mass markets, which once fueled growth, are approaching a saturation point. Meanwhile, advances in international communication and transport have made it easier for foreign competitors who have outgrown their own national borders to invade American markets. Many new industries, driven by the economics of rapid technological and market structure change, are global right from the cradle. Global industries today include telecommunications and computers, autos, pharmaceuticals, factory automation, steel, oil, farm and construction machinery, and finance.

At the same time, industrial technology has spread to many new lower-wage regions of the globe to intensify worldwide competition in older industries. This adds urgency to the pressure on the wealthiest countries to compete for an advantage in emerging industries. The total value of American imports and exports as a percentage of total goods (not services) production—a good measure of exposure of the United States to the world economy— was 12 percent in 1950 and 40 percent in 1980 before the dollar began its surge in value.[4] Some 70 percent of U.S.-produced goods are now subject to foreign competition.[5]

The easy days of uncontested American supremacy are over. Developing countries such as Taiwan, South Korea, Hong Kong, Singapore, and Brazil are moving up the development ladder to apply strong competitive pressure from below on the basic industries that were once the source of this country's prosperity. Meanwhile, Japan and the Western European countries have almost caught up in industrial competitiveness and living standards to the United States. They are competing in the knowlege-intensive industries of the future as equals.

The blue-ribbon President's Commission on Industrial Competitiveness, chaired by Hewlett-Packard Company President John A. Young, which issued its report in January 1985, concluded soberly that in the last twenty years the United States has been losing its lead in seven out of ten important high-tech industries. The nations whose citizens enjoy the highest living standards in the future will be those whose national economic systems adapt best to the rules of the new economic era.

As the United States prepares for global competition, it faces some deep economic problems, the gravest of which is the slowdown in productivity growth over many years compared with its main competitors. Manufacturing productivity growth has fallen steadily from an average annual 3.3 percent between 1947 and 1965, to 1 percent between 1977 and 1984. Manufacturing productivity growth in Western Europe was two and a half times greater in the latter period; over three times greater in Japan.[6]

Nor do the long-term indicators of future U.S. productivity suggest optimism. The capital investment rate (gross fixed investment to GNP) has been among the world's lowest for many years—about three-quarters that of European nations, and only half that of Japan. The rate of personal savings—the raw material of future productivity-enhancing capital investment—has also been far lower than its main competitors among the industrial nations. Finally, in advanced commercial technologies that will likely be the source of future economic competitiveness, U.S. Research and Development (R & D) spending (as a percentage of GNP) lags behind its major trading partners.[7]

In the last decade, the United States has been experiencing intensified global competition and the increased competitiveness of other nations in the form of huge increases in the domestic market share of imported goods in many industries— and ultimately in the loss of jobs in those industries. In the 1970s and early 1980s, the predictable environment large industry needed for making sound long-term investment strategies was disrupted by soaring inflation and interest rates, volatile currency rate fluctuations, and rising and uncertain oil prices. This further aggravated the U.S. productivity problem.

Trade unionism—one of the three pillars of postwar industrial prosperity—has been badly shaken by the decline in basic industries and has lost influence in the national economy.

Between 1978 and 1983, according to *Forbes* magazine, U.S. national net worth stagnated after thirty years of rapid growth.[8] Real incomes fell. Unemployment tapered off in the recent recovery to near 7 percent, a level normally associated with terrible recessions. This built dangerous pressures for protectionism.

With growth stagnating, the federal government, corporations, farmers, and consumers began amassing huge portfolios of debt to keep going. Record federal government and U.S. current account deficits have caused government debt to increase at a rate faster than GNP even during the 1983-84 recovery. This made the United States a net debtor nation in 1985 for the first time since World War I, mortgaging its future wealth to foreign investors beyond the reach of American sovereign taxing power in order to maintain its current patterns of living and investment.

Belatedly, large corporations have begun to adapt to the new technologies and the global economy. In some instances, they have abandoned U.S. production for lower wage, offshore plants. Others have increased their purchases of foreign component supplies. Companies like General Motors, Chrysler, U.S. Steel, and Kodak import finished foreign-made goods for resale under their own trademarks, and champion the antiprotectionist calls for free trade. This has been partly offset by the decision of Japanese and European corporations to set up plants in America. In the global economy, "buying American" no longer means "Made in America."

U.S. corporations in global industries have entered into joint ventures with foreign companies to strengthen their worldwide marketing capabilities. To improve response time in fast-changing markets, many are trimming middle-management layers and pushing more operating decision-making down the corporate management chain to decentralized locations. Factory automation systems are being implemented, although U.S. industry still trails Japan in this strategic area. Labor-management relations are being reshaped. Many corporations are dismantling their vertical production systems for greater reliance on suppliers—domestic and foreign—who can be easily cut out as conditions change. To avoid technological surprises, and to steal a march on competitors, large corporations are also increasingly investing in innovative small companies with promising research and development.

This country's main competitors, Europe and Japan, face difficult adjustments to the economic transition as well. Both have had more planning-oriented capitalism than the American free-market-oriented model. Planning is more difficult in times of rapid change. European nations are presently struggling to reshape their economic systems to combat debilitatingly high unemployment and to overcome the fragmentation of small nationalistic domestic markets. Japan, which has developed so explosively through export growth, must relinquish some of the controls which it has used so effectively in the past, and modernize the underdeveloped, mostly small business, domestic side of its economy. It must also demonstraate a consistent leadership capacity for making basic creative innovations in cutting-edge industries and not merely improve upon the innovations of other cultures, and it must do so without upsetting the rigid hierarchical, group-oriented social-economic system of consensus which has been so productive for it in the past.

As all the industrial nations struggle to adapt to the evolving global economy, each country is taking inventory of the economic assets in its national arsenal to discover overlooked elements which may pull it through the current period of transformation and enhance its national competitiveness in the coming economic era. In this context, small business provides one of this country's competitive advantages. It has been such a powerful productive force that Western European governments and Japan have endeavored artificially to stimulate the kind of performance U.S. small business has produced spontaneously.

The Small Business Achievement

The small business contribution has been most conspicuous in the innovative, glamorous, high-technology industries. No less an authority than Andrew Carnegie never tired of pointing out, "There ain't no profit in pioneering," but in the last decade, the pioneering efforts of small business entrepreneurs—many of whom have indeed gone bust—have made many industry-shaking contributions by commercializing some of the leading-edge applications of the technologies that are propelling the current economic transition. These include personal computer hardware and software, computer-aided-engineering (CAE), computer-aided-design (CAD), computer-aided-manufacturing (CAM), robotics, telecommunications, and biotechnology. Many have exploited undeveloped potential in government, university, and corporate research laboratories. Outbursts of entrepreneurial activity have also accompanied the deregulation of the railroads, trucking, airline, telecommunications, and financial services industries to abet experiments to provide more efficient organization.

Small business has also been promoting the efficiency of technological choice in U.S. industries through modern, small-scale, general-purpose reprogrammable machinery. Use of general-purpose machinery has been the traditional province of the craftsman and small machine shop, where cleverness and skill exert greater leverage on capital in producing smaller batches of specialized goods as required. The battle between mass production and craft technology was fought once in the United States and won in the late nineteenth century by big-business-managed mass-production technology. However, with the advent of computer-based technologies and the disintegration of some mass-production markets, the former dynamics have again shifted and the battle is being fought anew in some industries.[9]

Many of the young high-tech and innovative common-technology companies have been financed by the unprecedented development of venture capital and investor interest in small companies in over-the-counter markets. This has added dynamism to the economy and allowed some lucky entrepreneurs and venture capitalists to join America's club of one million millionaires, sometimes overnight.

"Entrepreneurs acting on their own or within established firms have done more to shake up American business in the past five years than for perhaps half a century," concluded *The Economist* in December 1984.[10]

Small business has also acted as an important economic shock absorber by making an unexpectedly significant contribution to new job creation. Two decades ago, scholars were making frightening calculations that the more than 20 million baby boomers who would enter the U.S. work force in the 1970s might compel the government to become the employer of last resort. Almost no one suspected that small business, which for many years had been a far less conspicuous job creator than government and big business, would be the major producer of new employment. But that is what happened. Between 1974 and 1984, at a time when Fortune 500 employment declined by 1.5 million, the United States created some 20 million net new jobs. Over three-fifths of them were created by independent small businesses with under 500 employees, even though this group represents less than half the private sector labor force. Job creation by small business continued during the recession in the early 1980s and at an accelerated pace during the recovery. Employment in Western Europe, by striking comparison, was stagnant throughout the same period.

To be competitive in the global economy, American industry must pare the size of its labor force and substitute more competitive factory automation in the current transition. Whereas today some 19 percent of the labor force is engaged in manufacturing, experts predict that little more than half that percentage will be needed to produce the same proportion of goods through enhanced automation in the next decade or so. Thus, in the short run, productivity gains that come from factory automation systems will exact a painful cost in employment displacement. New jobs must be found. Small business' prodigious job creation is a hopeful indication that it can be done.

The new jobs being created by the smallest businesses, mostly in service industries, have also been important in maintaining consumer purchasing power to keep the economy sufficiently buoyant through the transition period. In most industries, the new technologies are enhancing efficiency but are slow to produce new, growth-stimulating demand in the way that the combustion-engine technology of the early automobile industry did in superseding the carriage manufacturing empires of James Brewster, the Studebaker brothers of South Bend, Indiana, and others.

The large number of births and deaths of small firms has facilitated the transfer of assets from declining to growing industries. It has helped regions dependent upon declining industries to begin the process of rebuilding their economic base. It has also reduced the volatility of economic cycles. The efficiency of the small business–dominated domestic distribution network has allowed the United States to seed productivity-enhancing new technologies rapidly.

Finally, small business has made a visible contribution to the process of change by rekindling the enterprising spirit, by reawakening the animal spirits of capitalism. People today *want* to become entrepreneurs. Many of them are trying out their ideas in all kinds of businesses. It has helped touch off a creative entrepreneurial boom, akin to the ones immediately following World War II, in the 1920s, and at the turn of the century.

Record-level business start-ups have been accelerating for over a decade. Today, some 9.5 percent of working Americans are their own bosses. The trend toward self-employment has been driven by women, who now constitute over one-third of all entrepreneurs. So far, the affluent Woodstock generation's desire for an independent life-style and self-fulfillment appears also to have bred a taste for self-employment. Corporate executives are buying out divisions of the company in which they work as America's largest corporations proceed with asset real-location through a huge wave of new acquisitions and divestitures. Laid-off workers turn to self-employment when benefits end and until regular employment opportunities reemerge. Though not self-employed, some employees are getting a piece of the rock through everything from the stock ownership plans, which small high-technology firms offer to lure the best prospects, to 100 percent worker buy-outs of operations corporations are about to close down.

The urge for ownership and independence that has motivated American small business entrepreneurs has contributed to and been fed by the renewed economic emphasis in the industrialized world on creating wealth rather than on its equitable distribution. From the Great Depression to President Lyndon Johnson's Great Society, the primary emphasis of U.S. economic policy was to spread the prosperity generated by America's huge industries with the dual aim of maintaining a sufficiently affluent market to absorb the nation's industrial output and increasing social and economic equality as part of the fulfillment of the American dream. Now that the basic industries are struggling and America's creation of wealth has faltered under the hardships of economic transition, the emphasis has shifted back to basic wealth generation based on the simple fact that a society must first generate wealth to be able to distribute it equitably.

Privatization of public enterprises in Europe and around the world, U.S. industry deregulation and the contracting out of local, state, and federal public services to private companies are all signals of a broad shift in intellectual sentiment toward private sector and small business solutions, and away from big public project solutions, to economic growth. This is occurring not only in the major industrialized countries. Throughout the developing world, there is a new emphasis on small, labor-intensive industry and agriculture as a means of getting development back on track. Even in communist countries, there has been a turn to individual initiative to offset some of the inefficiencies of highly planned economies and to try to keep up with the dynamic changes occurring in the industrialized capitalist economies.

The thoughtful voices in America calling for a national industrial policy to help manage the country through the current transition have so far been overwhelmed by the tide of sentiment that wishes to permit the "invisible hand" and the entrepreneur to have a go at it first. The rediscovery of small business fits comfortably with the American ideal of the self-made man and idyllic economic notions of Smith's "perfect competition." President Ronald Reagan, speaking at St. John's University in Queens, New York, early in 1985, proclaimed a sentiment diametrically opposed to that of J. D. Rockefeller four generations ago: "We have lived through the age of big industry and the age of the giant corporation, but I believe that this is the age of the entrepreneur, the age of the individual. That's where American prosperity is coming from now, that's where it's going to come from in the future."[11] Speaking several years earlier, and in a distinctly pragmatic vein, Colorado Governor Richard Lamm, a Democrat, announced: "There is a tidal wave behind me. Its name is small business. Any politician who does not look over his shoulder at that wave will be a politician out of a job."[12]

This is not yet another book glorifying entrepreneurs or the catalytic role that a tiny handful of them are playing in the high technology boom. Innovation is a process to which small business entrepreneurs contribute, but which they by no means dominate. Likewise, most of the jobs small business is creating are not suitable for long-term prosperity. They are transitional. Both small business job creation and innovation derive importance by facilitating economic adjustments by the large corporations on whose international competitiveness American prosperity ultimately rides. In short, small business' importance lies in how, and how well, it complements the large economic entities that have been the main engines of American prosperity in the past and are likely to continue to be so in the future.

The aim of this book, rather, is to begin the long-neglected exploration of the broad dimensions, unique business characteristics and problems, and the specific economic functions of the U.S. small business economy. It is a subject that has been shunned by journalists and scholars seemingly in inverse proportion to the ritual praise that has been heaped upon it by politicians. The approach is that of a journalist trying to make common sense of details, trends, and broad themes of a necessarily fragmented story, not that of an economist making technically precise analyses from competing schools of economic thought.

The entry route is small business' role in the current transformation of the U.S. economy. Once small business' economic role is understood from this perspective, and the general principles governing small business economics extracted from it, we will project the trajectory of broad economic trends to try to foresee whether this wave of small business entrepreneurship ultimately heralds a new era of entrepreneurial American capitalism as some optimistic prophets believe—or conversely, whether, after helping the American economy adjust to the present period of transition, small business will resume losing share of total economic output at its rapid postwar rate, and perhaps, lose its ability to continue to perform its salutary functions in the general economy. Indeed, some of the new problems posed by the global economy and new technologies, such as the globalization of markets and enhanced computer-assisted organizational precison by large companies for penetrating small markets, pose grave threats to small business' long-term well-being. The answer, of course, ultimately leads us to consider the new forms small business itself may assume in struggling to adapt to the altered competitive balances of the dawning economic era.

2

The Position
of Small Business
in the Economy

In 1967, a small business entrepreneur named Wilson Harrell learned that multibillion-dollar giant Procter & Gamble, long the dominant force in the liquid household cleaner market, had designs to enter a profitable niche in spray cleaners that had until then been too small for it to bother about. At the time, Harrell controlled most of the spray cleaner market through Formula 409, a product made by a struggling company he'd bought four years earlier for $30,000. He had painstakingly built up the business—and the market—by trading equity to personalities like Art Linkletter for a cash investment and participation in pitching Formula 409 on discount TV spots in local markets. Given P&G's financial resources and its renowned marketing muscle, it looked as if Harrell's party was about over.

Determined not to go down without a fight, Harrell discovered that P&G's first assault would be a market test in Denver. He responded by not refilling store orders and quietly withdrawing Formula 409 from the Denver market just as P&G's test was getting underway. He also pulled all support advertising. P&G failed to notice the ploy. Buoyed by its fantastic reception, P&G confidently sank millions into a national launch.

This is just what Harrell expected—and wanted. Just before the launch started, he moved quickly to *overstock* store shelves with a discount offer the customer couldn't refuse. He sold the regular 16-ounce size Formula 409 with a half-gallon size for only $1.49. It was enough product to last nearly half a year. When P&G's new product reached the public, most customers were no longer shopping for spray cleaner. Stunned and confused by the contradictory results of the test and the launch, P&G withdrew from the market niche within a year, losing perhaps $25 million and firing several of its executives. Wilson Harrell was still king of the household spray cleaner market.

"Big companies are predictable and meticulously follow standard marketing rules," Harrell later explained. "To be successful, we had to take advantage of our maneuverability, be prepared to do the unexpected. . . . Let me add that 'risk-taking' is the term used when you are successful. If you fail, it's called 'stupidity.'"

In 1971, at the age of fifty-one, Harrell sold Formula 409 to P&G rival Clorox for $7.5 million, and moved on to other ventures. Harrell is an inveterate entrepreneur. This Southern-born World War II pilot entered business as a salesman, first selling simplified accounting systems to small businesses. He later sold insurance for Aetna Life Insurance. He reenlisted during the Korean War, and was shipped to England, where he managed officers' clubs around London, when the war ended. Now remarried to an Englishwoman, he stayed in London as a food broker supplying military commissaries and post exchanges. It was through these contacts that he eventually got wind of the popularity of Formula 409. After nearly a decade in Europe, Harrell returned to America, buying many companies, including the company that made Formula 409.

Using his money from selling the company, Harrell went right on buying a hodgepodge of companies, from cattle ranches and marinas to domestic food brokerages, and launching new products. He even returned to the household cleaner market with a product called 4 + 1. The product was a liquid concentrate to which the purchaser added water before use. The concept was that the consumer would be willing to do the extra work for a less expensive product. That, of course, was contrary to the dominant trend toward convenience products that were ever easier to use, but more expensive. Yet 4 + 1 bombed. Harrell and his investor group had to write off their $1 million tax-sheltered investment. It wasn't Harrell's only failure, but in the course of becoming a multimillionaire, his failures were comfortably outweighed by his successes. Meanwhile, this entrepreneur continues to sell old businesses and dream up new ones.

"The world is made up of pirates and farmers," he says in an analogy about two kinds of businessmen. "Pirates come in and kill all the natives, rape all the women, and level the landscape; farmers follow after them to till the soil, plant the seeds, build the communities. I realize you need both, but I was never much of a farmer."[1]

When Adam Smith published *The Wealth of Nations* in 1776 he was describing an economy in which local small businesses were virtually the only economic entities. Indeed, the era of the local economy was the heyday of small business.

Modern capitalism started in the small firm. It grew from the traders and runaway serfs who traveled the countryside selling goods to the nobility. They gradually undermined the nobles' authority, as wealth, then power, shifted to their hands. The small businesses they ultimately formed became the primary building block of economic development for today's industrialized countries.

In the United States, small business emerged in urban areas in the form of independent artisans and tradesmen, such as cobblers, tailors, silversmiths, and hatmakers. In rural regions, the archetypal small business was the country general store. It served as the mail depot, and often was the only ready source of supplies and available credit for the surrounding local farm population.

Successful small businessmen began to build domestic savings and smuggle in early industrial technologies from Britain, to build the first light industry. The Yankee ingenuity of Eli Whitney and Eli Terry, among others, found commercial fruition in small businesses. It was from this that business ethos and business skills were slowly disseminated through the young developing nation. It was small businesses that originally attracted the indispensable foreign investment which stimulated greater capital formation and growth.

Prior to 1850, there were no middle managers—that is, employees who supervised and reported to other employees—in the country. In nearly all businesses, the proprietor was intimately involved with the primary work of the company, which was typically carried out in a single location to serve local or regional markets.[2] But economic development was resulting in an important, subtle change: Increasingly, skill in *business,* rather than *craft* skill, was becoming the key to greater economic reward.

It was only in the post–Civil War period that the modern concept of small business—that is, as something distinct from big business—began to acquire significance. The era of the national economy, in which big business emerged as the primary economic force and small business' role became ancillary, begins in this period. Exploiting improvements in communication and transportation, the emergence of mass-marketing vehicles which had been given impetus by the Civil War, small businessmen like Carnegie, Rockefeller, and Cyrus McCormick succeeded in matching capital to evolving large-scale production techniques to speed production and derive economies of scale vast enough to produce goods at unit costs so low as to drive smaller competitors from the marketplace and yield substantial enough profits for reinvestment in still greater expansion.

The rise of the large industrial corporation was a watershed event in the history of small business, as well, of course, in the history of capitalism. Mass production altered Smith's "perfect competition." The disciplining mechanism of competition could work only where no firm could destroy all competitors. With mass production they could—and did. In industry after industry—farm machinery, office machinery, tobacco, automobiles, oil, and steel—scores of smaller companies were shaken out of the market until only a handful of the largest corporations dominated. In certain product lines within an industry supply was—and still is—even more tightly controlled. Through merger waves in the late 1890s, 1920s, the go-go conglomerate wave of the late 1960s, and the wave of megamergers in the 1980s, industrial assets were concentrated in fewer and larger corporate hands. The large capital requirements to compete in mass production provided an effective barrier to new competition from below.

With small businesses not only disciplined by the market under mass production, but in danger of being literally wiped out by it, small business gradually tended toward more labor-intensive lines of business, and other situations where big business had less or no inherent competitive advantage. Many of these arose from the new wealth created by the industrial economy. At the same time, small business often enhanced the efficiency of these mass-production industries through complementary activities. As the economy grew, retailers and wholesalers built the networks that kept the distribution side of the production-distribution equation of economics in equilibrium. Specialized small service firms continued to grow. Where there were production bottlenecks, small businesses, often run by the remaining independent and versatile skilled craftsmen who hadn't become skilled blue-collar employees, found profitable opportunities to start the kind of production that would unblock them. As the nation's work force migrated from the farm to the factory, small business swelled to fill the economic middle ground to help ensure an orderly transition.

This was the formative period for the economic position of small business in the twentieth century. Essentially, it undertook activities that big business could not or did not wish to undertake, using resources that big business overlooked or rejected. When big business gained the capacity or the desire to perform one of these functions, small business either found a competitive equalizer, moved into another line of business—or terminated operations. Sometimes small business applied effective competitive pressure. Occasionally it innovated. Often it poured into expanding areas of the economy; it fueled, for instance, the rise of many service sectors. As the retail and service sectors grew, big business began to dominate more markets within them. Small business demanded government protection and again searched for competitive equalizers. Again its influence declined—yet persisted.

U.S. economic development has created opportunities with uneven competitive balances between large and small economic entities. By and large, large business organizations have better exploited the major opportunities in manufacturing, mining, and transportation industries. Other businesses, mainly in services, retail, and construction, have been competitively or better exploited by small units with hands-on owner-management.

The private U.S. economy is not a monolith but a continuum of different-sized companies ranging from big businesses such as GM, IBM, Exxon, and GE at the top to Mom-and-Pop shops at the bottom. Before it is possible to analyze small business' role in the economy, or its problems and prospects, it is first necessary to answer the question, What is small business?

U.S. small business includes independent family business retailers and big-stake gamblers like Wilson Harrell. Some compete in small-business-dominated industries where the economics have not favored large size, such as in machine tools or in metalworking. In other industries, small business operates on the fringes of an oligopolistic core of large corporations. There are manufacturers, wholesalers, and service firms, each of whose business turns on very different considerations, and requires disparate skills. Some run one-man bands while others have hundreds of employees. The vast majority are private, but about 40,000 are closely held and publicly traded. A handful of these are high-flying, fast-traded high-tech companies, but most, including *The New Yorker* (recently sold), are rarely ever traded, and are ordinary product companies never listed in the newspapers or financial journals. Some small businesses have survived many years and have been handed down from generation to generation. Others are comparative toddlers, learning as they go, whose business life is still being measured in months.

With such a diverse population, any comprehensive answer to the question, What is small business?, must be elastic and leave room for exceptions. There have been as many different definitions as there are types of small businesses. Nevertheless, certain useful common parameters may be drawn.

A small business is privately owned or, if public, closely held.

There are two broad kinds of small business: (1) the very small business where the proprietor is the chief worker, and any employees work largely as direct assistants; and (2) the larger small business where the proprietor mainly directs the work of his employees.

The first kind of small business was well defined in a letter from a Georgia filling station owner to the U.S. Senate Small Business Committee in 1941 as "The little individually operated business, e.g., a grocery store, dry goods, merchant, filling station, shoe store, jewelry store, whose owner works himself, earns, or tries to, a small or fair living, and employs one or more employees to assist him."[3] The great majority of American small businesses fall into this class. One of their peculiar characteristics is that most—contrary to the famous observations of Adam Smith about his pin factory and assumptions of economic theory—*show little or no tendency to grow.*[4]

Larger small companies in the second category do indeed have growth tendencies although, to the distress of their owners, only a small percentage ever fulfill them. Only about 15 percent of all companies generate new jobs, and thus appear to have strong growth tendencies.[5] It is largely this growth group which creates effective competitive pressure from below on big corporations, and is sometimes the proving ground for new technologies or unusual entrepreneurial talent.

An entrepreneur—from the French word meaning "to undertake," applied to business in about 1800 by French economist Jean Baptiste Say to indicate someone who manages an enterprise, as opposed to the capitalist who controls the capital—will be used to refer to a businessman starting or expanding his own enterprise. Entrepreneurs are not necessarily innovators as well—in fact, only a tiny fraction bring to market products or business methods that are essentially new, and not merely efficient repetitions of what others have done before.

A small business must have few or no management layers. Many large corporations have five to twelve layers of management between the chief executive and the shop floor. Small businesses, on the other hand, are characterized by their owner's "hands-on" style of management. The owner is never far from knowing firsthand what is going on at all levels of his business. When the transcendentalist philosopher Ralph Waldo Emerson wrote, "An institution is but the lengthened shadow of one individual," he was of course writing before the age of big business when nearly all businesses that existed were small. Yet the description remains a suitable litmus test of small business today: Small businesses, in proportion to their size, reflect their proprietors' personal idiosyncrasies, styles, and talents.

A small business is unlikely to have sufficient resources to dominate its field of business. The Small Business Act of 1953, creating the Small Business Administration, says that "a small business concern shall be deemed to be one which is independently owned and operated and which is not dominant in its field of operations." The salient feature is that although a small business might from time to time be the dominant force in a small market (such as when it innovates or is the single producer in a highly specialized product niche), it is restrained from dictating critical terms such as price and application due to invisible pressure from potential competitors.

Small Business' Statistical Position

None of the quantitative definitions of small business are universally satisfactory. But they are useful in taking approximate measure of the position of small businesses in the U.S. economy. The federal government's Small Business Administration generally considers a small business to be one with under $10 million in assets or if it has under 500 employees.

Reliable data concerning small business is scanty, and often not directly comparable. Yet it often points in consistent enough directions to be able to draw a general picture of small business' economic position.

Small businesses come in three forms: sole proprietorships, partnerships, and corporations. From information that is available, it is believed that of the roughly 14 million nonfarm business tax returns filed with the Internal Revenue Service in 1981 all but a tiny fraction of 1 percent were for small businesses. These included 9.75 million sole proprietorships, 1.5 million partnerships, and 2.8 million corporations. Despite the large number of proprietorships and partnerships, corporations dominate the volume of business transactions in the United States.*

Gross revenues are so low for about half of these 14 million businesses (under $10,000 for sole proprietorships and $25,000 for corporations), that they are probably part-time enterprises. The SBA believes there are up to 6.7 million full-time nonfarm businesses in America.[6] Including full-time farm businesses, there are roughly 8 million full-time independent businesses of all kinds.

Some 4.5 million of the nonfarm businesses have employees and utilize the credit markets. A schematic portfolio of their population is as follows: two-fifths are in distribution businesses; two-fifths in services; and one-fifth in production industries.[7]

The broadest measure of the dimensions of the small business economy includes all but the *Fortune* magazine corporations which constitute the core of the nation's industrial superstructure. The largest 200 manufacturing corporations—the core of these *Fortune* corporations—control three-fifths of total U.S. corporate assets. At the start of the 1980s, 3,000 U.S. corporations had more than $250 million in assets. Together they accounted for 45 percent of total U.S. business revenue, and over half of all net income.[8]

Among these 3,000 largest corporations, however, are hundreds that are in reality large small businesses still run by their founders or family heirs. Many are hybrids in the process of undergoing the structural transformation between small business and large corporate enterprise.

Below the level of America's largest corporations there are about three-quarters of a million larger small businesses doing over $1 million a year in sales. Together with the largest corporations, they account for over four-fifths of the business done in America.[9]

Below $1 million a year is the universe of America's smallest full-time nonfarm companies, 6 million of them, dividing just one-fifth of the reported sales and net income of American business.

Measured as firms with under 500 employees, small business in 1982 accounted for 48 percent of total nonfarm U.S. employment, 42 percent of private sales, and 38 percent of GNP.[10]

There are three important caveats to such quantitative measurements of small business. First, the available statistics

*In 1981, for example, the 2.8 million corporations accounted for 90 percent of all U.S. business volume and 80 percent of all business profits.

are highly approximative. Second, they fail to distinguish those small firms which have grown into, or been acquired by, big companies. During the 1970s over 95 percent of the annual 2,000 to 5,000 publicly announced mergers and acquisition transactions (M&A), which included divestitures, with a value of at least $500,000, involved small companies.[11] Unreported M&A activity is much larger, of course. Between 1978 and 1980, the SBA believes that some 60,000 of America's smallest businesses with a single working establishment, became part of multi-establishment companies, either through growth or acquisition.

The third caveat to interpreting the aggregate statistics is that they fail to include the underground economy. Small business figures prominently in unreported underground economies throughout the world. Some $115 billion in revenue of the estimated $400 billion U.S. underground economy is believed to be due to cheating by self-employed businessmen. The underground economy is said to have expanded greatly in the last decade.[12]

Despite small business' relatively subordinate position to big business, it is an enormously powerful aggregate economic force in the economy. Driven by small businesses, the corporate population was expanding by over 20 percent a year, or 650,000 new incorporations by the mid-1980s. About two-thirds of these actually started business operations, the rest having been created for legal purposes. Noncorporate business start-ups total perhaps another 1.5 million a year.[13] Cumulatively, all business start-ups represent roughly $70 billion a year in new business investments.[14]

Of course, roughly 400,000 corporations (and an indeterminable number of sole proprietorships and partnerships) terminate their operations each year, too. In a normal year, 90 percent are voluntary, usually the result of retirement, where no family successor exists, or simply due to unsatisfactory profitability. Nearly all business closures—and outright failures—are small enterprises. In the economically distressed years of the early 1980s, a greater number have likely been victims of the highest level of bankruptcies since the Great Depression. Four-fifths of all failures are less than ten years old. A company's chances of survival—but not necessarily its profitability—increase with its size.

Trends in Small Business' Economic Position

Small business' share of both economic output and total employment has been declining throughout this century. Between 1958 and 1977 small businesses with under 500 employees lost an average of 1 percent of total private employment and sales to big business every four years. Declines have been sharpest among the smallest companies with fewer than 20 employees.

However, since the mid-1970s, there has been a noticeable deviation in the long-term historical trend: Small business' share of private business sales has continued to decline, but only modestly. Its share of employment has increased by 3 percent.

Most significantly, small business has maintained its share of private sales in the decade from 1972 in manufacturing and mining, reversing a long trend in these big-business-dominated industries. Big business' continuing overall gains have come in sectors where small business still predominates, such as retailing, services, construction, and wholesale. In nearly all sectors, large business' growth has come through increasing the number—not the size—of business units it operates.[15]

What has happened is that with traditional large industry growth constrained by the travails of economic transition and with government unable to provide the growth stimulus it had in the past, small business activity continued to pump up the economy.

Areas of Economic Significance

Small businesses are most economically significant in industries with the lightest burden of fixed assets and requiring the least amount of capital to set up shop. Historically, this has meant that as small business was unable to compete in capital-intensive industries like manufacturing, mining and transportation and utilities, it found opportunities in retailing, wholesaling, construction, traditional services, agricultural services, fishing and forestry, and in finance, real estate, and insurance.

Small business comprises the core of the nation's supplier and distribution networks. It also tends to gravitate toward the fastest-growing industries. In recent years, these have included legal services, oil and gas extraction, anthracite coal mining, forestry, security brokerage, pipeline transportation, air transport, freight, investment businesses, communications, various business services, and health care delivery.

It also, of course, includes new high-technology businesses, where small firms have played pioneering and early market development roles. However, high tech, an amorphous term, represents only about 2 percent of the GNP, and is restricted to a small corner of the small business economy.

Small business, in an unfamiliar guise, is also a significant force in the fast-growing not-for-profit sector. The reward in this sector, which includes foundations and public TV, is power and fulfillment of personal values. Yet the competition for available funding is fierce, and the winners are often those who exhibit a similar kind of entrepreneurial flair as successful small businessmen, as they often are. For some, of course, power from the not-for-profit venture is parlayed into profits through related private business associations the not-for-profit entrepreneur may have.

Retailing The nation's retailers, constituting about three-tenths of all businesses, have been a traditional stronghold of American small business. They include the archetypal corner grocer and candy store, restaurants and bars, hardware, shoe, building materials and garden supply and home furnishing stores. Many are family-run businesses. An increasing number are franchises and specialty shops catering to the American consumers' increasingly differing tastes for personal services and high-fashion clothes.

For many years the small retailer has been losing ground to large chains, such as those that fill suburban shopping malls. Between 1958 and 1977, the total retail sales share of single-shop retailers with under 20 employees fell from over half to one-third. The nation's top 50 retailers alone now account for one-quarter of all retail sales. Most big retailer growth has come through the dramatic addition of shop units.

Single-store independents that added even one or two additional stores have managed to hold their own. Franchising has been an important and increasingly popular means by which the small retailer has equalized his competitive position: By

1984, franchising accounted for one-third of all retail sales, with expectations that it would grow to one-half by 1990.

Services For many years, the fastest-growing of all small-business-dominated sectors has been services. Personal, legal, business, education, and health services; factors, collection agencies, leasing companies, repair shops, beauty parlors, hotels and motels and amusements of all kinds—a disproportionately large number of them set up as sole proprietorships—constitute a hodgepodge industry in which employment has doubled in 15 years.

Now that small business has set the pace in this growth sector, big business has been moving in. Although small service firms employ a growing percentage of service workers, large service firms have been winning a larger share of the sales growth. As in the retail trade, franchising has been an important trend by which smaller competitors have sought the benefits of larger organizations.

Construction Roughly two-thirds of the volume in the cyclical construction business is done by small firms with under 100 employees, who also hire two-thirds of the industry's employees. The smallest construction contractors build most nonurban single- or dual-family homes. The contract construction business, owing to its craft trade tradition, is marked by a constant movement between small-scale entrepreneurship and wage labor depending on fluctuations of individual fortunes.

Wholesaling Small business wholesalers account for two-thirds of industry employment and about three-fifths of total sales. Nevertheless, the small wholesaler faces a negative trend. In the last quarter-century, his big competitor with over 500 employees has tripled his share of industry sales and doubled his share of employment, largely through expanded volume at existing operating units. The main losers have been the smallest wholesalers, including agents and brokers who do not handle the commodities in which they trade.

Finance, insurance, and real estate This is the single general sector where smaller firms have been increasing both share of sales and employment, since the mid-1970s. The small business with under 500 employees accounts for half the industry employment and somewhat less than that in sales. This sector also includes a large number of real estate agents and independent insurance agents, many of whom are informally linked and strengthened through associations. An insurance giant like the Travelers, for example, is built upon a base of 10,000 small independent agents.

Some of the increase by smaller businesses is due to new activity in discount brokerage, commodities, financial advisory, money management, investment banking, and insurance stimulated by deregulation starting in the 1970s.

The United States has by far the largest number of independent banks of any industrialized nation—nearly 15,000 commercial banks and several thousand savings and loans. The vast majority are small, having under $75 million in assets. Traditionally, they have been a major source of financing for local small businesses.

Transportation, communications, and public utilities Transportation, since the days of the railroad, has been a big-business-dominated sector. Smaller companies with under 500 employees account for less than one-third of employment and about one-fifth of total sales. Nevertheless, such small companies are major forces in trucking and warehousing, various transportation, electric, gas and sanitary services, water transportation and local passenger train and air travel. At the smallest level, the sector includes local haulers and taxi drivers.

Mining In no industry is small business less significant than in the heavily capital-intensive mining sector. Some 80 percent of total mining sales are accounted for by a handful of giant companies with over 10,000 employees. From the late 1950s through the early 1970s, mining was marked by concentration. By 1972, the number of independent mining enterprises had dropped sharply along with industry employment. In the post-OPEC oil embargo period, however, a surge of activity in the oil and gas extraction and coal-mining sectors brought several thousand new small firms into the mining business—a great many financed by tax-shelter partnerships.

With the bust following the energy boom, many of them have again disappeared.

Despite the overwhelming trend to bigness, small mining operators have always been a colorful part of the industry, from the wildcat driller to those who lease an oil well or a "block" in a mine, which they operate on their own account and then sell the entire output to the lessor. Today, for example, there are some 3,000 companies with 6,500 employees mining two-man coal pits to extract the coal missed by mass-mining techniques.

Manufacturing Over three-quarters of manufacturing sales and slightly less than that of employment are accounted for by only 10 percent of all manufacturers that have over 500 employees. Manufacturing giants with over 10,000 employees alone account for over half the industry sales.

Yet since 1972, the gains of big manufacturers have slowed markedly. One striking phenomenon, which may in part explain why small manufacturers have been able to hold their sales shares in the past decade, is that manufacturing plant sizes in many industries, after generations of growing larger to benefit from economies of scale, have apparently begun to *shrink*. One study of 410 leading U.S. manufacturers showed that the average size of a plant built before 1970 and still operating in 1979 was 644 employees. For plants opened in the 1970s, the average size was 241 employees. Estimates for plants opening in the 1980s are 210 employees.[16]

Thus, rather than operate larger plants, big business, when it has been able to grow, has done so by acquiring or building more smaller ones. Between 1958 and 1977, large manufacturers increased the average number of plants they operated from 28 to 45. In the future, smaller plant sizes may offset one of small business' historical disadvantages in this sector and improve the competitiveness of some firms using the new technologies.

Despite its small share of sales, small business plays an important role as a components supplier and subcontractor to large manufacturers. It is also a major force in the strategic machine tools business, and flexible manufacturing based on craft skills in general. Other manufacturing sectors where small business has a significant part are in lumber and lumber products, printing and publishing, apparel and textiles, and stone, clay, and glass products. The celebrated small high-tech firm is in fact somewhat larger than most people realize: High-tech firms average twice the size of the average manufacturer, and are likely to have over 100 employees and more than one plant.[17]

In recent years, an overwhelming percentage of all the growth in number of manufacturing firms came from those working on their own without employees. Most of these are not archetypical small business entrepreneurs at all, but workers who have been laid off or whose wages haven't kept pace with living costs and thus must work catch-as catch-can as independents until regular employment prospects brighten.

Economic Characteristics of Small Business

The single overriding factor of the last century that has shaped small business and formed its fundamental economic character has been the general, superior competitive strength of big business. The march to bigness continues, at a somewhat slower pace, across almost every sector of the economy today. The history of American small business has been one of creative reaction to change and to disadvantage, of seeking competitive equalizers to the superior resources of bigger organizations—and simply, of enduring with little reward through economic tenacity. But why has small business managed to survive, and grow, in some businesses and not in others? What are the common economic characteristics of small business success?

In broadest terms, small business has succeeded where it has been able to offset big business' more favorable economies of size. These have included, above all, the complementary efficiencies of production scale and leverage of large organization. At small business' disposal have been its more modest advantages: quicker reaction time, economic tenacity due to the life-and-death nature of the business competition to an individual owner, personal relationships and, on occasion, superior cleverness.

Small business does well where technological innovation is economic on a small scale as well as a large. In contrast to manufacturing industries where advances in technology led to the mass production of standardized goods in such volume as to significantly reduce unit costs through economies of scale and, as a result, favored the eventual rise of a handful of dominant oligopolistic firms, there have been other industries where small business was able to offset the advantages big business derived from technological progress, and even cases where it was small business that was most advantaged from it. Today's electronic cash registers are probably a net advantage to the large retailer, since it helps him improve large volume inventory control and keep financial order over a large force of employees. But they are probably not so great an advantage that the enterprising small retailer can't adjust. On the other hand, the small personal computer probably helps many small businesses by bringing them a little of the big business power of the mainframe. In the more distant past, small businesses in many industries equalized a crucial disadvantage when it became possible to buy electricity from central generators rather than having to produce it on-site, which only big businesses could afford.

Small business tends toward businesses low in capital, and high in labor intensity. Because small business rarely has sufficient capital to be able to purchase the capital-intensive machinery that may give big business a decisive productivity advantage on standardized, mass-market products, small business has gravitated toward low-entry cost, labor-intensive businesses, such as retailing and services. By paying lower wages over longer hours, offering fewer benefits, minimizing exposure in slack periods by employing part-timers, and through the direct creative participation and dedication of the owner, small business has often been able to equalize, and sometimes beat, the advantages of larger size in labor-intensive businesses. In slow growth periods, small businessmen sometimes maintain their positions by "sweating" labor—as well as themselves and often family members—through longer hours or faster work.

Small business does well in businesses dependent upon a specialized skill or service. Where products or services must be designed to the particular needs of an individual or few clients, the advantages of mass-production technology and large organization are offset. Large organization thrives best where tasks can be divided into standardized procedures. Where they cannot, the personal supervision of an owner-manager may be an advantage. In the small machine shop, skilled craftsmen produce parts specifically designed for individual customers' needs. Repair work on factory machinery and equipment, automobiles, and home appliances requires individualized service. Real estate agents, public relations people, translators, tailors, and money managers render services that require specialized knowledge for particular needs. Specialized selling also sometimes offers small businesses a competitive niche to compete against better-staffed giants. That is what Robert Swanson, head of biotech firm Genentech, is hoping to do to succeed in a field crowded with giant pharmaceutical firms. Instead of spreading his sales resources thin trying to blanket Genentech's market, Swanson has targeted a highly select group of trend-setting medical specialists, who may provide a springboard to the larger market.

Small business often does well in small, isolated, overlooked, or "imperfect" markets. The economies of size are offset, even in producing standardized products, where markets are small and demand is relatively limited, as in, say, the artist's material industry. This is why small business generally thrives by filling niches in the marketplace, often regional, sometimes national, but rarely international. In recent years, small business has benefited from the segmenting of mass-consumer markets and the growing taste for expensive, high-quality, or unique products. Catering to local tastes or habits is another way small business succeeds in low-volume markets.

Small business does relatively better in rural than in densely populated areas because the efficiency of mass marketing is diluted when spread over great distances—advertising reaches relatively fewer people and transportation costs can become onerous, for example. Local small businesses producing for regional markets often succeed where their products cannot be efficiently transported because they are either highly perishable or sell for too low a price to justify the cost of carrying something of their dimension or weight. Plant nurseries, dairies, and lumber mills are examples.

In other instances, some small businesses thrive because big business simply overlooks an opportunity, or because the market temporarily misjudges the relative value of two competing products.

Small business often operates in little proven or unstable markets, or by filling marginal, fluctuating demand. Before a large corporation risks a major investment of resources and senior management energy, it needs to see a definite trend and a large enough potential market to significantly impact its bottom line. Small business, in the aggregate, often has the edge in little proven or developing markets because it can experiment often and react quickly to evolving conditions. Only when clear trends and large market potential emerge does the advantage switch decisively in favor of the resources at the command of a big enterprise.

Unstable markets, that is, those characterized by unpredictable wide swings in demand, or by fierce (especially price) competition, are unattractive to big business because they disrupt long-term planning and efficient utilization of the production capacity of large, expensive plants. Small businesses often fill this void, hoping to move alertly enough to avoid being hurt in difficult periods.

On the fringe of mass markets there is a margin of cyclically fluctuating, and therefore unstable, demand that small business often serves. This is true even in oligopolistic industries. It occurs because the leading competitors wish to target their production capacity efficiently. To do so, they must maintain capacity at a level sufficiently below peak demand to insulate them from cyclical lows.

A company with an absolute monopoly in the market, in other words, would carry too much unprofitable excess capacity in slack periods. Instead, profits are maximized by operating *less* capacity so that it can be fully employed throughout the business cycle.

In practice, of course, few corporations ever succeed in managing capacity so precisely. In any event, oligopolistic corporations, rather than compete strictly on price, have generally preferred to raise price umbrellas in their industry. This has sheltered many small competitors, and kept them viable. In especially severe downturns, some marginal small business competitors switch product lines, in effect skipping between markets to serve cyclical demand in each.

Small business survives by being closer to the marketplace and responding quickly and cleverly to changes in it. One of small business' significant advantages over its bigger competitors is its greater speed and flexibility of action. By virtue of his close vicinity to the market upon which he and his family's personal livelihood depend, the small businessman usually gets the first scent of changes in it. This gives him the first chance to act.

A sharp retailer, for example, can adjust his product offerings or his display to take advantage of changes in supply or among his customers. In recent years, a new class of retailer has evolved—the gray marketeer. The gray marketeer sells oversupplied, usually imported products like cameras and consumer electronics goods, at cut-rate prices without a license from the manufacturer to do so. The strong dollar has helped gray marketing to spread to industrial goods like construction equipment and semiconductors, as marketers exploit opportunities arising from the sometimes large disparities in product pricing around the world.

On occasion, a clever entrepreneur like Wilson Harrell can even outmaneuver a tough large competitor like Procter & Gamble, by knowing not only the plans of his competition but also how his customers are likely to respond to them.

Small businesses often survive by organizing their own countervailing economies of size. To counteract the advantages of big business, small businesses in various industries have with limited success in the past, lobbied state and federal politicians for protection. But more than through the largely ineffective "fair trade" (read "minimum price") laws passed in many states, small retailers offset part of the 33 percent cost advantage originally enjoyed by chain stores by organizing voluntary associations to obtain the economies of volume purchasing for themselves. The growth of format franchising in the late 1950s, typified by the fast-food restaurants McDonald's and Burger King but today applied to all kinds of retailing and services, including opticians, funeral parlors, and educational centers, gave small business franchisees many of the advantages of big size without sacrificing the advantages of small private ownership. Franchising stumbled temporarily under a tide of franchising scams, but since 1969 has expanded. In the 15 years after 1969 the number of format franchises increased by 133 percent to 282,500 outlets, and franchising is becoming a significant force in services as it already is in retailing. In all, franchising in 1984 employed 5.2 million at 462,000 franchise outlets for total sales of $460 billion.[18] Some existing independent retailers, such as hardware stores, are joining together in loosely organized conversion franchises, to link their identities by adding a common franchise name logo to their existing name on their storefronts, and then doing joint buying and joint advertising.

The Prototypical Small Business

Given the great diversity of small businesses, it is difficult, if not impossible, to characterize a prototypical small business. To the extent that it is useful to try—and separating out at the beginning the minority of great successes and larger small businesses—it is safe to say that the majority of small businesses are characterized by economic tenacity—long hours, willingness to endure bleak times, and the personal energy and resourcefulness of ownership—rather than any obvious economic advantage.

The majority of small business entrepreneurs tend to seek opportunities in industries that have low-entry barriers and where they have some personal knowledge of the field, rather than methodically searching out maximum profit opportunities. As a result, small businessmen confront constant competition from new entrants to the market.

The typical small company operates from one or possibly two or three locations, and deals in a single basic market. It is most often labor-intensive. It is likely to be undercapitalized, with a fairly low net worth and prone to a short life span. Due to its limited capital resources, it has short investment time horizons—if investments don't themselves back quickly, failure is the likely consequence. It is especially susceptible in recessions or cyclic downturns because, although it pays an average 20 percent lower wages than big business, it is already operating with a minimum number of employees and has little margin for making layoffs without impairing its economic efficacy.

Above all, the small business is run in a personal way. The smaller the business, the more casual the accounting is apt to be, with business and personal funds intermingled freely. Financing is likely to have been by family savings, often accumulated through years of sacrificing immediate gratification and augmented by borrowing from relatives. Family members may staff it or comprise the ranks of "top" management. When the founder dies, the business passes to his children, or dissolves. While he is alive, the profit motive yields results that tangibly and directly affect his family's standard of living. He lives and dies on cash flow—calculated as money in, money out, in his company checking account, not as depreciation plus net income as big corporations generally figure it.

In such a milieu, no problem can be too small not to worry about. An increase in a supplier's price very often cannot be passed on to the customer, as it often can in big businesses with more market clout. If rent goes up, it comes right out of the bottom line unless the small business entrepreneur can offset it with a newfound efficiency or exploitation of an opportunity. When a risk is taken, the small businessman throws every bit of his personal energy, intelligence, and heart into it. There is simply too much at stake in failing—simultaneously, it may be his shot at the main chance.

The Small Business Balance Sheet

The small corporation balance sheet differs substantially from that of the large corporation. On average, it has a lower proportion of assets to liabilities, and therefore a lower net worth than big corporations.[19] In 1980, small corporations with under $10 million in assets—that is, all but 35,000 corporations—had 19.7 percent of total U.S. corporate assets of $3.2 trillion; 22.7 percent of all corporate liabilities—and accounted for 16.3 percent of total net corporate worth.

Assets and liabilities Small corporations have a far higher mix of current to total assets than large ones. This partly reflects small business' constant need for working capital and partly the fact that small corporations, because they predominate in trade, services, and construction, hold a higher portion of shorter-lived equipment and fixtures. Holding a lower proportion of long-term assets, small corporations are more dependent on current debt. In 1980, current debt comprised nearly two-thirds of small corporations' total debt versus half at large corporations.

Sources and uses of funds Personal resources are the major source of funds for small business. Big business is financed by institutional capital. A survey by the National Federation of Independent Business, an association representing 500,000 small businesses, found that over two-thirds of the financing for small start-up companies came from personal resources or friends. Those purchasing existing small businesses were twice as likely to find an interested audience at lending institutions than those starting brand new businesses. Federal, state, and local government financing and venture capital financing together account for only 1 percent of all small company start-up financing.

It is commonly said that small corporations have higher debt-to-equity ratios than big corporations. This is misleading. It rests on a spurious—unequal—comparison. Much small corporation debt comes in the form of loans from the owner's personal savings. Thus, in reality, it is indistinguishable from equity. The only difference is how it is formally accounted. Big corporation equity, on the other hand, is swelled by equity raised on the public equity market. Small corporations typically have little access to such equity funding.

The small corporation's desperate concern for working capital, and its lower absolute cash balances, limits its cash-management options. In 1980, for example, big corporate treasurers were able to park nearly 20 percent of their companies' funds in T-bills, corporate bonds, and other high-yielding investments versus 10.6 percent in small businesses.

Two Private Economies

The different financial characteristics of small and big business are indicative of the fact that there are two private economies in the

United States: one of small companies and one composed of the largest 1,000 corporations. It is primarily the fortunes of the latter that have been chronicled for much of this century in magazines like *Forbes, Business Week,* and *Fortune.* While both are products of American capitalism, they coexist in different economic environments, often have differing goals, and serve distinctively different, though often complementary, economic functions.

To generalize: Big business is oriented toward maintaining a predictable, preferably homogeneous economic environment; small business, in the aggregate, thrives on diversity and change. One is the world of the manager; the other is the world of the owner. One strives to show secure, 10 to 15 percent earnings, usually accrual-basis, growth; maximum cash profits are everything for the other. One is financed substantially by external institutional capital; the other by personal savings invested at great personal risk. In one, success is rewarded with social prestige, power, and secure, attractive compensation; the other is driven by desire for personal wealth, the satisfaction of creating something from nothing, independence, and other secrets of the individual psyche. In one, success generally comes through skillful consensus building; in the other, through determined, lonely individual action. In one, a good idea must be sold; in the other, merely conceived and willed. One responds slowly with calculated minimization of risk for error, while the other often reacts swiftly and idiosyncratically. One operates in a world of price signaling, managed supply and influenced demand, negotiated labor, government, and often multinational accords; the other thrives at the sufferance of the often cruel "invisible hand" that guided Adam Smith's concept of perfect economic liberty. One largely manages the basic productive capital structure of the national economy; the other supplies, services, distributes, and tinkers with or tries to revolutionize it.

Of the two economies, John Kenneth Galbraith observed:

> The two parts of the economy—the world of the few hundred technically dynamic, massively capitalized and highly organized corporations on the one hand and of the thousands of small and traditional proprietors on the other—are very different. It is not a difference of degree but a difference which invades every aspect of economic organization and behavior, including the motivation to effort itself.[20]

Galbraith names the two parts of the economy the "planning system" and the "market system." Unlike the market system, the planning system does not conform well to the neoclassical economic model. The large corporate entities can influence, sometimes powerfully, the economic environment to their own best interests; small companies in the market system cannot. This enables the large companies to maintain a reliable flow of retained earnings and optimize their economic goals. Small companies, by contrast, are plagued with unreliable retained earning flows, and thus are highly dependent on favorable external economic conditions for adequate profitability. Significantly, beyond a minimum threshold of absolute profits, the best interests of the large corporations are served not by profit maximization alone—which remains the singleminded goal of the independent small business entrepreneur in the market system—but by the security of those earnings and by predictable, and preferably steady, sales growth.

Fernand Braudel, author of the magisterial, three-volume *Civilization and Capitalism,* likewise views the modern economy as a dynamic continuum of interlinked layers. The most basic layer, "Everyday Life," is comprised of custom, routine, and is a self-sufficient use-value, largely barter economy. The next two layers are monetary exchange economies: A market economy, governed by perfect competition and largely a small business world; and an economy he designates as capitalist, which occupies the domineering apex of the economic landscape and the highest profit zones. In the contemporary era, the capitalist layer is populated with large corporations and financial institutions. Braudel writes:

> There are two types of exchange: one is down-to-earth, is based on competition, and is almost transparent; the other, a higher form, is sophisticated and domineering. Neither the same mechanisms nor the same agents govern these two types of activity, and the capitalist sphere is located in the higher form.[21]

The domineering capitalist layer, Braudel argues, does not try to take direct responsibility for the entire chain from production to distribution. Instead it tries to occupy strategic links which give it effective control over the key parts of the chain and provide considerable freedom in setting prices and in international trade. As a result, there are many areas of economic activity with which big business concerns itself only indirectly, and prefers to leave the direct activity to the market economy and small enterprises. Moreover, the essential character and dynamics of the modern economy are shaped by the complementary dialectic going on at all times between the different economic layers. He notes:

It is sometimes said that big business tolerates small firms, although if it really tried it could sweep them aside. How generous! . . . The truth is that they need the smaller firms, first and foremost to carry out the humble tasks indispensable to any society, but which capitalism does not care to handle.[22]

For the purposes of the present work at hand, we can enumerate five principal distinguishing differences between big and small enterprise. It is their diverse economic responses according to these five characteristics which governs their complementary relationship in the U.S. economy.

1. **They foster change differently.** Small businesses, in the aggregate, foster change through a cycle of births and deaths. Big business' pattern of change is through expansion and contraction.

2. **Their risk/reward investment decisions are assessed differently.** In small business, the risk/reward calculation is directly motivated by the condition of an individual owner who stands to profit or lose enormously from it; most often the calculation is circumscribed by the potential fortunes of a single line of business. At large corporations, the risk/reward judgment is made by employee-managers without any direct livelihood stake in its outcome; most often, the judgment includes the long-range welfare of a large, perpetuating institution with diverse economic interests and fiduciary responsibilities to absentee owners.

3. **Their economic power is different.** Small business has little or no ability to influence its immediate economic environ-

ment. Big business, through its buying and selling power in the marketplace and its political leverage, does.

4. **They utilize different resources in the economy.** Because of its general competitive inferiority, small business must make greater use of the secondary resources—capital, human, and supply—of the economy. Big business, because of its superiority, has first call on the most desirable primary resources.

5. **They serve different markets in the economy.** Although there is some direct competitive overlap and much significant indirect competition, small business' size and relative competitive weakness has driven it to serve markets in the economy that big business either does not wish to serve or cannot serve effectively.

The differences between small and big business have grown more distinct over time as merger activity and economic maturity have caused the management of America's largest corporations to pass out of the control of its founders to a sophisticated bureaucracy of industrial managers with little or no equity at stake. This is one of the great trends in American economic history. In 1900, half of America's biggest corporations were still being run by the men who had built them. By 1925, this had fallen to one-third. By 1960, it was under 3 percent.[23] Andrew Carnegie, for example, held over 50 percent of Carnegie Steel in 1900; in 1929, the entire board of directors of U. S. Steel into which Carnegie Steel had been absorbed, held but 1.4 percent of the steel giant's stock. Organizational management skills, not personal risk-taking, had become the main route to power and material comfort in business.

In these trends, the economist Joseph A. Schumpeter, writing in the early 1940s, believed he saw the slow demise of the small businessman—and his unique entrepreneurial function in promoting the process of "creative destruction" by which innovative change works its way into the economy. He wrote:

[T]he function of entrepreneurs is to reform or revolutionize the pattern of production by exploiting an invention or, more generally, an untried technological possibility for producing a new commodity or producing an old one in a new way, by opening up a new source of supply of materials or a new outlet for products, by reorganizing an industry and so on. . . . To undertake such new things is difficult and constitutes a distinct economic function, first, because they lie outside of the routine tasks which everybody understands and secondly, because the environment resists in many ways that vary, according to social conditions, from simple refusal either to finance or to buy a new thing, to physical attack on the man who tries to produce it. To act with confidence beyond the range of familiar beacons and to overcome that resistance requires aptitudes that are present in only a small fraction of the population and that define the entrepreneurial type as well as the entrepreneurial function.

This social function is already losing importance and is bound to lose it at an accelerating rate in the future.[24]

Schumpeter believed the entrepreneurial function, as well as the small business entrepreneur, would ultimately be undermined for several reasons. First, technological innovation was becoming increasingly complicated and required cooperative effort by teams of scientific specialists rather than individual tinkering and inspiration. Second, growth of large corporations would eventually "socialize" the individualist, capitalist spirit. The consequences, he believed, would be the eventual transmutation of capitalism into a kind of bureaucratic socialism. "Can capitalism survive?" he asked rhetorically in *Capitalism, Socialism and Democracy.* "No, I do not think it can."

In the modern corporation, Schumpeter saw a kind of economic entity distinct from the small business of neo-classical theory:

From the logic of his position he [the modern businessman] acquires something of the psychology of the salaried employee working in a bureaucratic organization. Whether a stockholder or not, his will to fight and to hold on is not and cannot be what it was with the man who knew ownership and its responsibilities in the full-blooded sense of these words . . . .Thus the modern corporation, although the product of the capitalist process, socializes the bourgeois mind; it relentlessly narrows the scope of capitalist motivation; not only that, it will eventually kill its roots.[25]

He added:

The perfectly bureaucratized giant industrial unit not only ousts the small or medium-sized firm and "expropriates" its owners, but in the end it also ousts the entrepreneur and expropriates the bourgeoisie as a class which in the process stands to lose not only its income but also what is infinitely more important, its function. The true pacemakers of socialism were not the intellectuals or agitators who preached it but the Vanderbilts, Carnegies and Rockefellers.[26]

For the full drama to have its final curtain, Schumpeter allowed perhaps a century.

Although independent small businessmen have indeed been contributing less to economic output, Schumpeter's predictions have not yet been fulfilled, as most recently evidenced by the prominent role played by small business entrepreneurs in facilitating the current transformation of the economy. Technological invention does indeed require work by teams of scientists in expensive laboratories over many years, but big business has not yet managed to reduce the inherently disruptive innovation process to routine and predictability.

Even if many have not felt comfortable about the dominant power of a few big corporations, most have concurred that they were the principal agents of America's extraordinary prosperity. Schumpeter observed:

> It is not sufficient to argue that because perfect competition is impossible under modern conditions—or because it always has been impossible—that the large-scale establishment or unit of control must be accepted as a necessary evil inseparable from the economic progress which it is prevented from sabotaging by the forces inherent in its productive apparatus. What we have got to accept is that it has come to be the most powerful engine in that progress.[27]

Yet these large industrial enterprises that manage the basic capital superstructure of the American economy—both for the well-being of the general economy and to overcome their own problems according to their "socialized " bureaucratic institutional evolution—require, and seek, a large measure of economic stability.

From the point of view of general economic well-being, this is not a bad characteristic—contemporary criticisms of it notwithstanding—as much as it is a necessary one. Small businesses can, and do, start up and fail by the thousands each week, and aside from the personal trauma of the individuals involved, it causes hardly a ripple in the national economy. But when a major corporation stumbles it has the potential for being a regional or national event. Not only do thousands of employees lose their jobs, but so might the network of the corporation's suppliers and their employees. General Motors, for example, had 30,500 suppliers in the early

1980s. It is estimated that one of every six jobs in the economy is tied to the well-being of the auto industry. Every $1 of auto output buys 2 cents' worth of textiles, 7 cents' worth of iron, 1 cent's worth of glass, 8 cents' worth of screws, 1 cent's worth in engines, 1 cent's worth in miscellaneous machinery, and 22 cents' worth of motors, vehicles, and equipment. Rather than face the consequences of free market failure, it is easy to see why the government, as with Chrysler, Lockheed, and Continental Illinois, has felt compelled to move in to save it.

The economic laws inherent in managing huge capital-intensive production facilities also require that corporate managers do all in their power to create the conditions for a stable, low-risk environment.

In 1902, writing in *The Empire of Business,* Andrew Carnegie observed that the economic laws of classical theory did not strictly apply to the age of mass production. "Political economy says that . . . goods will not be produced at less than cost. This was true when Adam Smith wrote, but it is not quite true today."[28]

When Carnegie, the son of a Scottish handloom weaver who'd lost his job to machinery in the industrial revolution, expressed this thought, he had in mind the vexing economic problem posed by the new, huge factories and expensive machinery, namely, that the enormous fixed expense of these factories made it less damaging to run them at a loss than to leave them idle in times of slack demand or price cutting. As Carnegie put it, a small manufacturer-craftsman who worked in his home with two or three journeymen could easily stop production as demand fell, but, "As manufacturing is carried on today, in enormous establishments with five or ten millions of dollars of capital invested, and with thousands of workers, it costs the manufacturers much less to run at a loss per ton or per yard than to check his production. Stoppage would be serious indeed."[29]

The early history of large industrial business is marked by efforts to find ways of managing this vulnerability, and to avoid the fierce and destructive price-cutting competition which it tended to foment. In the early period of the "management" era the leaders of the mass-production industries eventually organized themselves through gentlemen's agreements, pools, trusts, and mergers to establish more price stability, while at the same time trying to rationalize supply and maintain customer demand through advertising, extensions of credit or any means other than price cutting. As oligopolies emerged from the trusts, the informal gentlemen's agreements (not always respected in a gentlemanly fashion) not to compete on price were often administered through a tacit acceptance of the prices established by the leading company in an industry. In steel, such understandings were reached at the famous dinners hosted by Judge Elbert Gary, chairman of U.S. Steel, and attended by leaders who managed 90 percent of the steel industry. Indicative of the spirit of the new, not quite free market economics, J. P. Morgan, the banking mastermind behind U.S. Steel and many other trusts, reputedly said, "I like a little competition, but I like combination better."

Combination, however, did not succeed in solving the basic production problem described by Carnegie. The vulnerability of the industrial structure was especially acute at low points in the business cycle. In the Great Depression, big corporations, carrying heavy and interlocked production capacity, were unable to adjust to the sharp fall-off in demand. The industrial system collapsed. The nation lost almost half its GNP between 1929 and 1933 and one-quarter of the work force was unemployed. It was only aggressive government spending—and the stimulus of war—that propped up the industrial structure again. Since that time, the government has regularly intervened in the economy through fiscal and monetary control, taxation, and market regulation to protect the industrial corporate structure's Achilles' heel and to maintain economic equilibrium for the benefit of the general economic welfare.

Other processes within and without have evolved to steer big business toward self-protective conservatism. Labor peace through most of the postwar period has been attained through undisruptive negotiated settlements instead of sending in the Pinkertons to bash heads, as in the Homestead Steel strike of 1892 (which resulted in a 50 percent wage cut for steelworkers) in the age of the owner-manager. Key settlements, such as the UAW-GM contract, through tacit acceptance, signal the parameters for labor-management relations in major industries and contribute to orderly national economic management.

The rise of institutional investors—through pension funds (which alone had $650 billion under management in 1983 up from only $2.4 billion in 1940), insurance company funds, and mutual funds—who own between one-third to one-half the equity on the New York Stock Exchange and like to see companies turn in predictable, unspectacularly increasing earnings as a condition of maintaining an equity investment, also influence the employee-managers of big corporations to avoid undue risk.

Small business, too, performs several strategic economic roles in offsetting big business' vulnerabilities that abets economic equilibrium. There is a symbiotic relationship between the small business and the big business layers of the private economy. While the aggregate small business economy benefits from the service, supply, and distribution needs of the large corporations, the big business economy profits by, in effect, shifting the economic fall-out arising from economic instabilities and uncertainties onto the small business layer beneath it. It can do this because their relationship, although symbiotic, is also hierarchical, with small business in the subservient role. Thus small business is powerfully affected by developments within the big business sector.

This relationship serves the interest of general economic equilibrium. Economic disruption (and the low profits and business failures that often accompany it) is better absorbed by the scattered cushions of the small business economy than the concentrated, capital overhead-heavy and interlocked big business economy.

Being partly unrestrained by perfect competition, the big business economy has less checked tendencies toward downward and upward economic instability. The small business economy is more or less self-adjusting. In practice, it tends to act as a cushion for the economy in a downturn and as a brake in inflationary periods. In an economic downturn, for example, small businesses respond to the fall-off in demand with lower prices and lower wages. This does not happen so readily among big businesses with their unionized wage contracts and their market power to make higher prices stick among customers. Many of those customers are small businesses. Throughout the economy, small firms run into large companies with greater buying or selling power—and thus the ability to pass on to them their higher charges. Small retailers must often buy from powerful distributors or compete against chain stores and department stores able to get volume discounts or buy directly from source. Small suppliers sell to more powerful distributors or producers. In home building, the price of a house is strongly influenced by the cost of building materials often produced by large entities. Small business, standing at the end of the chain and after absorbing all the higher costs, must try to pass on the higher costs to its customers. If it cannot, as is normally the case, it reduces its wage costs and often accepts reduced profits. Small business in this way is the "give" in the fabric of the private economy.

Small business also helps big business in more directly positive ways. By performing economically diverse functions that big business either cannot do well or profitably, small business furthers, in effect, an efficient division of labor in the economic system. This helps maximize the profits of big businesses operating in the highest profit zones of the economy.

Finally, small business, in the aggregate, helps big business and the economic system adapt to change. This is important because the long-term-planning–oriented big business economy does not adapt readily to change. Small businesses must adapt quickly. They haven't the resources to wait until the economic climate becomes evident before acting. No bank will lend them funds to help them through hard times—quite the contrary, bankers typically bail out in panic at the first bad news in a small company—and few see the merit of a good idea or a good man until everyone else does too. Since they cannot compete head-to-head against economic entities with greater resources and lower unit costs, small businessmen, in the aggregate, must try alternate strategies. In the process, a small but significant number of them probe and open future growth markets for themselves first and big businesses afterward.

One essential feature of small business' role in the modern economy is that much of the economic benefit of its most salutary functions do not accrue to it but to other components in the economic system, chiefly large business. In difficult economic periods, small business cushions the economic consequences by maintaining its economic activity, and often its employment, at the price of reduced profits or even for short periods, losses. Small business' share of overall private U.S. economic activity may even be maintained in such periods, since big-business growth is constrained by the sluggish growth rates in high-profit zones of each industry.

By and large, this is what has happened in the 1970s and the first half of the 1980s, the worst economic period since the Great Depression. The fact that small businesses are most heavily concentrated in domestically provided service industries, and big business in the traditional manufacturing industries that have been increasingly subjected to intense foreign competition as industries globalize, further accentuated small business' prominent economic contribution during this period. A tiny but highly celebrated and significant corner of the small business economy, of course, has helped pioneer the new industries upon which the U.S. major corporations will compete in the future.

This by itself does not add up to a renaissance for small business. Far from it. But it does mean that small business has been able to help prop up the economy during a transitional period when its traditional main economic engines have been unable to operate at full thrust. This is giving the larger and less adaptable economic corporations time to manage the disequilibrating shift of assets necessary to be competitive in the global economy driven by revolutionary new technologies. Indeed, perhaps the most striking aspect about the wave of mega-mergers in the first half of the 1980s is the lack of public outcry they've generated: Rather than worrying about diminished competition due to the mergers, as in the past, the overriding concern was that the basic industrial corporations themselves might be too weak to meet global competition or too lumbering to adapt to the new technologies.

In more stable economic periods when the largest economic entities are functioning profitably without a high degree or threat of disruption, small business' relative contribution to the general economic output generally diminishes. It continues performing its salutary functions, but obscured behind the booming productive output of larger entities. In times of transition or difficulty, however, when growth subsides, does its steady contribution and economic reserve functions emerge into visible prominence.

3

Small Business
and Employment

In 1980, Judith DeCrescente, an attractive woman aged thirty-six, got the good news: Her application for a $300,000 loan from the Small Business Administration had been approved. That year, Characters Typographic Services, Inc., a nonunion typography shop, was started with seven employees.

It had been a long haul up for Judith DeCrescente. Raised in the Hispanic South Bronx, one of the toughest ghettos in the country (it was the setting for the film *Fort Apache, The Bronx*), she learned Spanish on the street and raised hell in school. Her father, she says, "was a good-time boy, who knew Al Capone in Chicago" and an alcoholic. The family later moved, but after repeated battles with her teachers, and despite "A" grades, she was expelled from high school without graduating.

At eighteen she married. A year later, the first of her three children was born. For most of the 12 years of their marriage, her husband was in jail for auto theft and burglary. She supported her family by working first at Western Union, where she became the union shop steward. There she learned how to read the hole punches in the communication tape. That led to her first job in the typography industry at $125 a week. In all, she

spent 17 years learning her trade at a half-dozen small shops of
no more than 30 employees.

Typography was a male-dominated profession and the
typesetter assigned to train her refused to cooperate. "I had to
stand behind him at a distance, and I watched every move he
made," she says. She later quit when a far less skilled man was
raised to her salary level.

At successive jobs she rose to production manager of a hot-
metal linotype shop, learned phototypesetting, and volunteered
to do mathematical typesetting by minicomputer when one of
her employers couldn't figure out how to use the minicomputer
the company had bought a couple of years earlier. She knew
absolutely nothing about computers. Fortuitously, she and the
computer were in a private room where no one could see her
learning, textbook in hand, as she went along. Her reward: $75
more a week in pay.

That and other jobs ended in disappointment. Then she got
a break by landing a job as foreman at $450 a week—nearly
doubling what she'd been earning at the time—at one of the top
shops in New York. Today it is her archrival. In this period she
met her future partner at Characters, Harvey Karp, as well as
her second husband, Michael DeCrescente.

She and her partner at Characters agreed from the start that
the new typography shop had to be strictly nonunion. Their
common worry was Local 6 of the AFL-CIO, which had dominated industry work in the 1950s and 1960s. Known as Big 6, the
union had forced typography firms to accept rigid work rules
based on an elaborate array of job functions that could be done
only by workers assigned to that classification. As a result, in a
typical typography shop there would be many skilled employees
standing around for three to five hours a night—at full wages—
waiting for the work to reach them. Also, to safeguard its members' jobs against change, Big 6 refused to accommodate the
spread of the new, more efficient computer-typesetting technology. To cover the expense of the union contract, the shops had to
raise their fees.

This, however, provided a competitive opportunity for
small, nonunion shops. By the time the large corporate customers discovered them in the 1970s, these small shops dominated
the business. Many of the large union shops collapsed. Union

power collapsed with them. Although Big 6 was in decline, DeCrescente and her partner wanted to take no chances of a resurgence.

Obtaining the SBA loan hadn't come easily. Borrowing on all her assets and from relatives, she and her partner succeeded in raising the $130,000 they needed to approach the SBA. But when they visited the SBA officer at a Citibank branch in New York, he simply laughed at them. "He didn't want to hear from nothin'," she remembers. "He wasn't interested."

A few months afterward, she and her partner met a lawyer who promised he could make the necessary introductions to the SBA. The expense was worth it: They soon obtained the $300,000 loan at 15 percent plus a 2 percent floating rate.

The day she learned that the SBA loan had come through, DeCrescente canceled the vacation she'd been planning with her children and informed them, "From now on, we eat beans." She meant it. At the start DeCrescente often spent 24 hours at the office, sleeping first on a cardboard box and then on a $39 rubber mattress. She paid herself half her old salary. For a year, she was delinquent on her household bills.

She also required regular moratoriums from the SBA on the repayment schedule of the loan. Her problem—under-capitalization—is a common one for a small business—the loan plus capital they invested proved to be too little for equipment and an adequate cash flow. To their frustration, the SBA officer repeatedly vetoed the new equipment expenditures they wanted to make.

Financial strains notwithstanding, a good client list and sufficient receivables assets enabled them after a year to refinance the company with a factor—at over 20 percent interest—and pay off the SBA entirely. With the factor they had to meet every payment deadline, but they had more freedom to make business decisions. The company prospered. By early 1986 they paid off the factor.

Today, with about $8 million in sales, Characters is one of the five top typographers in New York. Its clients include Estee Lauder, Random House, Revlon, and a host of Fortune 500 companies. DeCrescente's business strategy has been to deliver timely, premium service at a premium price. She takes the attitude that the art director of a big corporation or advertising agency is willing to pay a premium, hardly noticed in the big corporate budget, for the rapid turnaround time and quality necessary for a competitive edge in the advertising business.

The sales effort requires a lot of wining and dining. Sometimes they accept work they'd prefer not to, such as low-profit annual reports, to prevent a major client from going elsewhere and risk losing him. At the insistence of one of their most important corporate clients they bought a telecommunications system. The client never used the system—but having the system won them new clients who did.

Within five years, Characters' employment spurted from 7 to 100. Many of its employees, like DeCrescente herself, don't have high school degrees. Almost all have been trained for their work on the job. DeCrescente personally trained the plant foreman. A young printout operator who eventually became a top typesetter used to make out a list of questions about typesetting each night and DeCrescente would answer them; today, he writes computer programs which an ordinary operator—at a much lower salary than a specially trained one—can use.

Characters keeps 15 messengers shuttling back and forth between the office and its clients. Most are eighteen- or nineteen-year-old black men from the ghetto. DeCrescente recruits some who express an interest in the first tasks of the shop. About half those recruited have succeeded. There was one unusual case. Late one evening, she was talking with a thirty-year-old messenger. Realizing he was quite intelligent, she asked him why he was a messenger. He'd been an alcoholic with a checkered employment history and no one would give him a chance with such a background, he said. DeCrescente discovered he had an interest in machine repair and sent him for a six-week course on the basics of typography and printout equipment. He later learned electronics. Within a couple of years he was earning $480 a week repairing Characters' equipment.

Early on, Characters discovered that being a nonunion shop had major drawbacks. Above all it made it more difficult to attract the best workers to the firm. While their wage scales were competitive, they couldn't match the group benefits offered by shops through a union. As a result, soon after they

opened they cautiously accepted a union local—not Local 6—
into the company.

At 100 employees, DeCrescente has reached a threshold
where the operation is becoming too big for her to maintain
direct, hands-on control over everything in the shop. She probably won't have to confront the problem, however, due to the
radical technological changes occurring in the typography industry. In the near future, the clients who now use typographers for routine work will be able to do the same work in the
office themselves using a $7,500 personal computer and a laser
graphic printing system. The survivors will become specialty
shops doing the high-quality esoteric work that cannot be done
in-house. DeCrescente figures that half the typography industry nationwide—and many of the jobs—will disappear within a
few years.

DeCrescente has been following the technological trends
from the beginning, and has developed the specialists that she
figures will give them the edge when the shakeout comes. Yet
come what may, DeCrescente is ready. "I've been poor once,"
she says, "and I'm not afraid to be poor again."[1]

The forces of global competition and new technology are
fomenting a reformation of the country's industrial structure. In
this transition workers are being relocated from declining, traditional industries to new, slowly rising ones. The need to adopt
more competitive management techniques and flexible computer-assisted production is reshaping the way work has been
done on the factory floor and in the office through the long and
successful mass-production management era. It is altering the
balance of power among management, labor, and government,
and is partly responsible for the worrisome long decline of U.S.
productivity growth and slow economic growth.

In the process, it is destroying individual lives and entire
economic communities which supported America's basic industries in their heyday. It is forcing workers and managers to learn
new skills, to shift to new industries and new jobs, often in new
locations and supporting a different—sometimes lower—standard of living. How well the United States adapts to the economic transition will depend partly on the responsiveness of

labor markets in easing the disruptive social and economic price of restructuring American business.

The transition from the farm to the factory a century ago also destroyed a way of life and caused a cultural crisis in this country's self-image. That transition, however, took place more slowly, providing time for those who couldn't change to live out their lives as farmers. The frontier farm, of necessity, had taught rudimentary mechanical skills that could easily be adapted to the factory, whereas complete retraining is often needed to adapt to the information technologies today. In individual cases of hardship it was always possible to fall back on subsistence farming; today, a century of industrialism has made workers dependent on society for their fundamental welfare. Finally, it took place against a backdrop of general economic expansion which made the change socially and economically palatable. The anemic growth of the last decade has meant that the changes have had to be made in a sluggish economic context where one man's gain was often literally the next man's loss and therefore tainted with a discomfitting social ethic. The new technology industries do not as yet have the uplifting economic dynamism the auto industry had early in the century. They can't absorb enough capital or create jobs fast enough to offset the decline of the older industries. The new technologies are being applied in many instances to first improving the efficiency of existing production; a surge of new products that will stimulate demand-led growth seem likely to appear only with a lag.

In addition to adjusting to the economic transition, the United States has simultaneously faced the strains of absorbing into the labor force over 20 million offspring of the postwar baby boom. This paralleled a steadily increasing number of working women, many of whom were wives forced to work to make family ends meet. In 1970, 43 percent of women held jobs; by 1984, 54 percent did. Net immigration of about 500,000 a year— half illegally—also continue to put pressure on the U.S. labor market.

In the last decade, it has become evident that American small business is an important regulating force of the labor market. It creates a vast number of jobs when big business and government can't, it enhances labor market flexibility, it serves a complementary function in skills training, and it is playing both a direct and an indirect role in producing the conditions for viable, future U.S.-based manufacturing. It has been a major factor in the great adaptability of the labor market to the strains of economic change.

The Changing Global Economic Order

In the current transition, America's economic system is competing on new terms against that of Japan and Western Europe, with a prudent eye on some of the industrializing nations of Asia. Past preeminence is no guarantee of future success: At the turn of the century, Great Britain enjoyed the world's highest per capita GNP; today it is one of the poorer industrial countries.

The post–World War II period to 1973 was the world's longest and most broadly shared prosperity in history. In that period Western European nations staged a rapid economic growth which raised living standards to near-U.S. levels and made them viable technological competitors in many industries. Japan was transformed from a nation exporting low-skilled, low-cost, labor-intensive products bearing the disparaged label "Made in Japan," to one that has become a world leader in the most sophisticated knowledge industries—computers, complex machinery, and specialty chemicals—where competitive success depends on superior research and development, engineering, and marketing. In 1984, it enjoyed an electronics (including computers) trade surplus with America of $15 billion.

Meanwhile, other low-wage nations, among them Hong Kong, Taiwan, South Korea, Singapore, Brazil, and Mexico, have followed Japan's trail up the development ladder. Purchasing Japanese, American, or European technology, some, like South Korea, are dislodging the Japanese in capital and machinery-intensive goods such as shipbuilding, steel, small appliances, consumer electronics, TVs, and are even challenging them in automobiles. At the same time they are ceding the simple products at the lowest rung of the development ladder— textiles, shoes, and simple electronic assemblies—to poorer countries like the Philippines and Sri Lanka, where hourly wages are in cents, not dollars.

Because technology, equipment, and expertise are spreading to the developing nations at an accelerated pace, the "Four Dragons" of Asia and other fast-growing nations will require less time to climb the development ladder than Japan did. Korea expects to be a major producer of sophisticated industrial and electronics goods by the early 1990s. Brazil is a world leader in armored tanks and is building business and commuter jets.

Faced with the prospect of being chased by a dozen would-be Japans, the United States has little option but to move ineluctably up the development ladder itself—and quickly. This requires constant innovation in knowledge-intensive industries like computers, biotechnology, telecommunications, and new materials. It means moving from commodity goods to specialized ones. It requires competing on quality and marketing ingenuity according to new economic rules. It means trying to revitalize some less competitive older industries with productivity-enhancing automation to try to offset the wage advantage of less developed nations.[2]

In 1973, one garment in seven worn by Americans was manufactured abroad; in the mid-1980s, one in two were. As a result, one million U.S. apparel and textile jobs have been lost to low-wage imported goods. Many of the surviving textile workers are employed in companies that have offset their uncompetitive wage differentials (average U.S. industry wages, including benefits, were a modest $7.80 versus 63¢ in China, 12¢ in Bangladesh, 30¢ in Indonesia, and $1.18 in Hong Kong) by improving productivity through installation of the most modern shuttleless loom technology, and by moving out of basic goods into specialized product niches. For many small manufacturers, the $50,000 cost of a new loom was simply too rich: In the last decade, the number of textile industry entrepreneurs fell from 25,000 to 15,000.

Walter B. Wriston, who pioneered electronic banking while he was chairman of Citicorp, points out that the world economy is operating under new rules:

We live in a global marketplace run on a stream of electrons carrying information. I know that sounds like a speech to the Rotary Club, and everybody agrees, "Yes, it's true." But what we have not yet absorbed in our gut is that it affects almost everything we do anywhere in the world. The gold standard has been replaced by the information standard. Not many people have intellectually jumped over that fence yet.[3]

Slowly, U.S. businessmen, politicians, and union leaders have begun facing up to the realities of this new economy. Economic adjustment to it, however, has been slowed by the painful symptoms it has been causing for millions of employees.

The unemployment rate rose from under 4 percent in the late 1960s to 11 percent in the early 1980s—the first double-digit unemployment since the Great Depression—before it leveled off at a historically high level of about 7 percent in the mid-1980s. Nor did this include the 7 million underemployed—those wanting full-time jobs who were making do with part-time work— or the 1.3 million "discouraged" workers who had given up looking altogether.

Median family income, which had risen steadily in the postwar period, *fell* in real (inflation-adjusted) terms between 1970 and 1983. The brunt of that decline was borne by the traditional single-income household, which in 1984 had only three-fifths of the buying power of the fast-growing, and visibly affluent, two-income families. Poverty rates climbed as well. American television showed painful images of homeless families in winter and undernourished children whose world views were being shaped by the dirty landscape of poverty around them.

At the source of America's painful economic adjustment process and its floundering living standard is its anemic manufacturing productivity growth rate. Productivity casts a shadow over all discussions of future U.S. competitiveness in the global economy. It lies at the root of wealth creation. When productivity growth stagnates, the economy is merely recycling existing wealth. In such an environment, the weakest and poorest are the usual losers, as they have been in America for the past decade.

Robustly increasing productivity, on the other hand, reduces the unit cost of each item produced, and thus justifies higher wages. Superior productivity is the reason Japan can still dominate world production with a commodity such as 5¼-inch floppy disk drives even though its workers earn three times more than their competitive counterparts in Taiwan and South Korea. Increased productivity ultimately produces economic growth, more wealth, better jobs.

Increased productivity depends on economic adaptability and organization: improved management of the workplace, the fuller use of existing resources, the appropriate skills and motivation of the worker, the innovative application of new technologies and sources of energy which permit the work to be done faster, with greater quality and more responsiveness to economic changes.

Yet productivity gains often cause disruption in the labor market since they frequently involve the displacement of workers. Since 1980, for example, employment in the wealthy, industrialized countries has more than tripled, yet along the way, mechanization has destroyed two of every three jobs.[4]

In a healthy, growing economy, the disruption is mitigated by an increase in shared wealth and the creation of new job opportunities, often in the very industries where productivity is rising fastest. But in today's older industries where growth is sluggish and automation replaces but does not create new or better jobs, opposition to automation and other measures that will yield productivity improvements is great.

Future U.S. international competitiveness and high living standards depend upon a resurgence of productivity growth relative to other nations. Productivity growth, as in the past, generally stems from fewer and more skilled workers manipulating more efficient (and generally more complex) machinery. Thus a prerequisite to achieving it is a labor market flexible enough to undergo the painful dislocations of workers from jobs they've performed all their lives and the learning of new skills and methods of working on the shop floor, as well as an upheaval of the labor-management relationships that have evolved throughout the long mass-production management era.

Restructuring of the Labor Market

In the economic transition, the U.S. labor market has been undergoing a huge restructuring: Basic manufacturing jobs are emigrating overseas and being eliminated by automation at home. In Hong Kong, in 1983, some 800 U.S. companies employed 50,000 nonunion workers to make and export $13 billions' worth of goods—42 percent of it to the United States. Typical of many multinational giants, General Electric added 5,000 to its worldwide employment force in the 1970s, but did so by cutting U.S. employment by 25,000 and increasing foreign labor by 30,000. In response to the collapse of its export sales following the sharp appreciation of the dollar in the early 1980s, Caterpillar Tractor slashed its U.S. export-related work force from 31,000 to 15,000, stopped manufacturing certain products itself and began reselling those purchased from companies in West Germany, Norway, and South Korea in order to maintain its leading world market share in construction equipment.

As always, the activity of large corporations has had a deep effect on small companies and their employees. Consider the case of small Isaacson Steel: A few years ago, when bids were solicited for a steel contract for a multimillion-dollar office building in Seattle, financially troubled Isaacson, which had a small fabricating plant only five miles from the construction site, seemed the likely winner. Isaacson's bid was indeed low. But it was beaten by U.S. Steel, which soon announced how it could bid even lower—it planned to buy the steel in Japan and have it fabricated in South Korea. Soon after construction began, Isaacson shut its plant and 270 more U.S. iron workers were out of jobs.[5]

Tens of thousands of jobs have been lost to automation. Corporations such as IBM, GE, and GM spent $30 billion on factory automation in the United States in 1984. The total is expected to exceed $100 billion by 1992.[6]

In the factory of the future, there will be fewer people and more robotic, "steel collar" assistants. Human workers will do less of the easily specified, routine assembly and other monotonous tasks. Instead, they will have to be retrained to do more monitoring and programming of robots and other computerized machinery, more troubleshooting and maintenance. A general understanding of overall operations to maximize flexibility will become an indispensable skill.

As a result of industrial restructuring, the Great Lakes region lost 2 million jobs between 1973 and 1982. The textile-producing regions of the Carolinas were also pounded. Some

200 shoe factories, most small, closed between 1979 and 1984. West Virginia lost 29 percent of its manufacturing jobs, Illinois 25 percent, Pennsylvania 21 percent, Michigan and Iowa 20 percent, and Ohio 19 percent. Even in the mid-1980s recovery, business leaders meeting in Hot Springs, Virginia, announced that big business wouldn't be hiring back as strongly as usual— only 60 percent of the manufacturing jobs lost in the recession were ultimately reinstated in the recovery. Some 107 of 139 major manufacturing industries had fewer employees in 1985 than at the start of 1980.[7] As a result, U.S. manufacturing employment in 1985 was below 20 million—1 million fewer workers than in 1970.

The strains of restructuring the U.S. labor market has caused a breakdown of the traditional working cooperation between business and labor unions which helped provide a stable economic environment in the past. Symbolic of the situation was the 1978 rupture of the Labor Management Committee, formed under the auspices of the federal government to deal with the economic crisis of the 1970s, when big business leaders helped defeat the AFL-CIO–supported Labor Law Reform bill.[8] Being concentrated in declining mass-production industries where it couldn't protect workers' real wages or preserve employment levels, and unable to penetrate new, growing ones, union membership rolls fell far faster than the decline in overall employment in industry. From 1980 to 1984, total union membership fell from 23 percent to well under 19 percent of the work force—little more than half of the 35 percent on union rolls in 1954.

With decreasing presence in declining industries, unions lost the critical mass necessary to hold together industry-wide agreements. In 1985, the steel industry ended 30 years of coordinated bargaining with the United Steelworkers, citing competition from nonunionized smaller steel companies paying 25 percent lower wages. In recent years, similar master labor-management agreements have come undone in the airlines, trucking, copper, aluminum, and meat-packing industries.

Givebacks—where labor trades back benefits gained in prior negotiations in exchange for job preservation—became a regular feature of labor bargaining in many industries. One key giveback demand, as in the typography industry, has been work rule and job classification reform on the shop floor. Influence in setting work rules and job classifications has long been the very core of industrial union power. Yet by the 1970s, it was growing evident that the job classification and work rule system appropriate for the mass-production era had become an obstacle to further productivity growth.

The organization of work in other nations, notably Japan, appeared to be better adapted to the changing world economy. Big Japanese companies, for example, compensated for their shortage of skilled workers after World War II by rotating workers among jobs so that they became multiskilled and could perform various tasks as economic opportunities warranted. In a fluid world economy of rapidly shifting competitive balances, the ability to efficiently switch workers between jobs—and in and out of industries—appears to be a competitive advantage. It is also more conducive to producing the kinds of multiskilled workers needed to run automated factories.

U.S. union leaders and corporate managers are gradually moving to adopt less rigid working patterns. The most celebrated experiment is GM's $5 billion experimental Saturn small-car project. At Saturn, which is the byproduct of research done with UAW cooperation, work rules will be extremely flexible, workers will share in Saturn's profits, pay scales may increase as workers develop additional skills, and new technology may even permit the abolition of Henry Ford's moving assembly line. Instead, cars may be shuttled on automated vehicles from work station to work station where large finished sections of the car will be added. One expert estimates that success at Saturn could cut the number of man hours it takes to build each U.S. car from the current 200 to 40. That would catapult GM's productivity past the 100 hours per car in Japan and possibly wipe out the $2,000 per small-car cost advantage the Japanese currently enjoy over U.S. automakers.[9]

GM and the UAW have also taken the lead in searching for a cooperative means to ease the dislocation of workers who lose their jobs due to progress in adjusting to the economic transition. In the autumn of 1984, they reached a landmark accord in which any autoworker with a year's seniority who is displaced by new technology, productivity gains, or other efficiencies of modernization in the ensuing six years would be entered in a

$1 billion Job Opportunity Bank. The bank, which is to be funded by GM and administered jointly with the UAW, will finance retraining or transfer of the worker to a new job at full wages. In addition, GM agreed to invest up to $100 million in job-creating ventures, many of them small businesses, in auto communities like Flint, Michigan, Green Island, New York, and Oklahoma City, which have been hardest hit by layoffs in the industry.

The adjustment, however, has been too slow for the millions of existing workers—blue collar and white collar—who face immediate displacement from their jobs. Automation is expected to so reduce the number of factory workers that it is conceivable that sometime in the twenty-first century, the United States will need only the same number of traditional factory workers as it needs farmers today.

Before the end of the 1980s, some 10 million factory jobs will have been destroyed. Others will have been created to replace some of them. But they will be *different* jobs, in *different* locations, requiring *different* skills. Pay scales will be different. Many of the new jobs will be more knowledge-oriented.

Since early in the nineteenth century, the number of production jobs, such as factory workers, retail salesmen, and bank tellers, has been slowly decreasing relative to those who rely more on their brains, including bank presidents, nurses, real estate agents, and secretaries. The technology of the late nineteenth century speeded this process by augmenting human muscle with machines; the technology of the current transition is doing so at an even faster pace by extending the reach of the brain.

Yet the 165,000 steelworkers who lost their jobs in the first four years of the 1980s don't care that 150,000 new jobs were created in firms making computer hardware. Nor does it add any joy to the lives of the 200,000 laid-off autoworkers and their families to know that 200,000 others found jobs writing computer software. The town of Ware Shoals, South Carolina, where half the population of 1,800 lost its employment when the Riegel Textile cotton mill shut down, and the 50 other similar towns in South and North Carolina where 12,000 textile workers had their livelihood and careers terminated by mill closures in 1984, weren't any less depressed because the unemployment rate in the neighboring "Research Triangle" of North Carolina, with one of the highest concentrations of Ph.D.s in the world, is only 3 percent.

In Homestead, Pennsylvania, where a welcome sign as late as 1984 still claimed it was "The Steel Center of the World," over one-third of the town, mostly its sons and daughters, have emigrated in search of new jobs and new lives while their parents, stuck with unsalable homes and without any hope of ever finding an income as good as the one earned in the dirty, sprawling Homestead Works, get food from a soup kitchen organized in an abandoned restaurant. The same scene goes on in many of the downtrodden steel towns along the Monongahela River Valley.

A way of life in America is being destroyed in the economic transition. The blue-collar version of the American dream is dying. It is the ethnic, community-oriented life of industrial America, where for most of this century union working men gave their eight for eight—eight hours of honest work for eight hours of honest pay—so that their sons, when they grew up, could inherit their right to the union card and join an upwardly mobile middle class. Now their sons are moving away, often far away, to look for work. Families are breaking up. Entire ethnic communities are becoming memories of the last industrial generation.

The technology of the current transition will not spare white-collar managers either. To adapt to the new, more competitive environment, and to make the best use of computer and telecommunications technologies, large corporations in all industries, such as Xerox, U.S. Steel, Uniroyal, and Procter & Gamble, have already begun to slash away tens of thousands of paper-pushing middle managers. Experts say that in the coming years, the office work revolution may even bring changes as great as those occurring in the factories.

Finally, the historic farming trend to fewer and more productive farmers continues, through a farming crisis, to force hundreds of thousands of farmers to other professions.

There is a painful social cost for any major economic change. How hard the burden becomes—whether, in fact, it becomes hard enough to retard the transition America must make from the older, uncompetitive industries to the growing, knowledge-oriented ones of the future—depends on how many interim and long-term jobs are created to ease the passage. It depends on how well and how fast workers can be trained and retrained in the new skills. It depends on what use can be made of the skills that are no longer in high demand and, very practically, on how mobile Americans can be in moving to where the new opportunities arise.

Small Business and Job Creation

In the United States, the labor market has been lubricated by the unparalleled creation of almost 20 million net new jobs in the 1970s, and 8 million more in the first half of the 1980s. No other industrialized nation came close to creating new jobs at such a rapid rate.

A disproportionately large share of the new jobs was created by small business. The smallest companies created most: Firms with fewer than 20 employees created nearly two-fifths of the jobs even though they represent only one-fifth of total private sector employment. Small businesses with under 100 employees, which accounted for little more than one-third of all private employment in 1976, accounted for over half the new jobs. In total, small firms with under 500 employees created over three-fifths of all new jobs although it employs only half the U.S. private labor force.

Nor do these figures include the fast-growing companies that surpassed the 500 employee threshold. A McKinsey & Company study shows that these mid-sized companies, those between $25 million and $1 billion in sales, added jobs at three times the rate of the entire U.S. economy from 1970 to 1983.[10]

Small business' share of job growth fluctuated depending upon economic conditions, but exceeded its over 500 employee competitor between 1976 and 1982 in *every* major sector of the economy except retailing.[11] About 7 million of the 8 million net new jobs created in the first part of the 1980s were in the broad services sector. The Fortune Service 500 gained, but not as rapidly as smaller businesses.

The small business job creation performance is remarkable in view of the fact that government and big business, whose proportion of total jobs in the postwar period had been growing steadily, stalled under the economic difficulties of the last decade. Government, nearly all at the state and local level, hired 3 million of the 20 million who found jobs in the 1970s; since 1981, it has created no new jobs. The payroll of the Fortune 500, the nation's largest industrial corporations, shrank by 9.5 percent, or about 1.5 million, in the decade from 1973. As a result of this unexpected performance, small business reversed its long-term declining employment share and regained 3 percentage points lost in previous decades.

By creating so many new jobs, small business helped create an economic environment that has permitted assets to be reallocated to future growth industries and invested in productivity-enhancing automation, instead of being tied up preserving jobs in ones that must eventually shrink. Big corporations, in other words, have been able to proceed with the business of transforming the industrial core because small business was creating enough jobs on the perimeter of the economy to absorb employees laid off by rationalization as well as those entering the work force for the first time.

The creation of so many jobs by small business also helped to maintain adequate levels of purchasing power to facilitate a stable process of economic adjustment. Mass-production industries, keyed as many are in consumer-durable and related industries, are particularly sensitive to levels and distribution of consumer purchasing power. Inadequate levels and distribution of purchasing power was a principal cause of the Great Depression.

Small business helps maintain purchasing power both as a direct customer of big business' products, and indirectly as an employer. The total employment payroll of small businesses with under 500 employees, roughly estimated, is about $600 billion a year.[12] This figure, of course, is exclusive of the unknown multibillion dollars small businesses put in the consumers' pockets through the underground economy.

Small business jobs are one reason why the United States has been able to get through the most difficult economic decade since the Great Depression without many of the visible miseries of that period.

How good were these new jobs? That is a matter of some controversy. Nearly half were professional, technical, and managerial jobs. Many of the rest, however, paid comparatively low wages. [13]

Some critics are concerned that the current economic transformation may be causing the work force to polarize between the very highly and the very poorly paid, with the middle-level earners gradually disappearing. Others argue that the decline is only temporary or that it's not happening at all.

The growth of small business jobs in the last decade would tend to increase the proportion of low-wage and part-time employees. This is because small business, on average, pays 20 percent lower wages than big business and employs a greater percentage of part-timers.

Nevertheless, the creation of so many new jobs by small business has meant that the nation's human capital is being productively invested. Most of the baby boomers have found jobs. Not the best or the most productive jobs in too many instances, but they have cleared the first major hurdle of being absorbed into the productive job market. Women, too, with a high representation in the service sector, have continued to get two out of every three new jobs. Some of the laid-off workers have found makeshift—temporary, they hope—jobs. Except for Japan, America has the fullest employment in the industrialized world. Nearly 60 percent of the working-age population is at work.

Many of the jobs are being created in no-tech businesses that support or utilize high-tech products. The personal computer industry, for example, has spawned thousands of no-tech jobs in computer retail shops, among producers of simple computer accessories, in the trade press, as well as generating a small, growing force of computer repairmen. Users of the new technologies include young private air-freight businesses which depend upon sophisticated communications and information systems to manage routing schedules efficiently. Many of these are not high-paying jobs. But they are building the distribution and service networks, and creating the product demand high-tech manufacturing industries need to grow rapidly in the future.

With the number of baby boomers entering the work force tapering off, the pressure on the labor market is easing somewhat. For the 1980s, about 15 million new jobs are needed—over half have already been created. Yet until the year 2000, no more than 10 to 15 percent of the jobs that must be created to absorb new entrants to the labor market are likely to be generated in the high-technology manufacturing growth industries of the future. This is less than the heavy smokestack industries are likely to lose in that period. Thus, for the foreseeable future, the task of job creation will remain heavily on America's small businesses.

Small Business' Role in Job Creation

There is nothing mysterious about small business' disproportionate contribution to job creation in the last 15 years. The inner economic dynamics of small firms—abetted by market conditions—simply favored it. Small business creates jobs under different economic conditions from big business—and, of course, differently from the government as well. In addition, there is a body of highly publicized research suggesting that small business may inherently tend to create a disproportionately large number of new jobs.

Under stable growth conditions, such as prevailed during much of the postwar era, big-business employment tends to expand. So does small-business employment. But measured as a proportion of total employment, the relative significance of small business' contribution is lower.

In uncertain, slow-growth economic environments, however, such as has been caused by the current transition, big business is more cautious about adding employee costs. As the numbers of workers looking for jobs rises, wages tend to fall— low enough that cash-poor, labor-intensive small businesses can afford to hire them. They may not hire the specific workers that have been laid off; rather, the surplus of available labor tends to depress wages in the general market. It is from this pool that small businesses find employees they can afford. Quite often, it is the very existence of low wages (and low rents and other costs) which encourages new small businesses to be born.

It is easy to see that the labor market conditions of the 1970s and 1980s—uncertainty for the big industrial corporations plus the huge influx of low-wage, new-job entrants from the baby-boom generation—were just right for the abundant creation of jobs by small businesses.

A large number of unemployed workers willing to work at low wages creates a competitive environment that favors labor-intensive businesses—which are generally small businesses—over capital-intensive ones. High interest rates were another disadvantage to (usually large) companies needing heavy financing for the large plants and equipment on which their competitiveness depends. Finally, the environment favored job creation by small labor-intensive businesses because the oversupply of some goods due to competition between foreign and domestic producers kept prices low, while consumer demand in the service sector where small business predominates remained high.

The same conditions may not prevail in the future. For example, as the number of new entrants tapers off and as American big business gradually adjusts to the economic transition and robust economic growth resumes, the supply of available labor will shrink. Wages will rise. Small business, whose jobs tend to be less desirable than big business', will have a harder time competing for workers and it will likely again account for a lesser proportion of absolute job growth. Of course, if other conditions favor it or industry competitiveness considerations, as today, demand, a business may prefer to invest more aggressively in automation than in rebuilding employment. Thus paradoxically, to the extent that big business grows more efficient than its small competitors through greater investment in automation or other organizational economies, big business may tend to create fewer jobs per dollar of sales growth than small business.

Both phenomena are at work today. They can be seen in the employment figures in the business cycle of the early 1980s. In the recession at the start of the decade, small businesses with under 20 employees accounted for all the net increase of nearly 1 million jobs; in the recovery of 1983–84, big business, led by manufacturing companies, accounted for a greater (although still a minority) portion of the total net new jobs.

This phenomenon is not simply a function of small business' greater representation in the service sectors. It is matter of the different dynamics between small and large firms in all industries: Large companies tend to optimize output—includ-

ing management of its labor force—to the most reasonable fore-
cast of economic demand; small business tends to fill
proportionately more of the marginal demand above and below
the line of such forecasts. The fact that big business can optimize its economic output and that small business cannot is one
major reason why small business profits tend to be both lower
and more volatile than big business.

Through the business cycle, it means that big-business
employment levels are generally better matched to variations in
sales than small business. In a downturn, small business lays
off fewer employees, relative to the decline it experiences in
sales, than big business. In a recovery, it hires back proportionately fewer as well.

This happens because small business and big business
make hiring and firing decisions according to different criteria.
Big business, being more capital-intensive, tends to make hiring
and layoffs in a series of large discrete jumps tied to a decision
to open or close a production line or a centralized decision to
alter employment levels in large numbers of stores based on
broad business trends. Small business, being more labor-intensive, and having lean, proprietor-owner managements, adjusts
employment levels according to more transitory fluctuations in
business. But after the initial layoffs are made, employment in
small business, which depends on a minimum threshold of
employees simply to continue in business at all, stabilizes. Employees are sweated; profits often disappear. But the small businessman endures until the bitter end, waiting for the recovery
to bring back his customers. Big business, meanwhile, has
greater leeway to make further adjustments with a new round
of production-line closings or staff firings.

As a result, existing small businesses are quicker to make
layoffs earlier in a downturn—and quicker to hire back any
vitally needed employee who may have been lost in the re-
trenchment. Big business' first layoffs come later and are deeper.
Likewise, in the earlier part of the recovery, big business rein-
states those laid off more slowly; when recovery trendlines
become clear, however, it once again becomes the major contributor to employment growth.

Research bears this pattern out. In the manufacturing sector, small business is squeezed harder in recessions but enjoys

wider profit margins early in recoveries than big business since its employment levels fluctuate less than its sales. As soon as demand resumes normal range levels, big business' various economies of size quickly rebuild its profitability advantage and it again becomes the major force in employment growth.[14]

A similar pattern exists in the traditional service and retail sectors. Between 1976 and 1982, small service firms added employees at a faster rate than large ones, even though large service company sales grew faster. It created proportionately most, however, in the recession. In retailing, where the economics have favored big firms for a long time, big retailers' job share growth exceeded that of small business in every two-year period except during the recession.[15]

Research into job creation in recent years has added other information that sheds some light on other ways in which small business functions in the labor market. It has been discovered that job creation and destruction in the economy is continuous and more violent than previously known. For instance, a net 12 million jobs were created between 1976 and 1982. However, to arrive at that result, a total of 39 million new jobs were *created* and 27 million were *destroyed*. In other words, in that period about 40 percent of all the jobs in the United States were destroyed. They were replenished by new ones, with 12 million added for good measure, but in that brief period 40 percent of all Americans had to change jobs. As a general rule, over time, 8 to 10 percent of the jobs in the country are destroyed and recreated each year.

Small businesses, however, added and lost proportionally more jobs by going in and out of business at an extremely high rate. The nation's largest corporations, by contrast, did so more through expansion and contraction.

This makes small business an expeditious agent of change. Small businesses in sluggish industries quickly fail and their employment is lost. Yet immediately other new small businesses start up in growth industries to regenerate the lost employment. Big business faces the slower task of shifting assets within an ongoing institution.

The different criteria by which large and small business create jobs also cause small business to act as a shock absorber on the labor market in economic downturns, and help more structurally depressed regions begin the task of revitalizing. In this manner, small business serves as a spontaneous market economy equivalent of unemployment insurance.

In old industrial states and regions that have been hardest hit by the transition, small business is often the first lifeline for displaced employees. Although a declining industrial community's wealth may not make it an attractive market, the oversupply of available labor and services entice small businesses to start up there.

Big business' contribution to employment growth is far greater in fast-growing regions. To be sure, small business creates a greater absolute number of jobs in fast growth regions. But its relative contribution is measurably far greater in slower growth ones. Between 1976 and 1982, for example, all the net new employment in the middle Atlantic states of Pennsylvania, New Jersey, and New York came from small businesses with under 100 employees. In the industrial-belt states of Ohio, Indiana, Illinois, Michigan, and Wisconsin, the pattern was the same. Large companies with more than 500 employees increased employment by less than 4 percent while small companies with under 100 employees grew by over 11.4 percent.[16]

In the last decade there has been a celebrated body of research which suggests that small businesses, young ones in particular, may have a greater innate propensity for job creation than big business. In the early 1980s, the notion that small business created most of the nation's new jobs was so popular with politicians in Washington that it became something of an eleventh commandment to aid and protect small business for its job-creating powers. The most influential research supporting this notion came from researchers at the Massachusetts Institute of Technology led by David Birch. The MIT report, which concluded that small companies of under 100 employees in the period 1969–76 generated about four-fifths of all new jobs, gained such widespread fame in the Capitol that several Democratic presidential hopefuls, including Senator John Glenn and Reubin Askew, former governor of Florida, considered featuring the issue in their campaigns.

A couple of years later, however, the SBA commissioned another study, this time from the Brookings Institution, covering the period 1976–80. The Brookings' research found that only two-fifths of the jobs created in that period could be attributed to small business.

Influential economic journalist Robert Samuelson, writing in the *National Journal,* noted the discrepancies in the two studies. The politicians got nervous and backed off the issue. Small business lobbyists were furious. Most of their anger was directed at the SBA, an agency whose purpose is to promote small business, for jeopardizing the political safety of one of small business' best issues.

When the dust settled, the MIT and Brookings researchers got together and discovered that a large part of their differences had to do with technical assumptions that each had made about the data they were using.[17] The MIT approach had introduced a bias favoring small companies; Brookings had erred in the other direction. With revised assumptions, Brookings ran the numbers again. It came up with the now generally accepted conclusion that in the period 1976–80, small businesses with under 100 employees created 51 percent of the new jobs even though at the start of the period they represented only 36 percent of the business population. The MIT and Brookings researchers have been supported by further research done at the University of California at Berkeley.

If small business has been creating a large portion of the new jobs in the decade—and if, as the job creation data suggests, it may have been creating more in the past than previously recognized—why has small business' share of total private employment not increased over the last twenty-five years? The reason, say the researchers, is somewhat the same as why the proportion between adults and children, who account for all the new births, is a constant one: natural growth statistically turns them into big companies before very long.

These research findings also concurred on other discoveries about job creation in the United States. Among the most interesting is that all new jobs are created by only 15 percent of companies. Young companies less than four or five years old, such as Judith DeCrescente's Characters Typographic Services, seem to create a disproportionately large share of these. Indeed, some 350 of the 500 fastest-growing private companies on the *Inc.* 500 list in 1984 were less than eight years old. The total employment of the 500 companies had increased by 400 percent to 58,600 employees in five years. If this research holds up for periods other than the period of the 1970s when the studies were conducted, it means a significant number of America's future jobs will come from companies that are not yet in existence.

The researchers also found that job creation occurs in bursts, or oscillations, rather than at a steady pace over time. A company may go through a long period of quiescence and then suddenly, due to a new product innovation, a new production process, or a change in the marketplace, go through a sharp phase of growth. There is as yet no known way to predict which companies are part of that 15 percent club of job creators, or when a sudden growth phase may begin.

It is still too soon to conclude that the research of job creation in the 1970s provides a firm basis for believing that the innate characteristics of small business cause it to have a greater natural propensity for job creation than big business. The 1970s were an unusual period—not a good time for big business anywhere in the industrialized world.

Nor have other variable effects on job creation, such as the relative costs of labor, energy, and capital, or the impact of tax policy assigning a relatively higher burden on corporate profits than on (employee-based) payrolls, been sorted out. By and large, the economic environment in the country throughout the 1970s and 1980s has favored a greater use of labor. This may have magnified small business' role.

For example, high real interest rates and declining real labor costs gave companies a greater incentive to substitute labor for capital and throughout the period dissuaded them from capital investment in new labor-saving machinery. The same conditions did not prevail in Europe—real unit labor costs in Europe increased 35 percent faster than real capital costs between 1973 and 1981—and in fact European capital investment in the period increased more rapidly than in the United States.

Whether or not it can ultimately be demonstrated that small business may be responsible for a greater degree of job creation than previously believed may be far less important than the discovery that small business *can* create a disproportionate number of new jobs when other important economic entities like big business and government can't. This makes it an important complementary safety net built into the U.S. labor market—particularly as big corporations are counting on factory automation to enhance their competitiveness in the global economy.

Small Business' Employment Profile

Small business and big business make distinctly different use of the U.S. labor market. Small business is manned by a high proportion of employees from the secondary labor market, those who, for one reason or another, are less desirable to large corporations. It employs a high percentage of first-time job market entrants, those who have been out of work a long time, the least formally educated, the formerly self-employed, part-time workers, women, certain minorities, workers who stay on the job for shorter durations, and correlatively, fewer prime-age employees. They tend to work long but irregular hours, are not organized in unions, and receive lower pay and poorer benefits than employees of big corporations. In this way, small business adds several complementary dimensions to the American job market. It provides the first step into the labor force and up the job ladder, a safety net for those who tumble down it, and an accommodation for those, such as semiretirees, working mothers, or artists who otherwise don't fit easily into big business' and government's more rigid employment hierarchies. In effect, the small business employment rolls constitute a reserve labor force that big business can draw upon as needed. This is something big business has desired to stabilize its labor costs since the days Henry Ford helped trigger a labor migration to his auto factories from the South by advertising then-princely wages of $5 and later $14 a day.

Age The under twenty and over sixty-five-year-old work force comprises 16 percent of the work force at small businesses, but only 6.6 percent at large ones. Large companies prefer those employees who are in their prime, that is, between twenty-five and fifty-five. These generally higher-wage, more productive employees make up two-thirds of the big business work force; those who remain work for small firms, where they constitute slightly more than half of all employment.[18]

First jobs Two out of three Americans find their first job in small business. Part of small business' lower wages often goes to cover the cost of basic skills training on the job, for the best workers who will likely move on to better-paying jobs in big businesses as they open up.

Level of education College graduates are most likely to be found at big companies. High school dropouts usually get their further education on the job at small companies. They constitute over 26 percent of the work force of small businesses with under 100 employees but less than 16 percent of those at large companies.

Long-term unemployed One of the most insidious tragedies of job displacement is that those employees who are unable to find new jobs easily and provide for their families begin to lose their skills, their self-respect, their hope, and become increasingly unemployable. The longer an employee is out of work, the more would-be employers doubt his appetite for work.

The Bureau of Labor Statistics tracked 5 million of the 11.5 million workers displaced by factory closings or layoffs during 1979 and 1981–82 who had been employed for at least three years prior to losing their livelihood. By January 1984, only 60 percent of them had found new jobs—almost half at lower wages. Those who fared best possessed high skills, a white collar, and white skin. Three-quarters of the 700,000 managers found new jobs. A quarter of the women simply dropped out of the work force altogether. Semiskilled blue-collar workers fared very poorly. About 3.5 million received unemployment compensation, but since benefits lasted only six months in many states, half were still looking for work when their benefits expired.[19] A Congressional follow-up study found that government efforts to assist displaced workers served no more than 5 percent of the millions who needed help.

For those who had reentered the ranks of the employed, small business was more likely than big business to have been the avenue. Nearly 14 percent of the employees in small firms had been unemployed during the previous year versus 9 percent for those working in big companies with more than 500 employees. For those who had been out of the labor force altogether, small firms were almost twice as likely to provide the opportunity for work than big ones.

Part-time employees Small business is in the vanguard of the part-time work revolution. Only about three-quarters of jobholders in small businesses with fewer than 100 employees work full-time as against 90 percent in big companies. Employees of small retail companies and certain service firms that work only at peak hours are composed of many who work part-time. Many are women with children trying to help make ends meet or semi-retirees looking to keep active. Many are waiters.

Women Women compose about 43 percent of the small business work force, and about 36 percent of all large business employees. In part this reflects women's prominence in the general service sector work force.

Racial minorities Small business hires a lower proportion of blacks, but a greater proportion of Hispanics, particularly men, than big business.

Supervisory personnel Due to the personal nature and size of small business, it operates with fewer supervisors per production worker than big business. Companies with over 25,000 employees have 44 percent supervisory staff positions while small business under 500 employees have only 32 percent.[20]

Hiring practices Not surprisingly, small business tends to fill its modest labor needs informally and without great difficulty through personal contacts and recommendations from current employees. As a result, at a small business it is a common sight to see several members of the same family working side by side. Big business, with its large and complex work organizations, relies far more on formal personnel departments.

Job tenure On average, new employees in the smallest firms stay on the job 1.9 years versus 2.4 years for large corporations with over 5,000 workers. At initial jobs in retail, mining, or the selected services, tenure is likely to be shortest.

Wages and benefits Since it employs a larger percentage of the least desired employees, average small business compensation is significantly lower than big business. Wages vary directly according to the size of the employer. In 1978, 61 percent of those employed at small businesses with under 25 employees earned less than $5 an hour. At the average big company, only 33 percent of the work force earned this low wage. Those earning over $10 an hour were only 10 percent of the small business work force, but 17.8 percent of that of big companies.

Pension plan coverage and group health insurance follows the same pattern—the smaller the firm, the less likely is the employee to be part of a pension or group health insurance plan and the less comprehensive is the plan likely to be. In 1983, only 14 percent of employees in firms with under 25 employees were covered by pensions versus 72 percent of big business employees. Less than two-thirds of those employed in the smallest American companies are included in an employer's health plan or covered by a household member's policy compared with over 90 percent at big companies. The chief reason for this is that the same small business is less generous on wages and salaries—small business' lower profitability.

Union representation Employees at small businesses are far less likely than big business or government employees to belong to a union. As the experience of DeCrescente's Characters in introducing a union into the company in order to be able to offer competitive employee benefits suggests, union representation increases the likelihood that a company will offer employee benefits.

Less than 5 percent of the employees at firms with under 25 employees were covered by union contracts in 1983. That increased to 19 percent for companies with between 100 and 500 employees. The largest companies, with over 500 employees, had 30 percent of their employees under union contracts in 1983. Big business was more likely to be unionized in all sectors of industry and services.

While private sector union representation has been falling in recent years, it fell fastest in small businesses. The exception was manufacturing, where the decline was led by big business.

The small businessman resists unionization to preserve his autonomy, and his freedom in managing the workplace, which is one of his few competitive advantages over—and sometimes his only means of surviving against—big business. Flexibility to reduce wages in sluggish periods is sometimes maintained by nearly matching union pay scales to defuse union sentiment among the work force and to dissuade union organizers from going to the expense and trouble of organizing a small shop when economic conditions favor the sellers of labor. When unemployment levels are high and employees are at a relative disadvantage, the greater wage flexibility of nonunionized small companies often provides them with a significant competitive advantage against large unionized ones.

The small scale and family atmosphere of many small businesses also helps discourage unionization. Where plants are organized the employees are more likely to be oriented to the circumstances of their own company—somewhat akin in spirit to Japanese unions—than to the general industry. Although working conditions at small businesses run the gamut from squalid to almost familial, in general, small companies are less prone to experience labor-management conflict than big ones.

One small company that has experienced the full gamut of labor-union relations is electronics parts maker Robinson-Nugent of New Albany, Indiana. The company was founded in 1943 as the Robinson Machine Works by J. D. Robinson, who for a decade. worked out of his garage, mostly fixing valves and trailer hitches and building custom parts from metal pieces. If there was work, his two sons helped him on weekends. Gradually, he gained a reputation for quality maintenance, and hired a few employees. In the mid-1950s, the Robinsons accepted a proposal from a customer, Byron Nugent, to design some sockets and connectors for transistors, which Nugent would market. At the time, no one thought transistors would ever fail and used to solder them in place. Nugent died shortly thereafter and it took until the mid-1960s before transistor failures finally brought Robinson-Nugent some of the big clients it had been waiting for. Sales topped $1 million. By 1969, the company had 120 nonunion employees.

That's when the union trouble started. Aware that their compensation was inferior to that of nearby big-business plants, the company's employees, with the help of the UAW, organized. The Robinson family was horrified. A seven-and-a-half-month strike ensued, with the company calling in scabs and the employees responding with almost daily vandalism, such as slashed tires and smashed windshields. The union was accepted.

As it turned out, unionization wasn't nearly so threatening as the Robinsons had feared. In the mid-1970s, following the Japanese custom considered heresy among large U.S. corporations, they even began recruiting blue-collar members into management ranks as sales continued to grow. A turning point came in 1979. A deluge of orders required that the company boost production output by 20 percent in the following months or risk losing the orders to competitors. To enlist employee support, the Robinsons handed each of its 220 hourly workers a $100 bill. With union encouragement, plant production exceeded 20 percent.

Since then, "productivity" has become the sacred byword between management and the union. Management meets monthly with groups of 20 employees to apprise them of the status of company orders, how customers are using their products, and to discuss various economic conditions. Increased productivity helped make Robinson-Nugent a highly profitable $41 million company by 1983. It was also responsible for the three-year contract providing 9 percent annual wage increases and improved benefits which the company gave its employees during the depths of the recession in mid-1982—a time when its less productive competitors were laying off workers.[21]

Small Business and Job Skills

For America to make the productivity gains needed to succeed in the new economic era requires more than simply reallocating capital assets and getting new technologies in place. It also involves something equally difficult—the training and reallocation of employees to the appropriate jobs. A skilled work force to manage automated machinery, above all machinery based on the new "information" technologies, is essential to raising industrial and national competitiveness. In a global economy, it is a significant inducement to multinational corporations to locate their production facilities in one nation or region over another.

One of the causes of the U.S. productivity problem is that skills and jobs are currently mismatched. The severe shortage of manufacturing engineers who are familiar with machine tools, computers, and production planning is so seriously impeding progress toward factory automation that many of the corporations in the field, such as IBM, GE, and Rockwell International, are making sizable grants to universities across the country to set up academic programs in manufacturing engineering.

Some of the destruction and re-creation of 10 million jobs every year represents a reallocation effort by the marketplace to match skills and appropriate jobs. The extremely high 7 percent recovery level of unemployment is attributable, at least in part, to the mismatch of skills.

The acquisition of skills is a cumulative, building-block process based on a combination of social environmental factors and personal experiences—initial learning begun in the family, community, and school forms the individual's values, attitudes, behavior, and general learning skills. These are then applied to specific knowledge which may be acquired in further academic training and ultimately in on-the-job experience through imitating fellow workers and direction from a supervisor.[22]

New skills disseminate through a society only over time. The early growth of the consumer electronics industry, for example, was retarded by the shortage of salesmen who understood the new products well enough to educate—and sell to—retailers and then the general public. It is the education of the general population that makes economic development so difficult. In a premechanical society, even simple machine repairs are beyond the skills of the general labor force. Similarly today, productive utilization of computer technologies grows only to the degree that the general work force learn how to operate computers.

Small business plays an integral part in developing many of the skills that facilitate economic growth. Through on-the-job experience, small business' lessons begin at the most rudimentary level of learning work responsibility and how to be collaborative with co-workers, bosses, and customers. Gradually the employee is introduced to the basic concepts of business and may develop special skills. The most adaptive learners often use the low-wage experience of small business as a first step toward upward mobility.

In imparting fundamental general skills, small business is providing a remedial workshop for the failures of the present education system. In 1983, the U.S. National Commission on Excellence in Education reported that the number of functional illiterates—those whose skills are so low that they may have difficulty finding employment—was between 18 million and 64 million. Cutbacks in public education in the last several years heightens the importance of small business' service. Some of the responsibility for the nation's high unemployment rate lies with the failure of the education system to teach the basic skills an employee, and an economy, needs to build upon.

Big business is the chief training vehicle for certain highly specialized skills where training costs are prohibitively high for a small business to incur—in such cases, small business routinely waits until the employee has been trained on the large corporation's budget and then raids them with competitive salary offers.

This country solved its skill shortage problem in the late nineteenth century by dividing labor into many component job functions that could be repetitively performed in ignorance of the broader operation year in, year out, by semiskilled workers. In production and in management, the information technologies require a more general knowledge. Productivity gains come not by further subdivision, but through the skillful adaptation of production and management to rapidly changing conditions. It is estimated that in the computer industry, fundamental job changes requiring retraining are probably needed every 18 to 36 months.

Of necessity, workers who have graduated from small businesses, as in the major corporations of Japan, are likely to have shifted tasks from time to time. The flexible production techniques which U.S. corporations are trying to develop have an indigenous tradition in the Yankee ingenuity of the small shop craft-based industries which flourished in America before the rise of the mass-production industries. They have survived to the present day in several sectors, such as metalworking and other fields where high quality is required. Vested in these small shops are the general-purpose skills which, in the past relegated to small, specialized markets by the course of American capitalism, may become the nuclei, in one form or another, in the application of the information technologies of the future. Certain of the reviving traditional craft-based industrial regions of Japan, Italy, and Germany, for example, have quickly and productively adapted the computer technologies to the production of goods to make them among the world's most competitive today.[23]

In these shops, the machine has always been a tool used creatively by skilled craftsmen to produce a wide range of products; it has never, as in the mass-production industries, dictated the pace and mode of work to an assembly line of workers who were little more than its adjuncts. In America, it has frequently been associated with ethnic and family shop traditions where the boss, often a skilled immigrant who, after some years as an employee, opened his own shop, was the master craftsman passing on the skills to various apprentices. Many of the versatile machine shops flourishing today in the Boston area are owned by skilled immigrants who learned their trades in Germany, Portugal, and Greece. In the steel industry, production by the minimills, which produce a variety of simple shapes, is based on the flexible, craft system tradition. Nevertheless, in comparison with some other industrialized nations, America has a relatively fragile base of remaining traditional craft skills upon which it can draw in the new economy.[24]

Throughout American history, small business has helped preserve skills in declining industries. Sometimes it puts them to new and productive uses. Such is the case of the Timberland Company, which makes an immensely popular line of high-quality, high-fashion rugged footwear. What makes Timberland so unusual is that it earns good profits in an industry all but conquered by imports. The company origins date to Nathan Swartz, who emigrated from Russia in 1918, got a job in Boston as an apprentice stitcher in a small shoe company there, and by the 1950s owned a small, private-label shoe company which he ran with his two sons. Although the Swartzes sold just about the cheapest shoe on the market, hoping for a profit margin of a nickel or dime on each pair, foreign competition in the 1960s undersold them. They barely survived the ensuing industry shakeout. In 1968, however, they scraped together $16,000 to buy injection molding equipment which would streamline costs. But skilled labor was still a problem. So they moved out of their plant in South Boston to an old mill in Newmarket, New Hampshire, a worn little town with one big attraction—an abundance of skilled labor left over from New England's shoemaking heyday. To escape the commodity business in which they knew they couldn't compete with the imports, they launched a brand-name shoe, Timberland, whose special appeal was its durability, comfort, and—thanks to its skilled craftsmanship—high quality. It happened, fortuitously, to coincide with the 1970s fad among well-off, well-educated young urban professionals for the outdoorsy look, which the Swartzes exploited.[25]

Small Business and Occupational Mobility

In addition to providing essential training and skill development, small business also facilitates the fluid commerce of employees from job to job, which renders this training practical.

This is important because U.S. capitalism has always been a disruptive force involving the constant rise and fall of industries, thereby requiring a continuous mobility of people between occupations, and sometimes geographical regions. Early in the nineteenth century the great mill towns of New England were booming, only to be later abandoned when economic conditions changed. Industrial mining in the mid-nineteenth century built the Western mining towns, which likewise were exploited and abandoned. Shipping gave way to the railroad, and expressways and air travel superseded trains. Urban downtowns have decayed as suburbs flourished, and then risen again. The center of the U.S. steel industry over the years migrated progressively westward.

Today, the New England region is reviving, thanks to the high-technology boom centered on Massachusetts' Route 128 and the renewed demand for high-quality crafted goods that had been the specialty of the region's traditional machine tool shops. In North Carolina, the fall of the textile industry has paralleled the rise of the Research Triangle. In Texas, the decline of the oil refining business in the "Golden Triangle" is being offset by the rise of several other industries.

To keep up with the constant shift of economic fortunes, the United States has the highest occupational mobility rate in the industrialized world. About 30 percent of all working Americans change jobs every year. Since 8 to 10 percent of those jobs turn over with normal economic attrition each year, about two out of three who changed jobs did so voluntarily in search of something better, or because they were fired.

One in four Americans lives and works in a region other than the one in which he was born. In part because of the traditions of westward expansion into the frontier and to large immigration, geographic mobility in search of improved opportunity is strongly rooted in the American economic culture.

In very few countries other than America can many people seriously consider quitting their jobs to search for something better, least of all in another city or town. In America, it is small business which provides a great part of this mobility.

When a person uproots himself in search of opportunity in an unknown city, more likely than not he will find his first job with a small business. Small business hiring procedures are rapid and receptive to the broadest range of backgrounds, and the new native needs money fast. He'll likely upgrade quickly to another small business, which will begin to train him in some more marketable skills. This job, too, will be only a stepping-stone, as he looks to trade up, perhaps to a better-paying big business, as he discovers more about the opportunities in his new region. But it is small business that lubricates this process of mobility, and thus provides America with one of its economic strengths in adapting to change.

Throughout history, migration has always been one of the final defenses against human poverty. Americans moved en masse from the farms to the factories, and in the first 30 years of the century, the Northeast Central states—today's Rustbelt—flourished with an immigration boom. In almost all cases, those who migrated did better than those who stayed behind.[26] In the 1970s, 5.2 million Americans moved to the fast-growing Sunbelt states from the slow-growing ones in the North and East.

Yet this large number was comprised largely of younger people and well-educated professionals. The displaced, middle-aged industrial workers were largely left behind. Many had invested their savings in homes that couldn't be sold because they were in declining regions. Some had working spouses earning just enough money to make life manageable. Others had strong attachments to their family roots, even if their sons and daughters had moved away from their crumbling ethnic communities in search of work. Many felt just too plain tired to start over again.

For many, the best hope now remains in finding an opportunity in their local communities—often a small business. This may be an existing business, or one that is part of young industry that may be sprouting alongside the declining one, as in Waterbury, Connecticut, once America's "Brass City." The industry got started in the 1830s when Israel Holmes managed to smuggle modern brass-making machinery out of England by shipping it in pieces from different British ports. Brass eventually became the plastics of the nineteenth century, used for everything from sleigh bells to pots, buttons, screws, and eyelets for shoes. Yet since World War II, brass industry employment, centered on the Mad and Naugatuck Rivers, which run through Waterbury, has declined from 20,000 to 1,500. In early 1985, the last of the Brass City's big three brass companies closed after its employees angrily refused to make wage and benefit concessions. Workers, whose pay averaged $9.50 an hour, received no severance pay. But unlike workers in other parts of the country who have been forced to take cuts in compensation to save their jobs, the Waterbury braziers were able to say "no" because a renaissance in Connecticut led by small technology companies and the service firms that have sprung up around them has driven the unemployment rate down in Waterbury from 16 to 6.8 percent in the last decade. Jobs were being offered in the newspapers want ad columns.[27]

Many of the small businesses in the region were attracted by the low costs of setting up and the proximity to craftsmen who had acquired their skills in the old brass plants and machine shops and had, of necessity, opened shops of their own in diverse new fields that are hard to find elsewhere in the country. Ralph Crump, an ex-Californian, for example, founded Frigitronics, Inc., a manufacturer of advanced diagnostic and surgical devices, because within a 50-mile radius he could obtain all the important specialized manufacturing processes he needed for his business, such as high-quality machining and electronic-beam welding.[28]

Small Business and Wage Rigidity

Small business facilitates efficient adjustment to economic change by helping to create wage flexibility in the labor market. It does so by injecting the mediating free market forces of "perfect competition" into a modern economy which tends to drive wages too high or too low, for economic well-being.

According to neo-classical economic theory, the level of wages is inversely proportional to the availability of labor: A shortage of labor will drive up wages, while an oversupply of labor will drive them down. High wages, which are not offset by still higher gains in labor productivity, as in many old American industries today, lead to an erosion of that nation's international competitiveness. In trying to assuage the British crown on one of its major preoccupations in granting independence to the American colonies, Benjamin Franklin and other patriots argued that the existence of the U.S. frontier, by constantly siphoning labor from the Eastern Seaboard cities, would cause labor costs to be prohibitively high for the independent colonies to compete with England in industrial production.

Like other free-market mechanisms, the theoretical wage mechanism balancing wages and the availability of labor applied more perfectly to the age of small business—as well as to the small business part of the economy today—than it did to the era of big business. Before the Great Depression, mainstream economists believed mass unemployment was impossible. When the impossible occurred, it was held that the malfunction in the labor market must have been due to the fact that wages were stuck at levels that were too high, since the availability of labor was in such palpable oversupply. This, of course, was absurd. What had happened was that the neoclassical model of the economy didn't apply to a mass-production industrial economy requiring broad and relatively steady levels of demand for stability. In a very real sense, wages were too low and narrowly dispersed to maintain this demand. The power of purchasers in the economy was insufficient to support the industrial superstructure.

In the postwar period, big business, government, and labor unions cooperated to make sure the same circumstances didn't recur through minimum wage laws, the welfare state, and labor settlements with cost-of-living adjustments. Yet this system introduced certain wage rigidities—such as automatic wage increases and the increased power of labor unions to win broad wage gains for all, including the plentiful semiskilled workers—which in the 1970s exacerbated the new economic problem of inflation. This introduced an inflationary, rather than deflationary, instability in the economy.

Efforts to reduce inflation produced a disconcerting increase in unemployment. Rather than reducing the wages of many workers, corporations and unions agreed to keep fewer workers at higher wages. This propensity has been largely counteracted by small business. As unemployment rose, small business moved in to create millions of new low-wage jobs and to cut real wages of existing workers. This created competitive pressure for wage cuts by bigger businesses.

As a result, while unemployment was rising in the late 1970s, U.S. real manufacturing wages were falling sharply; as unemployment rates leveled off, so did real manufacturing wages—just as neo-classical theory predicts it should. This has helped the United States reduce inflation without paying a punitive price in unemployment. In Europe, where wage rigidity tendencies were not counteracted by small business, real wages have continued to climb at a time of sharply rising unemployment, which is injuring Europe's ability to adjust competitively to the changes in the world economy.

Wage rigidity has hastened the decline of some basic U.S. industries by preserving real wages at levels that are too high, given the rapid productivity gains of foreign competitors. Small business helps break up wage (and work rule) rigidities in some of these industries by essentially functioning as the domestic equivalent of foreign imports. Where wage structures are uncompetitive over a sustained period, small business gradually wins a market share based on lower wages.

This occurred in the beleaguered U.S. steel industry. Big steel companies attributed the breakdown of the industry-wide bargaining in 1985 to the fact that some nonunion steel companies, paying $4 to $5 less an hour in wages in an industry where labor is 35 to 40 percent of total costs, were hurting them in the marketplace. Thus they wanted to fend for themselves in company-by-company bargaining. Minimill competition in some steel products, for example, spurred Bethlehem Steel to convert its Johnstown, Pennsylvania, bar, rod, and wire unit into a minimill. To match minimill labor costs of a maximum $17 an hour contingent upon output (low enough, until recently, for minimills even to compete with imported steel), Bethlehem eliminated one-fourth of the 2,100 wage workers in the mill and half the 800 salaried staff; the hourly employees also deferred $4.91 an hour in wages and benefits in exchange for stock as part of a profit-sharing plan. Flexible work rules now permit carpenters, welders, riggers, and bricklayers to do one another's work if they have the skills, as a further means of reducing labor costs.

As a general rule, the greater the degree of concentration within an industry the less efficient small business will be in exerting the kind of pressure that breaks up wage rigidities.

Another way small business breaks wage rigidities in older, less competitive industries is by permitting the large corporation to shift some of its highly paid in-house component-making to less expensive, outside suppliers. This has been the growing trend in the auto industry, where the wages paid by nonunion suppliers are often one-third that for the same work in the unionized auto company shop. In 1984, Ford was farming out 42 percent and GM 22 percent of each car's production (some to foreign suppliers as well).

While small business tends to undermine wage rigidities in industries with declining international competitiveness, the force of organized labor is often sufficient to prevent it from doing so in growth industries or during temporary cyclical downswings. This is important. Where an industry is internationally competitive, small business' tendency to undermine wages would be undesirable for an economy concerned with economic equity and maintaining adequate purchasing power. Indeed, the exploitive capacity of small business in fiercely wage-competitive environments is in all too graphic evidence in parts of the textile and circuit-board assembly business which employs illegal Mexican immigrant labor at below the legal minimum wage.

New growth industries, because they abound with small, often newly created companies and therefore present a moving target for organized labor, are rarely unionized. This is healthy in the early stages, since it lowers the barriers for new entrants to foster competition which will eventually winnow the field to winners with the maximum competitiveness. Once the growth trajectory of the winners becomes clear and the industry achieves sufficient critical mass to sustain a few dominant companies which either enter from outside or arise by growth from within the industry, the variables in the economic equation begin to favor the organization of the work force in order to guarantee both equity and stability.

At this stage it is often advantageous to share some of the increasing wealth in exchange for a productive and highly motivated work force rather than to sweat labor for every last penny. Likewise the market share won by smaller competitors on lower wages will be but a trifling nuisance hardly worth bothering about, and likely to be offset by economies of scale, marketing prowess, lower capital costs, other efficiences of bigness, and the superior ability of large companies to raise prices to their customers to reflect their increased costs—including those arising from settlements with labor unions.

The great challenge to the organized labor movement today, if it is to continue to be a significant force for economic equilibrium, is to regroup from its present disarray and adapt strategies relevant to the new economic era and the personal stresses of union members who must suddenly learn new methods of working or face being discarded by the job market. If labor unions fail to meet the challenge, the prospect of a polarizing work force—or perhaps worse—becomes a greater palpable danger. Some consequences of polarization can already be seen in some of the industries being restructured by deregulation.

Although small business often undermines wages, in certain circumstances it actually enhances wage flexibility by firming wages in an orderly fashion.

Many of the jobs created in the last 15 years by small business, full- and part-time, were created by marginal capital, that is, capital that would otherwise have been idle had not a low-wage or part-time employment opportunity been available to bring it into use. Marginal capital may be nothing more than an amount needed to hire another waiter in a restaurant, or for a retailer to hire part-time help for the busiest store hours. There are many layers of marginal capital—as wages gradually fall with labor oversupply it becomes economic to employ more marginal capital to create more lower-wage jobs. In this way, while undermining existing wages over time where there is labor oversupply, small business simultaneously constructs several floors beneath the labor market as it does so, thus providing for an orderly deescalation in wages.

Furthermore, once economic growth resumes and the number of available jobs expands and the number of job seekers diminishes, wages escalate. Each floor of marginal jobs disappears one by one as many low-wage-dependent small businesses will be unable to continue to compete. Their exit from the market will be painless to the national economy since the jobs they provided have been upgraded and their output taken on by competitors. Indeed, the existence of these floors provides relatively full employment as the expansion proceeds, thereby helping to propel wages gently upward. Gradually, rising wages alter the relative costs of labor and capital, impelling business to increase its investment in labor-substituting automation—but in a healthy, full-employment environment where it is less economically disruptive.

The large influx of new employees to the work force in the 1970s brought much marginal capital into use to create low-wage jobs. Now that the number of new job entrants has begun to taper off and the new job entrants of the baby boom have acquired on-the-job experience, wages will likely begin to firm, then rise. In the 1970s, some 300,000 teenagers entered the work force every year. In 1983, only 150,000 did. Despite 7 percent unemployment in 1984, many minimum-wage jobs located in prosperous suburbs were going unfilled. To fill them, some localities were offering free bus service to tap unemployed inner-city employees, while businesses offered $50 bonuses to workers who stayed on the job more than six months, or compensation starting 10 percent above the minimum wage.[29]

Small Business and Future U.S. Jobs

In addition to being a likely major direct creator of jobs for the foreseeable future, small business is adding the flexibility and skills to the U.S. labor market which may indirectly help attract multinational corporations to locate their future generation of factories in this country. The "automate or emigrate" decision is not being faced by U.S. corporations alone. Western European and Japanese corporations face it, too. America is still the world's largest and most receptive market, and certain strategic factors (including the fear of protectionism) make it attractive for foreigners to build plants within its borders. In the future global economy the 500 or so leading corporations of the world from various industrialized nations are likely to have so many operations spread over the globe that the current passions over national origins will become moot.

While the overseas adventures of U.S. multinationals have been an understandably passionate economic issue for many years, less attention has been given to the growing significance of foreign—including Japanese—multinationals setting up shop in America. Foreign direct investment in physical U.S. operations since 1973 has leapt 900 percent to $130 billion in 1985. Foreign investment has created an estimated 2.5 million new American jobs.[30]

For the first time in 30 years, the U.S. will soon have ten auto companies making cars in the United States: GM, Ford, Chrysler, American Motors, Volkswagen, Honda, Nissan, Toyota, with Mazda and Mitsubishi on the way. By 1990, Japanese companies expect to be producing one million autos or approaching 10 percent of all U.S. car production. The Japanese are not just assembling components shipped from abroad. At least 30 Japanese suppliers have followed them. Honda plans to build engines at its Ohio factory. Within a decade or so, it is possible that these assembly plants will develop into true auto manufacturing companies, like GM's Opel in Germany or Ford of Europe, where major components are manufactured and cars for local production are designed on-site.

Whether this happens or not depends partly on the U.S. labor market. An Arthur D. Little survey of three dozen Japanese firms found that the most sought-after employees were those whose past experience was not limited to performing a single function in producing a single product because they wished to train them in the more flexible production methods and family-loyalty-type management techniques used in Japan. Compensation bonuses are tied to company profitability. There is more integrated teamwork, more interaction, between managers and line workers, and an open-door policy to hear suggestions for improvement from blue-collar workers. When an employee has a personal family crisis, such as major surgery on a spouse, someone from management may take a personal interest during that period. The salient point is that these are the very qualities and work habits that are more likely to be found and recruited from among small U.S. business employees than among large ones.

So far, the Japanese reportedly have been largely satisfied with their U.S. production work forces. If the Japanese and other foreigners, using U.S. labor and supplier resources, succeed with their U.S.-based manufacturing strategy, it will cause large U.S. corporations that are presently fleeing to offshore production to reevaluate their strategies.

Small manufacturers are themselves probing the global economy for competitive niches that will permit them to remain U.S.-based. One major weakness of offshore production is its sheer distance from the large United States market. As a result it often takes many months to respond to changes in the U.S. market. This was the weakness exploited by R.J.M.J., a $20-million maker of women's slacks and shorts located in New York City's garment center. In early 1984, R.J.M.J., like most of its competitors that manufacture offshore, ordered a fabric called French canvas for its product line. At the height of the selling season it unexpectedly got hot, causing customers to clamor for more. R.J.M.J. President Robert Shipman immediately ordered more French canvas from the company factory in Westminster, South Carolina, and through two subcontractors in Florida and Georgia. Within three weeks he was able to start making new deliveries. Because ordering more material from offshore plants required a six- to eight-month lead time, the offshore-dependent firms couldn't meet the demand before the season—and the opportunity—had ended. The upshot was that R.J.M.J. won 35 new accounts and its sales of French canvas increased from $60,000 to $3 million.[31]

Small businesses are also playing a role in trying to figure out how to penetrate the notoriously inbred domestic Japanese market, which, once broken, might help to balance out U.S.-Japanese trade to the benefit of U.S. employment. In the first five years since the Ministry of International Trade and Industry, under international pressure, in 1980, dropped a rule which made it easier for foreign companies to set up operations in Japan, some 500 small U.S. companies have rushed into the market.

The outline of a general world pattern is beginning to emerge where future production facilities will be located. Products that are labor-intensive and depend upon fairly standard and slow-changing technology seem, in the long run, likely to find their way to Third World nations. But those with relatively low labor content of 10 to 15 percent of total costs, and especially where competitiveness turns on changing technology, skilled labor, engineering control, and proximity to quality suppliers, seem likely to locate in the environment where these are most likely to be found—the advanced industrialized countries.

The future U.S. share of such facilities and jobs—and the level of future U.S. living standards—will ultimately be determined by the relative competitiveness of the entire U.S. economic system to that of Japan, Europe, and the fast-developing nations of the Third World. America has the most free-market-oriented capitalism of all the major industrialized nations. But in the postwar era, new, highly productive forms of capitalism have arisen in Japan and Europe. This country's competitiveness advantage has dwindled. The issue now is which of these forms of capitalism will adapt best to the new economic rules being molded by the current transition.

The labor market, of course, is a critical component of the economic system. How well it adapts partly determines the future competitiveness of the entire economic system.

Japan, with an unemployment rate of less than 3 percent and large company employee compensations linked directly to company profits, has thus far not only adapted its work force flexibly to new conditions, but the dynamics of its labor market have actually favored rapid factory automation and flexible production systems.

The rigid labor markets of Western Europe, on the other hand, have produced no net new jobs and have retarded job mobility for over a decade. This has resulted in an average unemployment rate of 11 percent—two to three times higher for youths under twenty-five in some of the countries—and lengthy, skill-eroding stays on the unemployment rolls, which is hostile to economic adaptation. European governments' economic options have been hamstrung by the large amount of social welfare they must pay to the unemployed.

Despite many problems, the U.S. labor market has adapted relatively well to the stresses of transition and the unparalleled absorption of so many new workers into the job market. Small business has been a significant complementary force in enhancing the U.S. labor market's general flexibility. This flexibility is helping the country to make the changes necessary for its economic system to be competitive in the future economy.

4

Small Business and Innovation

In 1980, Aryeh Finegold, then thirty-three, quit his job at Intel. Finegold, a former Israeli officer who had led paratroopers behind Syrian lines in the 1967 and 1973 wars without losing a man, knew something about calculated risks. He and his fellow managers had sometimes discussed the problems they were having in speeding up the process for designing semiconductor chips. He knew that a new generation of microprocessors from Intel and Motorola were powerful enough to permit a desktop computer to perform some mainframe functions, such as doing high-quality graphics and running design simulations. He also knew that research at Stanford and Berkeley on creating a complex software to permit engineers to work through an integrated hierarchy of diagrams to design, among other things, semiconductor chips, had resulted in 1979 in four engineers at the Lawrence Livermore National Laboratory building a working model of a huge computer in only six months rather than the five years such projects had required in the past.

Fitting the pieces together, Finegold came up with a commercial opportunity to create computer-aided-engineering

94

(CAE) systems. In 1981, backed by venture capital, his company, Daisy Systems Corporation, introduced the first commercial CAE system. Within four months, the company was profitable.

Finegold, however, wasn't the only entrepreneur to see the opportunity in CAE. The same year Jared Anderson, forty-three, a cowboy-boots-wearing Ph.D. who had once designed an IBM-compatible computer by hand, launched Valid Logic Systems. He managed to hire two of the inventors of the innovative CAE software used at the Livermore lab for his design team.

The field was rounded out by the entry of Mentor Graphics, founded by Tom Bruggere, thirty-five, and Gerry Langeler, thirty, two former Tektronix executives who had quit to go into business for themselves but without any idea what it might be. By systematically polling various experts in the technology field, including senior scientists at Bell Labs, the CAE system concept was virtually designed for them.

By early 1985, the "Little Three" pioneers had 83 percent of the booming, $260 million CAE market, whose volume is expected to reach $2 billion by 1988. Attracted by those prospects, large corporations like Hewlett-Packard, Tektronix, and General Electric have been muscling up to enter the market in a big way. At the same time, dozens of small start-ups are flocking to fill the fast-forming niches as the market takes off.

CAE is on the cutting edge of the new technological revolution. A cousin of the more than decade-old computer-aided-design (CAD) systems which are used mainly by draftsmen to convert engineers' designs into production drawings, CAE is a tool for the engineer. It comes in the "front-end" of the product development cycle, where engineers conceive the product. Its most urgent use has been in the design of semiconductor chips—the building block for all kinds of electronic products—which have become so complex that design engineers, until the arrival of CAE, had commonly to labor for years to design a new product. But it has applications for design of many other products as well. In competitive high-tech industries like semiconductors, computers, test and measurement equipment, aerospace, and consumer electronics where product lives are short and the demands of quality are highest, having a CAE system is becoming a matter of survival in the marketplace.

CAE's attraction to Finegold and the other Little Three entrepreneurs is that the system liberates engineers from having to design, build, redesign, and rebuild prototypes to work out the bugs of their product designs. In the past, an engineer did all this by hand. Starting in the late 1970s, mainframe computers were used to simulate prototypes to work out the bugs before building the physical prototype.

The system had limits, since the engineer couldn't interact with the computer to fix errors during the simulation process; he also had to wait until all his colleagues working on other aspects of the design were ready with their changes before revising the design. CAE removed these obstacles as well as made the system very much simpler to use and allowed engineers to run "what-if" scenarios in search of more creative designs.

The result is that higher-quality products can be designed much more quickly—often in one-fourth the time. In fast-moving high-tech industries where products rapidly become obsolete, speedy design time can make the difference between getting to market for a good return on investment and getting there when profit margins are on the downward slope. For this reason, CAE, when used with CAD and CAM (computer-aided-manufacturing) is at the heart of greatly enhanced U.S. productivity in manufacturing. CAE systems in 1985 were selling for $35,000 to $100,000 and falling, with less powerful versions running on PCs being developed to sell for under $10,000.

So far, the big corporations have had problems knocking out the Little Three. Size confers advantage in marketing and other aspects of business, but not so much in design of complex, knowledge-intensive software-based systems like CAE. Hewlett-Packard spent $30 million to develop CAE for its internal use and $30 million more to develop a commercial product. It also trained a special sales force of several hundred (as against 100 salesmen for the Little Three). But in late 1984 it disbanded its CAE development division in Silicon Valley and split it into two locations in Colorado. Several key executives defected to start-ups or to one of the Little Three.

Both Hewlett-Packard and Tektronix, which sell special instruments for debugging prototypes, are threatened by the Little Three's CAE systems because they eliminate the bugs (and, in some cases, the need for the prototypes) and thus the need for special debugging instruments. To get into the market pioneered by two of its former executives, Tektronix paid huge premiums, in one case nine and a half times *sales*, to acquire several tiny CAE companies, and even put the head of one of them in charge of CAE software development to keep its engineers from quitting. But as of early 1985 delays had prevented it from coming to market.

GE's effort to get into CAE through a CAD firm it had bought in 1981 had also run into snags. There was repeated raiding of its specially trained sales force by new start-ups, which offered equity or profit-sharing schemes to entice the salesmen. Two presidents and two years later there was still no product. Computervision, the pioneer of the CAD market now directly threatened by CAE systems, has also had personnel problems in getting into CAE. The toughest CAD competition now seems likely to come from Huntsville, Alabama-based Intergraph Corporation, which was the only CAD company to gain market share against IBM in 1984.

It is possible that there mightn't have been a CAE market or a Little Three at all had IBM decided to commercialize its in-house CAE technology, which is reportedly several years ahead of what is available on the market. But IBM didn't want to give away the technology to a product that was giving it competitive advantages in designing products for other—bigger—high-tech markets.

The greatest danger in a fast-growing, low-capital entry barrier market like CAE, in fact, might not be from the big corporations, but from the dozens of small start-ups from below threatening to find new applications and more efficient technologies that would make the existing CAE systems obsolete even while they continued, in the short run, to grow. To head them off, the Little Three are expanding in all directions of the market, particularly down into less expensive PC-driven CAE systems. Meanwhile, ever vigilant against the forays of the bigger competitors, the entrepreneurs of the Little Three deftly pick off the best salesmen and executives trained by the large corporations.

Through 1985, profits were quite handsome, particularly for the two market leaders, Daisy and Mentor. In calendar year 1985, Daisy earned $22.6 million on $133.6 million in sales.

Mentor earned $8 million on $136.7 million. Indeed, business was so good that Finegold once fired a salesman who had surpassed his target by 50 percent because he suspected he should have done even better.

Nevertheless, by early 1986, market conditions and the strain of rapid growth finally caught up with the Little Three. Daisy stunned Wall Street security analysts who had been touting its stock just days earlier by announcing it expected a $4 million loss in the first quarter of 1986. All the Little Three had been hurt by the prolonged electronics industry slump, while large and small competitors were squeezing margins. Rapid expansion and more intense competition had caused Daisy to sacrifice quality control, and products were being shipped hastily in incomplete packages or before being perfected. Most of all, Daisy was caught in the middle of trying to make a difficult product line shift: To meet customer demand for IBM or DEC compatible computers, Daisy was trying to sell too many products, the newest of which effectively obsoleted its earlier products to the detriment of total return on investment. Valid, meanwhile, had disruptive top management changes and, despite highly regarded technology, had fallen behind in market share. As of early 1986, only Mentor, which unlike Daisy, purchased its computer systems from outside manufacturers rather than get locked into any system by manufacturing itself, had not shown any visible signs of stumbling.[1]

Flexibility in the labor market alone will do little to enhance the competitiveness of the U.S. economic system unless it is accompanied by industrial innovation. Only by moving up the development ladder to develop, commercialize, and apply rapidly evolving technologies through innovative business strategies can the United States add sufficient competitive value to its economic output to offset higher wage costs and thus maintain, or enhance, its high standard of living.

That superior industrial innovation confers global competitive advantage and higher living standards has been understood since the first steam-powered industrial revolution in the eighteenth century. Over 200 years ago Britain unsuccessfully attempted to prevent the export of its revolutionary textile technology and the emigration of its skilled textile workers. It soon learned how hard it was, even in that slow-moving world of merchant sailing vessels, to hold onto its advantage for long against smugglers and foreign inventors.

More than any other nation in history, America has thrived by applying innovation to commerce. Yankee ingenuity, driven by Eli Whitney's invention of the interchangeable part and with it the "American system" of manufacturing, embellished early technology to create thriving small industries in machine tools, gunmaking, clocks, textiles, and axes. In 1859, 15 years after the invention of the sewing machine, America had 15 times as many sewing machines as Britain.[2] Innovations in farm equipment by McCormick, Deere, and others vastly multiplied U.S. agricultural output. Andrew Carnegie seized upon the converter invented by England's Henry Bessemer to build the world's greatest industry in steel.

The late nineteenth century was the world's last great period of innovative upheaval. Such epochal inventions as the electric light, the phonograph, various electrical appliances, the telephone, radio and television, industrial grade rubber, plastics, synthetic materials like rayon, pharmaceutical drugs, the automobile, and the airplane were born of the technical breakthroughs made preceding the period. Nearly all the major commonplace products and industrial processes of the twentieth century have been derivations of those technical breakthroughs.

The innovations of the late nineteenth century overthrew old rules of business competition. They created new fundamentals based on production speed and economies of size. America's economic strength today is due in large part to the fact that it found the world's most efficient and innovative ways of developing, commercializing, and applying the technologies of that epoch.

The current economic transition is driven by a burst of technological innovations which are creating a whole new era of products and processes. They, too, are creating new laws of business economics which are superseding those of the mass-production management era.

To prosper in the new economy, the United States must make three related transitions: (1) Innovate in the rapidly evolving technologies; (2) Apply the new technologies to American industry as rapidly and innovatively as it did in the past; and (3)

Quickly grasp the changing business economics of the new economy and adapt them to appropriate new business strategies and business organizations. To effect such a transition is enormously difficult because it requires a fundamental reorientation—and overthrow of powerful vested interests—of the American management, labor, industrial, and financial systems which grew up to master the economics of the former era.

The New Economics

A major feature of the new economic era is the acceleration of time—the acceleration of time in which innovation makes new technologies obsolete, the accelerated time in which industries mature, and the acceleration of time in which industrial advantage passes from developed to developing nations on a globe greatly contracted by modern transportation and communications technology. As a result, rapid development, commercialization, and application of innovation may confer as great a competitive advantage as did economies of speed and scale in the era of heavy industry.

Accelerated obsolescence is shortening product lives—and the period during which investments can be recouped and yield profits. A sophisticated electronics product might take eight to ten years from conception to market, but the entire return on investment must often be realized in only two years. The old electromechanical telephone switch had a sales life of over ten years; the new electronic ones, which cost $500 million to $1 billion to develop, become technologically obsolete within five years. The rapid obsolescence of electronics is now extending to many mechanical engineering industries where development often used to take at least ten years.

Failure to innovate and commercialize rapidly sharply reduces a product's commercial life and the profits necessary to invest in R&D for the next round of innovation. One recent study suggests that a 12-month delay in introducing a high-tech electronics product could slash the earnings over its life by 50 percent.[3] A semiconductor production line costs $100 million today and may become obsolete within three years or less. To recoup such an investment, companies must sell in huge volume. Global marketing is an important means to do this. So is enhanced flexibility through manufacturing automation. Computer-controlled design permits Japan's leading auto components manufacturer, Nippon Denso, for example, to make radiators to fit any car made in the world. The vulnerability of mass-production industries to shifting demand and technology is greater than in the past.

Where technological change is stalled, competitive advantage shifts to low-wage developing nations which quickly master the technology. The most modern rolling mills, paper machines, or numerical control tools are for sale throughout the world; skilled technicians are for hire; technology is available through licensing; and, as Britain learned 200 years ago, and America knows from trying to prevent sophisticated technology with military applications from reaching the Soviet bloc, efforts to prevent the transfer of competitive technology at best can be successful only in creating short delays. The fact that several dozen disk-drive companies can start-up within months of one another underlines how rapidly "advanced" technology spreads.

As a result, large corporations must be ever more alert to entry opportunities into growth markets, many pioneered by small firms, where oligopolies will likely form at a more accelerated pace than in the past. It took the auto industry 20 years for the boom in new companies to start to fade into oligopoly early in the century. In the United States the microcomputer—personal computer—market, where an average product lasts but 18 months before becoming obsolete, it has taken less than five years for IBM to dominate with over 40 percent market share and for all but two or three companies to face losses and imminent shakeout.

The new technologies of computer-aided-engineering/computer-aided-design/computer-aided-manufacturing, among others, provide the vehicle by which American companies can competitively accelerate the process of innovation—indeed the very existence of such a machine and its availability to America's global competitors makes it a requisite of success that they do so—and also improve product quality.

Such technologies also reduce the initial investment cost of many new products. This encourages experimentation. In the future they will permit almost anyone who designs anything from a space station to a toothpick to try out his idea without the expense and burden of committing a prototype to metal or to wood. The design will be drawn with an electronic pen on a terminal using the computer to correct any mathematical flaws. The computer can test out how the machinery can be programmed to produce the design in the most cost-effective way. Potential customers can test out the engineering quality of the design on their own computers, then decide whether to place an order.[4]

Two young men who have turned the new design technology into an enterprise are Ted Bickford and Peter Arnell, both in their mid-twenties. Using a computer design system, they created a reproduction of a silver-plated bowl designed in 1906 by Josef Hoffman, a Viennese architect, as a gift for Albert Einstein. They have sold over 100,000 of them at $120 apiece. Remarkably, the two young men worked only from a photograph, since the original bowl has disappeared. By way of historical comparison, starting in 1919, Walter Gropius of the Bauhaus School of design in Weimar Germany had experimented with mass-manufacturing craftworks using the electric motor, but gave up the effort because of the insufficient precision of technology.[5]

There are two tendencies within the new manufacturing technologies: one that improves industrial productivity in mass production industries by reducing break-even points and improving quality through integrated, factory automation systems; and another, associated with the craft industries exemplified by Bickford and Arnell, which enhances the economics of short production runs. In some cases so-called batch production runs of 50 units or less have become economical. This may help highly specialized industrial and consumer markets to flourish in the future.

CAE/CAD/CAM systems can be reprogrammed for many purposes, which means that technical and marketing ingenuity is more highly leveraged by the new technology than sheer size, as in the past. Falling costs, increased computer power, and the availability of time-sharing are pushing these new technologies into the hands of a greater number of people. This, too, increases competition—and opportunities for small business—as well as accelerates the innovation process. Because knowledge is cumulative, it might take only two hours, for example, to write a new software program by building upon an older program that took three weeks to write.

Many countries fell behind in the last economic transition because they remained attached for too long to the economic strategies that had brought them success in the past. The current transition poses a similar challenge. According to the report of the Commission on Industrial Competitiveness, the United States over the last 20 years has squandered a big lead in industrial competitiveness. Most alarming, the erosion extended to seven of ten "sunrise" high-technology industries that will provide future competitive advantages, including industrial chemicals, plastic and synthetic materials, pharmaceuticals, medical instruments, electrical equipment and components, engines and turbines and scientific instruments.[6] In 1984, for the first time ever, the combined electronics sector trade balance was negative, and by $6.8 billion. Early estimates for 1985 were worse—$12 billion.[7]

The pattern of the eroding competitiveness was also disconcerting: In industry after industry, the United States would make a product-engineering innovation, while other nations, notably Japan, would quickly swoop in with efficient production and marketing techniques to apply and commercialize it more successfully. Japanese corporations often introduce new high-tech products in one-half the time it takes American competitors. Robotics and factory automation were first developed in this country, but more effectively applied in Japan. The commission reported:

> It does us little good to design state-of-the-art products, if within a short time our foreign competitors can manufacture them more cheaply. The United States has failed to apply its own technologies to manufacturing. . . . The Japanese have been the most aggressive in applying process technology, and the results have often been lower cost and superior quality products—attributes well accepted by both American and foreign consumers.[8]

The failure of U.S. corporations, and the U.S. economic system, to respond effectively to the challenges of Japan and, in some technologies, to European and other nations, has created a realization in America that in the new economy technology is a precious resource to be managed as efficiently as oil was after the OPEC-induced oil shocks of the 1970s. Dr. George Keyworth II, science adviser to President Reagan, recently said that America's technological lead, once taken for granted, is "fragile." Spreading awareness of the new economics has touched off a debate in the research community about technological innovation policy—how to better manage the American advantages in product technology and overcome deficiencies in process technologies—as extensive as anything since the launch of Sputnik in 1957.

In Search of an American Solution

Thus far, Japanese capitalism has adapted faster to the new economics than American capitalism. Japan calls its capitalism "plan-oriented." In practice, this has meant that the Japanese government, often acting through the Ministry of International Trade and Industry, tries to guide Japan's independent economic entities to produce results that are in the best national interest.

This includes identifying certain strategic growth industries through consultations with industry and other sectors of society, then nurturing some of them—but by no means all—through incentives and coordinating cooperative early stage R&D efforts by the leading corporations. When the research is sufficiently advanced, the Japanese corporations compete among themselves to develop commercial applications from it. At the early stages, the government sometimes helps the market develop by protecting it against foreign imports and by making government purchases. The large competing corporations then organize for rapid commercial expansion and high-quality production to launch the product globally at a low price. From global selling they quickly build market share and derive economies of scale and low unit costs few foreign competitors can match. Throughout this process, MITI strives to create an orderly market with a limited number of strong competitors. If excessive competition or cyclic conditions begin to cause market chaos, it attempts to mediate alliances among the competitors (who sometimes reject them).

In the past, Japan's success has come mainly by taking advantage of the undervalued price of technology moving around the globe by commercially exploiting basic R&D done by other nations. Today, it is trying to adapt its system to produce the original innovations, which the Japanese perceive as a necessity for staying ahead in the new economy.

Among the "guided" capitalisms of Europe, which has always had strong basic science, governments and "national champion" corporations are also more closely coordinating their innovation policies. Although Europeans perceive they suffer a dangerous technology gap with Japan and America, some of their industries provide stiff competition. The Airbus, for example, sometimes beats Boeing and McDonnell-Douglas. The Ariane rocket is competitive against the U.S. space shuttle for launching satellites. Its telecommunications, nuclear power, and various mechanical engineering industries are world competitive as well.

The U.S. approach is more laissez-faire: Although it spends about half the world's annual $200 billion spent on R&D, it depends on the informal interplay between the laboratory and the marketplace to provide competitiveness in applying new technologies to commercial products and processes. Japanese and European nations, among other countries, also regularly tap U.S. university laboratory achievements.

What national industrial policy exists in America is run through the military and space R&D programs. Commercial applications result as spillover. In the postwar period, federally funded, military-based R&D provided important catalysts to the development of commercial industries such as electronics and aerospace. Today, however, as reported by the Commission on Industrial Competitiveness, the catalytic relationship between military R&D and commercial applications may be significantly less in many fields, like electronics, where military and commercial technologies have diverged greatly. One such area is semiconductors. Dr. Gordon Moore, co-founder of semiconductor leader Intel, and who was on the team that introduced the first silicon to Silicon Valley in the 1950s, reports:

When I first got into the semiconductor business, the military applications were driving some of the technologies. That stopped happening before the mid-1960s. But the government hasn't understood that yet.

Radiation resistance, for example, a major military requirement, has no commercial counterpart at all. So it forces the technology in unnatural directions. On balance, it is a very inefficient way to do research because such a small portion of the funds go directly to things that help your economic competitiveness.[9]

In recognition of the changing global economy, the government has taken some measures to encourage commercialization of inventions made under government funded sponsorship.[10] The Justice Department now looks favorably upon R&D consortia among industry competitors in what is a tacit acknowledgment of one of Japan's successful industrial policy methods. J. Paul McGrath, former assistant attorney general in the Reagan administration responsible for antitrust, said that in the technology war with Japan virtually any consortium of competitors within an industry would "pass muster."[11] Consortia have been formed in semiconductors, chemicals, and computers, among other industries. The government has even helped steel corporations fund research in cooperative development of new steel technologies.

Yet the basic thrust of the U.S. response, in keeping with its long economic tradition, remains laissez-faire. Major U.S. corporations have slowly begun to respond. In 1984, corporate R&D spending increased 14 percent, raising the R&D share of total sales to 2.9 percent, up from the 2 percent level of the preceding five years.

But it is small companies—from the biotech firms of Southern California to the computer companies of Massachusetts' Route 128—that have responded most energetically to the opportunities of the current transition. As a result, many U.S. (and foreign) corporations have been establishing new kinds of links to small U.S. companies as a means of keeping abreast of the outpouring of commercial innovations. Many of these innovations are occurring in markets and are based on technologies that are as yet far too unstable to merit a large corporation's prudent commitment. Yet they are often critical elements to rapid and efficient commercial exploitation of innovation.

Small business cannot afford to do the years of basic research involving many scientists that is integral to the innovation process. That must be done by larger, more stable institutions, such as big business and government. Likewise, only in rare instances can small business itself commercially exploit an innovation on a worldwide scale. This, too, is most efficiently done by larger economic entities.

Today, small business' chief role is complementary: First, to seek out and rapidly commercialize new products and processes from the basic research and development carried out by government, big business, universities, and independent research institutions. Second, once a major technological breakthrough has been made, to push its development, applications, and dissemination along rapidly. Third, to experiment with innovative business strategies and organizations. In these matters it prods the investment power and efficiencies of the large corporation, essential for future international competitiveness, in the most promising directions.

Small business is abetting the search for an American solution to the new economics by helping resolve a central paradox of innovation in the modern economy: how to manage the disorderly process of innovation in an orderly manner without jeopardizing the fundamental stability of the economic entities which underpin the economy. Central authority intervention strives to help resolve it in Japan and in Europe. In the United States an important part of it is managed by the complementary free market competitive force of independent small enterprise.

The Innovation Process

Industrial innovation is a process. To enhance its productivity and competitiveness in individual industries, the United States must efficiently manage all the major components of the process: basic research and applied research; product and process development; commercialization and application. This involves managing both scientific and business risks.

What is an innovation? A true innovation does something in a way that hasn't been successfully done before. An innovation may be a product or a business strategy. Product innovations are of little value to enhancing competitiveness unless they are exploited commercially. Exploitation can only be optimized through efficient application, effective business organization and strategy, and adequate investment.

The scientific phases in the innovation process are inherently unstable and sloppy. They advance by a myriad of small steps of trial and error leading to an occasional roadblock which may prove to be intractable. It is never possible to know beforehand which problem may become a dead end. The innovation process migrates back and forth between laboratories and often across national borders, with breakthroughs frequently coming unexpectedly from people following different technical experimental tracks.

Pure accident sometimes plays a role in the innovation process. Teflon and nylon were discovered on different occasions by Du Pont scientists in the course of looking for something entirely different. The oral contraceptive—the Pill—was also discovered accidentally by an industrial chemist in the late 1930s, although it took 23 years before it won Federal Drug Administration approval in 1962. So were countless other common products.

Basic research in particular is very expensive and risky because it often benefits potential competitors as much as those who actually perform it. If science is dealing with essentially new technologies, as at present, it can take two to three decades before viable commercial products can be developed from it. Such was the experience with the invention of the internal combustion engine to the development of the commercially viable automobile, and the invention of the first operational computer in 1946 to its widespread and industry-wide profitable dissemination in today's computer revolution.

Finally, proven genius and past success are no guarantees that an innovator is pursuing the most commercially applicable line of development. Even the prodigious Thomas Edison, the Wizard of Menlo Park, sometimes bogged down on suboptimum technologies. While Edison stuck obstinately to research into direct current (DC) electrical systems, George Westinghouse, inventor of the air brake, challenged him with an alternating current (AC) system, which ultimately proved less expensive over long distances. Westinghouse Electrical & Manufacturing Company, founded in 1885, went on to become one of the multibillion-dollar core corporations of the industrial superstructure.

The business phase of the innovation process also presents risks that are difficult to manage. Once a prototypical product has been developed, the practical uses and commercial ways to apply it are not at all obvious. They may seem so in hindsight once the markets have developed, but the inventors themselves are the products of ages whose imagination was formed without the invention. Thus Edison, for 15 years after inventing the phonograph, insisted that its widest and perhaps only large-scale use would be for dictating letters. Although he foresaw an application for musical recordings, he had little musical knowledge and was partially deaf and thus found it hard to believe such an application could have mass appeal.[12]

With marketable applications so unpredictable, leads earned on the scientific phase of innovation can easily be squandered in commercialization. Technical merit must be matched by business acumen. When the first computers were invented, conventional wisdom held that they would find a natural market in scientific research. This is where Univac, which had the most advanced machine, concentrated its efforts. But the interest of scientific researchers was scant. Instead, unexpectedly, business showed an interest in using it for payrolls. IBM noticed this opportunity and, using a redesigned Univac machine, took the lead in the computer market within five years.[13]

Cyrus McCormick, who manufactured 500 of his mechanical reapers for the 1848 wheat harvest, succeeded in building the precursor to International Harvester because of a business innovation other reaper inventors (and there were others) hadn't made: installment selling. Installment selling made the reapers affordable—cash-poor farmers paid $30 down, and the remainder of the $120 price in periodic installments thereafter. McCormick continued to make business innovations by creating the first modern sales organization to support his franchised dealers, mostly local liverymen and storekeepers.[14]

The commercial success of an innovation requires two triumphs. The first is the initial stage of market introduction, when the entrepreneur is involved in the life and death struggle of trying to find, or carve out, a market niche, and the market itself is becoming educated to the innovation's potential. The second occurs once the innovation has begun to establish itself.

At that point, future success depends more on business organization—commonly big business organization—to produce, market, and finance it with maximum competitiveness.

Ultimate commercial triumph, however, may be dependent on still another factor beyond the innovator's control, namely, the unforeseeable impact of other innovations on the commercial marketplace. Even an innovation as historically significant as mass production depended on a series of precedent innovations which created an environment in which it could be commercially viable: First, the evolution of an extensive mass distribution network, which arose from the urban department stores built by wholesale distributors like Marshall Field, the discount chain stores pioneered by Frank W. Woolworth, and the mail-order trade spearheaded by men like Aaron Montgomery Ward and Richard Sears; second, technical feasibility, which grew from the streamlining of the manufacturing production system in response to the Depression of the 1870s; third, financial control, which came from the innovative adaptation of railroad cost-accounting methods to industry; and fourth, a mass marketing mechanism to provide a means by which large corporations could attempt to maintain adequate consumer demand to support their huge production overheads, which arose with the first modern newspaper ads placed by department stores such as Macy's, Lord & Taylor's, and Wanamaker's to become today's $100 billion advertising industry.

In our own time, the OPEC-triggered oil crises of the 1970s and the pollution controls on coal burning resulted in probably the most important innovation in coal use in a century. Commercialization, which has recently begun, may ultimately provide America an ecologically safe access to its 500-year coal reserves and restructure the economics of the energy business.

With so many uncertain variables even a company—or a nation—that develops the most technologically efficient products has no guarantee of winning the business competition. Carnegie's emphatic opinion that "there ain't no profit in pioneering" is usually correct.

The final arbiter, of course, is the marketplace. The competition takes the form of economist Joseph Schumpeter's concept of "creative destruction," the process by which innovation supplants old products and methods, enhances productivity, and ultimately leads to economic growth. By its nature, it is an unruly, at times seemingly ruthless, process. Creative destruction in the retail trade, for example, is seen in the rise in different periods of the department store, the chain store, the mail-order house, the supermarket, the convenience store, and the format franchise.

Creative destruction is going on at all times. It is responsible for the surges in new product contenders and the winnowing out of losers. The failure cost of innovation is very high: The vast majority of entries fail; countless others survive, such as the companies known in Silicon Valley as the "living dead." Even venture capitalists, whose expertise is supposed to be finding winners in the creative destruction process, are happy if out of every ten investments they strike a big winner in one.

U.S. capitalism is more dynamic than is sometimes realized. Yesterday's winners often lapse into stagnancy and are surpassed by competitors. Fully 14 of the 43 corporations cited by Tom Peters and Robert Waterman, Jr., in their best seller, *In Search Of Excellence* ran into trouble only two years after the book's publication. To stay on top, even dominant corporations in oligopolistic industries need to make, or at least quickly adopt, innovations.

Yet innovation is hard to institutionalize. Very often a corporation will rise on the strength of a major innovation only to find that as it rides on its past glory it is overtaken in the marketplace by more innovative competitors. Such is the case of Xerox, which in 1970 was cited by *Forbes* as one of America's blue-chip companies and only 15 years later stood near the bottom of *Forbes'* profit rankings. Xerox President David T. Kearns says it was 1979 before the company woke up to what had happened: Japanese competitors had nibbled away at its position in the low-cost photocopier market and were about to launch an assault on its highly profitable middle-price copiers with sales prices that were equal to Xerox's manufacturing costs.

For most of the twentieth century, the United States dominated all phases of the innovation process. Future competitiveness depends on how the interrelationships between the economic entities which manage the innovation process evolve to manage the new economic environment.

Innovation in the Two Private Economies

Research and development in America is carried out in five chief locations: the federal government laboratories, university laboratories, corporate laboratories, independent research laboratories, and in private garages across the country. The federal government finances about half of the $120 billion spent these days on R&D. Corporations finance most of the rest.

One of American industry's greatest innovations was building the first bridge between science and industry in the late nineteenth century. Until then, industrial inventors had had little connection with the scientific establishment of the day. The origins of modern R&D date to Thomas Edison's "invention factory" in Menlo Park, New Jersey, in 1876. Edison was the first major scientific inventor to clearly conceive his inventions' merit in terms of commercial applications. Of his role as scientist, Edison stated:

I do not regard myself as a pure scientist, as so many persons have insisted that I am. I do not search for the laws of nature, and have made no great discoveries of such laws. I do not study science as Newton and Faraday and Henry studied it, simply for the purpose of learning truth. I am only a professional inventor. My studies and experiments have been conducted entirely with the object of inventing that which will have commercial utility.[15]

The first industrial corporate R&D laboratory was established in this country in 1900 by General Electric, which had grown out of Edison's company. By mid-century, there were some 200 major industrial R&D labs and 2,000 smaller ones. Their purpose was innovation, because only through purposeful innovation could large corporations thrive as institutions once their founders—their guiding spirits—passed away. The pioneer organizer of GE's first industrial lab explained its mission:

Our research laboratory was a development of the idea that large industrial organizations have both an opportunity and a responsibility for their own life insurance. New discovery can provide it. Moreover the need for such insurance and the opportunity it presents rise faster than in direct proportion to the size of the organization. Manufacturing groups could thus develop their continuity beyond that of the originator because the accumulated values of knowledge and experience became generally recognized. No one yet knows the possible longevity of a properly engineered manufacturing system.[16]

Today, 15,000 U.S. companies conduct R&D of some sort. The overwhelming part, however, is carried out by the nation's largest 1,000 companies. They account for 95 percent of all corporate-financed R&D. The largest 15 R&D spenders account for about two-fifths of the nearly $60 billion in total corporate R&D.

In other words, virtually all U.S. corporate spending on R&D is done by big business. Small business accounts for next to nothing. In 1984, IBM and GM, the nation's two biggest spending R&D corporations, each spent about as much as the *total* invested by the venture capital industry in potential small-growth firms.

Yet small business has always played a prominent role in the process of creative destruction. It has excelled at R&D requiring low amounts of capital and high degrees of specialized knowledge, almost always with the single-minded aim of getting a promising technology out of the lab and into the marketplace as rapidly as possible. Quite often, this has involved merely identifying, obtaining, and bringing to the marketplace unused or rejected innovations through various business strategies. Some of these strategies themselves have been important innovations which have given the United States early commercial leads.

Viewed as part of the innovation process, small business' role amounts to a low-cost extension of big business and government-financed laboratory testing to trial-and-error commercial applications of the myriad variations that might lead to competitive advantage. Once an advantage is found, it opens the market and sends market signals where larger investments might be merited.

A classic example is the case of Milton Reynolds, who played a catalytic role in introducing the first ballpoint pen. His innovation was nothing more than discovering an overlooked invention, the ballpoint pen, and marketing it in the mid-1940s to Gimbel's department store. They sold for $12.50 each, and in just six months, Reynolds parlayed an original investment of

$26,000 into an after-tax profit of $1.5 million. This success paved the way for bigger competition, such as Bic and Gillette, which soon rushed in and drove down the price with great economies of production scale. Reynolds took his windfall and gracefully bowed out of the market a very rich man.[17]

The small business innovative function, then, is not chiefly that of inventor, but of exploiter of inventions that have been made by others. This is as Schumpeter perceived 40 years ago when he wrote:

[T]he entrepreneurial function . . . does not essentially consist in either inventing anything or otherwise creating the conditions which the enterprise exploits. *It consists in getting things done.* (Italics added.)[18]

As Schumpeter perceived, the business of scientific invention has become increasingly complex and expensive, generally requiring specialized equipment and teams of scientists. To perform such research and early development is beyond the financial and human resources of all but a scant few.

Yet in hindsight, even in this age of atom smashers and genetic engineering labs, the large corporations which manage the industrial superstructure have yet to do away with the entrepreneurial function and reduce innovation to a routine— economically predictable—process. They remain dependent on the complementary, catalytic role of small business entrepreneurs to help resolve the paradox of managing the disorderly process of innovation in a relatively orderly, free-market way. Walter Wriston points out:

Kodak should have invented the Polaroid camera, but didn't. RCA should have invented the computer but it didn't. We at Citibank, I suppose, should have invented the credit card, but we didn't. It was the Lands and other entrepreneurs. It's the entrepreneur that still makes this country go. That's where the rubber meets the road.[19]

Big U.S. tire manufacturers, intent on increasing volume and product standardization, disregarded innovations in radial tires that reshaped the industry. Appliance-makers missed the technical advances in microwave ovens. GE and Allen-Bradley, which dominated the numerical controls (NC) business until the 1970s with hard-wired controls, failed to switch to solid-state electronics until it was too late and their customers had turned to Japanese NC suppliers. RCA and Zenith and most of the other U.S. TV manufacturers fell irrecoverably behind when the Japanese invaded the U.S. market with solid-state television by having assumed that the TV business was already mature with little room for technological leadership. Americans likewise completely missed the opportunity to produce a low-cost videocassette recorder, which was invented in America by Ampex Corporation in 1956.[20]

The list of innovations introduced by small firms in the twentieth century is impressive: It includes the aerosol can, biosynthetic insulin, double-knit fabrics, dry chemical fire extinguisher, heart valve, pacemaker, helicopter, safety razor, quick frozen food, soft contact lens, continuous casting, oral contraceptives, vacuum tube, zipper, and the personal computer.*

Small businesses have played instrumental roles in launching many major markets. Xerox launched a multibillion-dollar industry. Texas Instruments, then a tiny firm making oil-finding equipment, played a galvanizing role in the development of the computer industry when it paid $25,000 to license the transistor technology from Bell Labs, which it used to invent silicon transistors.[21]

Small businesses today continue to play a market pioneering role in nearly all the new technologies of the economic transition: computer hardware and software, local area networking, telecommunications, factory automation, robotics, and biotechnology.

Big business has been unable to usurp small business' role in managing the innovation paradox because its inherent economic and organizational characteristics, in some instances, are not as well suited to doing so as small business:

Large corporations need a clear indication of sizable and enduring market potential to justify a significant investment in an innovative product or process. The large corporation, whose strength is its planning and its efficiencies based on its large organization, is at its most vulnerable in unstable markets

---

*Innovation here is defined as first sale. The list excludes such epochal inventions made early in the century as the airplane and the assembly line. For a more complete list, see *The State of Small Business: Report of the President 1983*. (Washington, D.C.: U.S. Government Printing Office, 1983).

where conditions are in flux. It may try to minimize the risk of failure by funding many different potential R&D approaches to a new product. But even if successful in the laboratory, the risks multiply when a product moves into the uncertain arena of the marketplace, especially where defined markets have yet to form.

The risk/reward ratio is such that a multibillion-dollar corporation cannot afford to enter markets so small that even success would make only a marginal impact on the corporate bottom line. Markets that may emerge quickly but be short-lived abnegate big business' advantage of continuity and planning, and in the long run, profits from such markets are more disruptive than they are worth. By the same token, large corporations can rarely afford to waste the organizational effort of an early commitment to products or technologies that may soon become victims of creative destruction.

Instead, it is sound economics where uncertainties are especially great for big business to wait until clear trends toward a large, enduring market emerge and then to use its vast resources to plan a long-term strategy to dominate the market.

Big business has many valid ancillary reasons to avoid the potential failure of market pioneering. In an ongoing entity like big business, a commercial failure, even of small size, has repercussions beyond the actual financial risk. Supplier relationships or distribution networks that may have been utilized in the failed small venture may endanger other company products. Failure may cast a long, negative shadow on the corporation's reputation in the marketplace or on Wall Street, which may endanger future projects or the company's ability to raise equity or low-cost capital. Thus the failure risk for a large enterprise is more complicated than for a small one which suffers a clean and final death.

Big business can rarely afford to make big gambles. Unlike small companies, only on the rarest of occasions can it afford to bet the entire company on an innovation. IBM did it in the mid-1960s when it gambled on making all generations of mainframe computers compatible. Had it failed, it probably would have gone bust; instead, because of one great risk, it won two-thirds of the mainframe market by the 1970s and by 1984 was the world's most profitable company with a net of $6.6 billion—70 percent of total U.S. computer industry profits.

Under almost all other circumstances, the innovative process at large corporations is circumscribed by caution, and an overriding sense of responsibility to the shareholders, society, and to the perpetuation of the corporate institution itself. In the course of this caution, many worthy ideas are aborted or languish.

A new investment must fit overall corporate strategic objectives. Even if a large corporation possesses the R&D to develop and commercialize a product which promises to be successful, it often won't do so unless it is closely related to one of the corporation's product lines. Product-line extension is the easiest kind of management decision in a large corporation. The most difficult to make—and to enact—is the decision to initiate an investment beyond the carefully developed corporate plan. The market studies upon which big business relies are most effective when extending a product line or introducing a product with which consumers are already familiar, but they are next to useless when trying to identify markets for truly innovative opportunities.

Vested organizational interests may block innovation inside a large corporation. The risk/reward ratio of corporations that already have major investments in, and are earning handsome returns from, existing products often mitigates against an innovation that might supersede or endanger one of those products.

There are sound economic reasons for wishing to avoid innovation. Retooling costs for a new product can be huge and it could severely cut into the life of the existing product and thus the return on investment to switch to the innovation. Profits are necessary to finance new R&D. One of the most difficult decisions in any company is to know when to phase out an existing, still profitable product—and even more so, a process—and replace it with a new one to maintain company competitiveness. IBM hadn't marketed its reputedly superior CAE technology because it was benefitting more by using it to develop other products with greater profit potential.

Corporations also have some unsound reasons for avoiding innovation. A successful product is the source of livelihood and power for a cadre of managers within the corporation whose objectivity in assessing the merits of an innovative replacement may be colored by selfish interests, and move them to oppose it. Many corporations develop a hostile stance to outside innovations as part of a "not invented here" syndrome.

The nature of the corporate bureaucratic organization itself often resists innovative change. To reach commercial fruition an innovative product which challenges—and threatens—the existing organization often needs a committed chief executive officer with vision at the top, a product "champion" in the organizational ranks, and an integrated departmental project development team. Barring that, good ideas often fall victim to the institutional conservatism of big business.

In any big organization there are many layers of committees and managers from which an innovative proposal must gain a string of approvals to proceed, although a single "no" may kill it.

Some innovations are killed because decisions to stay with a particular project that fall out of line with budget forecasts are often close judgment calls honed by customer contact and intuitive technical feel. Yet many of the corporate managers whose support must be won lack the customer contact or the engineering background to make that evaluation.

When a good project at a big corporation is killed, one of three things happens: (1) It dies; (2) Its boosters leave the company and commercialize it through a newly founded small business; or (3) They bootleg it inside the corporation. Arthur K. Watson has testified that IBM owes the important development of the disk memory unit to the willingness of its scientists to risk their jobs in defiance of management directives to drop the project:

> The disk memory unit, the heart of today's random access computer, is not the logical outcome of a decision made by IBM management. It was developed in one of our laboratories as a bootleg project—over the stern warning from management that the project had to be dropped because of budget difficulties. A handful of men ignored the warning. They broke the rules. They risked their jobs to work on a project they believed in.[22]

Dominant corporations sometimes suffer from myopic decision-making. In concentrated industries, there has been a tendency for large corporations to go along with the pack rather than to risk being wrong on an innovative technology. Aware of each other's R&D plans, large U.S. corporations often took their cues for their new investments based on what their U.S. competitors were doing. In part it was the blindness of auto and steel executives to the evolution of the global marketplace with other strong competitors, because of their historic fixation on each other, that permitted foreign companies to take a quarter of the U.S. auto and steel markets. The myopia of RCA and Zenith caused them to refuse to produce black-and-white television sets for Sears 20 years ago; Sears turned to Sanyo and supplied it with the TV-making technical knowledge to enter a business in which they are today one of the world's five largest competitors.

None of this is to say big corporations are not innovative. Quite the contrary. Those cited here for their failures to perceive major markets, as well as others, continue to bring forth some other innovations and move in to commercialize others as they emerge, which brings the innovation process to fruition. What they have not done is to reduce innovation to a predictable routine.

In an economic landscape bursting with thousands of innovative projects, most will die off quickly, victims of scientific snags or competitive shakeout. Only a tiny elite will thrive to abet the process of creative destruction. But the central enigma of the innovation paradox remains as vexing as ever—which ones? In normal times, it is hard enough to pick the eventual winners. In times of technological upheaval it is harder and much more dangerous.

Fortunately for the U.S. economy there has always been a large number of entrepreneurs ready to ferret out or recycle unexploited innovations that may be the fruit of large corporate or federal R&D in search of commercial gain. The mechanism serves big business and the economy well, too, for in the course of trying to commercialize, the small business entrepreneurs open doors to new growth markets through which large corporations later pass at reduced risk to endow it with the organizational strength to compete in the global market.

The most celebrated recent case is the birth of the personal computer industry. When Steven Jobs and Stephen Wozniak, both barely out of college, offered the desktop computer they'd designed together during their off hours to the Silicon Valley corporations for which they worked, Atari and Hewlett-Packard, respectively, they received a cold "no." Whenever a big company says no, it often gets a competitor. In 1977, encouraged by friends and an environment that welcomed entrepreneuring, they formed a company; then, using readily extant technology, launched the first desktop personal computer under the corporate logo, Apple Computer. By 1984, the PC market was worth $14 billion—the same volume it had taken the mainframe market to reach in 30 years—and served by several dozen catch-up, me-too manufacturers, among them Hewlett-Packard.

In the euphoria of the early, heady days of the PC boom in 1979, Adam Osborne, a former trade journalist for a computer magazine who had built a $100 million business in three years by bringing forth the first portable PC, predicted triumphantly in his book *Running Wild:*

> In its most famous business, run-of-the-mill business computer systems, IBM will soon cease to be a significant force . . . hundreds of new companies are bursting into existence.[23]

At the time, IBM, which was built up by Ohio farmboy and former NCR supersalesman Thomas Watson, Sr., trailed the many small entrepreneurial computer firms racing into the market. Yet very quickly IBM, perceiving the potential in the PC market, impressed the business world by organizing a "skunkworks" (a temporary team of engineers, technicians, designers, and others working separately from the corporate bureaucracy) at a Louisiana plant. By 1981, in under 18 months—a far shorter development time than it would have taken within the corporate bureaucracy—it launched a personal computer.

Utilizing IBM's vast economies of scale and its peerless marketing strength, the PC line dominates the American—and the world—market. By 1985, its U.S. market share of 40 percent was more than twice that of number two competitor Apple and its success was shaking out scores of smaller competitors from the market. Even Apple, which had found its most receptive markets in the small business and home segments but was all but frozen out by corporate purchasing managers mesmerized by the safety of the IBM name, was struggling. In 1985, Jobs and Wozniak left the company. Among the earlier victims of the portable PC shakeout, Adam Osborne.

Should William Hewlett and David Packard, who, after all, had started in a Palo Alto garage with $500 between them in 1939 to make scientific instruments, have been more alert to the desktop PC one of their junior employees was offering them? (Hewlett, by the way, did donate some components to help them build their prototype.)

In hindsight, it would obviously have been a fortuitous hunch. But it wouldn't, given the facts at the time, have been an appropriate decision. Over the years, Hewlett-Packard had grown into a very profitable, $4 billion corporation with important interests and organization to nurture. Its management style had evolved appropriately. Of the hundreds of ideas inside the corporation it had to choose those few which best fit its market strategies.

Was IBM wrong for not developing the PC before Apple? After all, it had once turned down the first working "xerox" photocopy machine that patent lawyer Chester Carlson had developed in the late 1950s in a lab over a bar; worse, it had been caught unawares in minicomputers in the sixties and now had a multibillion competitor in Frank Olsen of Digital Equipment Corporation.

Of course not.

IBM executives and engineers had looked at the possibility of making a PC, but had rejected it because its performance capacity would have been far less than the smallest mainframe and it didn't seem to have an obvious market. In fact, the problems IBM foresaw have afflicted the market. What IBM could not have predicted, however, was that children and their parents would become utterly smitten in spite of the problems and go on a PC buying binge that triggered wild growth.

For speculative innovations where market potential is unknown, it normally makes better economic sense for the biggest corporations to hold back at first. For their own safety, however, they must remain alert to opportunities pioneered by small entrepreneurial firms.

In this way, small companies absorb much of the extremely high failure risk of early commercial innovation. Once an innovative opportunity becomes evident enough to meet its investment criteria and the economics of the marketplace begin to swing from small to big business' favor, it can use its superior capital resources, management organization, marketing, production scale, and R&D teams to enter the market, either directly or through acquisition. Then along with a few innovative survivors like Apple, DEC, and Xerox, which grow into big firms themselves, it can dominate the market.

This process facilitates U.S. competitiveness as well. Small firms, although they do little or no R&D themselves, help give the country a quick start on commercializing the technical innovation accomplishments of its laboratories. The risk/reward ratio for this activity is very highly leveraged, but since the cost is spread over thousands of economically insignificant small companies, many with only a handful of employees, it is easily absorbed by the economy.

Moreover, because the failure costs are isolated in small single-purpose companies that quickly die, it does not weaken viable ongoing enterprises which might compromise the competitive strength of U.S. economic entities vital to the industrial structure. By winnowing out the failures according to the rigors of the marketplace, they signal market's judgment of promising trails crucial to future competitiveness. Sometimes, pressure applied on industry powers from below shakes up comatose corporations to improve their own innovation efficiency, or spurs a big corporation to commercialize an innovation it has developed but is holding in abeyance.

That small businesses often either innovate at the price of their own extinction or become big themselves likewise enhances the competitiveness of the U.S. economy because, in an increasingly global economy against foreign competitors advantaged by government involvement, the resources of big business are usually a requisite of successful competition in big markets.

This pattern is evident not only in microcomputers but also in other new technology industries small business has pioneered. Now that small companies have pioneered many first generation biotechnology products and promising directions have been staked out, almost all the large pharmaceutical corporations, such as Eli Lilly, Bayer, and Hoffmann LaRoche, have entered the field. They will do battle with chemical giants such as Monsanto and Du Pont which are making $100 million investments in new laboratories to get a piece of the biotech frontiers as well as with the myriad small biotech survivors and new entrants. Now that the big corporations are participating, R&D spending is in the billions of dollars. That's the kind of spending necessary to build leads into competitive advantages.

In 1984, there were $4.3 billion worth of computer software company mergers and acquisitions. Big companies were buying their way into promising markets, and small companies, like Lotus and Software Arts (developer of Visicalc) were trying to scale up their marketing muscle by merging to meet the competition in the next phase of the innovation process. Big corporations which have moved into CAD/CAM are now starting to muscle into the CAE business pioneered by the Little Three. As robotics begins to signal the future technological and commercial directions it will take, big corporations are entering this field, too.

Small Business Innovation

Small business brings innovations to market faster than big business. It also commercializes more innovations per R&D dollar than big business. These facts are not surprising given small companies' capital constraints—small businesses can rarely afford a long and complicated R&D program.

One of the most comprehensive and recent studies of the small business role in product innovation in the 1970s covered 121 industries and innovations selected from such trade journals as *Industrial Research & Development, Product Engineering, Tooling & Production,* and *Review of Scientific Instruments.* [24] It found that small firms under 500 employees needed 2.22 years to bring an innovation to market as against 3.05 years for large businesses.

In every phase of the development process—product engineering, development of prototypes, setting up production to starting up sales—small businesses moved faster than large ones. Only in the setting up of the production process was big business nearly as fast. Similar patterns have been found in other studies of the subject.

The study also found that 40 percent of the product innovations tracked were made by small firms or by independent inventors. This is an extraordinarily high rate of innovation considering that small businesses spend well under 5 percent of the national corporate R&D dollar.

Another recent study of small business' role in process innovation in the food processing and manufacturing industries found that between 1971 and 1977 small businesses with under $10 million in sales received 45 percent of Putnam Awards made by the editors of *Food Processing* magazine.[25] Small business innovation was particularly high in machinery manufacturing, instrument and controls manufacturing, and plant maintenance, sanitation, and design.

Such findings notwithstanding, it is important not to overstate small business' role in the innovation process. The product innovation study, for example, pointed out that small companies produced 2.5 times as many innovations as large firms *per employee*. When distilled to popular discussions of small business and innovation, this finding sometimes has been inaccurately translated as meaning that small business is 2.5 times more innovative than big business, or that it produces 2.5 times more innovations as big business. Other studies have credited small business with innovative capacities up to 24 times greater than large corporations. Such comparisons are spurious.

Of course large corporations which manage the existing industrial superstructure and employ thousands of people having nothing to do with new product innovation will have a lower rate of innovations per employee than a small business whose entire existence may be hinged on commercializing a new product!

Moreover, innovation is a process. Crediting 100 percent of an innovation to a small company that makes the first sale may be utterly misleading since many small business innovations were either built on R&D—and sometimes on completed innovations—financed and carried out by the government or big business.

The salient point is that U.S. small business and big business each have complementary roles to play in the innovation process. This in turn has an important impact on American industrial productivity growth and competitiveness. By entering the innovation process at the stage where the bridge is being built between scientific R&D and early commercial application, and in experimenting with new commercial strategies, small business facilitates and accelerates innovation.

Characteristics of small business innovation Most small business innovations are dependent upon a special skill or knowledge. This is because such qualities often do not gain much leverage from large amounts of invested capital. An innovation may come because of a special talent for marketing, or for writing computer software, or for designing a new drill bit. The innovation that eventually propelled the growth of machine tool maker Robinson-Nugent, was to devise, at the suggestion of a client, socket plugs and connectors for transistors. The two young Apple founders' significant innovation was designing, at little capital expenditure, a concept for a desktop personal computer from existing technology.

Studies indicate a notably high incidence of small business innovation in the manufacturing and wholesale sectors. Instrumentation, consumer goods, and medical devices are subsectors where small business is also a major contributor.

Indeed, it is in many of the pioneering knowledge-intensive, small business industries, such as software engineering, that the United States holds its strongest technological leads over the global competition.

By contrast, it is in manufacturing processing that small business is less able to apply pressure to advance the innovation process because the large costs and long times often required are beyond its means, where U.S. corporations suffer their greatest competitive disadvantages against the Japanese.

Although small business innovation is most common in the business phases of the innovation process, small business fills roles in product and processing development. While much scientific R&D is performed by teams of technicians grinding away on expensive lab equipment trying out variations of a basic breakthrough in scientific knowledge for offshoots that might yield commercial possibilities, there is another type of scientific R&D. Its approach is just the opposite. It attempts to solve a particular problem by deducing the solution from facts known about the problem itself. Such R&D is far more knowledge-intensive—and more risky—than the former kind. It can be carried our efficiently by small teams of scientists on relatively low budgets.

For example, take R&D in the pharmaceuticals industry. The primary approach to drug research starts from a base of knowledge and, using perhaps teams of 200 scientists, screens thousands of compounds for therapeutic effects. The second approach, requiring a small team of experts, starts by analyzing the chemical processes in the body and attempts to design products to modify those that cause a specific disease. Tagamet, the anti-ulcer drug that is the world's best seller, was discovered in this manner.[26]

Perhaps the archetypal low-budget, knowledge-intensive innovator is the garage tinkerer, the basement inventor, whose precursors were the village blacksmith and the farm mechanic of the era of Yankee ingenuity. In the age of advanced scientific instrumentation and subatomic physics his role in innovation has diminished. Yet even he, like the small businessman, has persisted against the odds.

A case in point is maverick inventor Stanford R. Ovshinsky, who started as a teenage scientist in Akron, Ohio. He was too poor to go to college, yet pioneered Ovonics (a neologism coined half after himself and half after electronics), a noncrystalline or amorphous material. It has taken the better part of a lifetime and persistent efforts to commercialize his work, but the industrial scientific establishment at last has acknowledged him. Various applications of his work, notably in new solar power processes, are receiving big corporation investment.

The tools of the lone garage inventor have changed and their costs and sophistication have increased. But technology, even as it drives him into an ever quainter corner of the innovation process, is always creating new tools for him to work with. The advent of the PC and powerful software to run it at modest cost, likely soon to include variants of CAE/CAD/CAM, for instance, may open the door to new fields of opportunity in which the garage inventor can go on persisting against the odds.

Small business' characteristics cause it to abet the innovation process in a variety of situations:

Responding alertly to shifting market conditions By nature of its economic fragility, small business is highly attuned to shifts in its markets. Big business, by contrast, often needs a stampede before a change will be noticed by enough executives for something to be done about it. Nothing rivets big business executives' attention like a flamboyant small business success or a raft of start-ups and a flow of venture capital in sectors in the big company's backyard.

When an innovative opportunity arises due to a change in the structure of an industry or market, it rarely fits the way established companies are organized to serve—or the way industry executives have been conditioned to think about—the market. This gives the innovative newcomer time to try out promising alternatives before his success wakens the large established companies.

Quite often, small businessmen spark innovation in trying to solve a dire personal business problem. In the great Los Angeles sardine shortage of 1903, sardine canner Albert P. Halfhill, in desperation, began processing and canning experiments with other kinds of fish. He discovered that the "junk" fish albacore, nicknamed by the poorer classes living around San Pedro Harbor where the albacore then ran, "hog of the sea," because it ate everything in sight, was tasty enough. When steam processed it came out looking a palatable enough snow-white. He packed 700 cases at $5 a case. He went around to the local grocery stores, opening a can to let shopkeepers and customers alike sample with a toothpick. Thus was born the billion-dollar canned tuna-fish industry, which has made profits for the three major companies—Heinz (Star-Kist brand), Ralston Purina (Chicken of the Sea), and Castle & Cooke (Bumble Bee)—that have come to dominate it. Albacore, now rare, is the premium variety of tuna sold in American supermarkets.[27]

In response to the energy crisis and the conservation drive, small companies created services in installation of home insulation, new kinds of thermal windows and heat regulators, windmills and solar heating systems. Small business responded quickly to materials shortages by pioneering numerous substitute materials.[28]

Exploiting overlooked, neglected, or rejected opportunities
Small business provides a competitive spur to innovation by taking advantage of overlooked opportunities. The pioneering

of the market for CAE is illustrative. Aryeh Finegold of Daisy connected his knowledge of research going on at universities in the San Francisco Bay Area with a problem he and other managers at Intel were having in speeding up design. The founders of Mentor, Bruggere, and Langeler, learned of the opportunity by polling scientists and others at places like Bell Labs who actually designed the product for them. In other words, the technology already existed and the commercial opportunity was sufficiently ripe that it was obvious from a polling of two dozen people in the computer graphics field that the opportunity was simply not being exploited.

In this way, small business acts as a reserve guard for the United States in rescuing innovations that big businesses or government organizations, for one reason or another, pass up. Chester Carlson finally found a licensee for his photocopier not among the nation's top corporations, but in a small Rochester, New York firm, Haloid Corporation. Haloid's chief executive hocked everything he had to bring the machine to market in 1960. From these licensing royalties and stock, Carlson has earned $50 million—and Haloid grew from a $37 million company with 3,000 employees into Xerox, the $9 billion giant with 100,000 employees, now one of the mainstream corporations of the U.S. economy.[29]

Keeping fast-growing new industries on track Small firms play a critical role in sustaining the innovation process in industries where the growth rate is so fast and innovation so dynamic that the structure of the industry alters.[30] In such cases, many companies are selling innovative products that are already obsolete, but because they are prospering due to the extraordinary growth rate, they fail to notice it. New entrants do. Thus new start-ups drive innovation rapidly when there are new ideas—this is one of the economy's greatest competitive strengths.

Serving small or specialized markets Nearly all markets start small. Many of them remain small—too small ever to interest big business. But not too small for smaller enterprises.

Some markets are socially important as well. For example, so-called orphan drugs—those which benefit only a thousand or so patients or those whose patents have expired and aren't being used—are not worth the effort of the big pharmaceutical companies. Small computer software and peripheral companies have flocked into the limited markets to serve the mentally handicapped, the motor-impaired, the deaf and the blind.[31]

It is important to keep innovation alive in small markets, because the unforeseeable twists of the innovation process sometimes may suddenly make part of the mainstream. The market for supercomputers, the largest computers on the market costing between $5 and $15 million apiece, has always been small and specialized. (A top-of-the-line IBM mainframe costs $3 million, and a powerful Digital Equipment Corporation minicomputer $300,000.) In the early 1970s, the only supercomputer manufacturer was Control Data. It got competition when its top designer, Seymour Cray, left the company to build supercomputers for himself. Today, the world has six supercomputer competitors—Cray Research with 40 percent of the market, a Control Data spinoff, small Denelcor of Aurora, Colorado, and the three Japanese computer giants, Fujitsu, Hitachi, and NEC. Supercomputers have suddenly gotten to be one of the hottest segments of the high-tech boom. If demand reaches just 1,000 supercomputers a year by 1990, it would be a $2 billion market with a very different price-performance curve than it has today.[32]

Providing innovative supplies In many industries, such as textiles, materials, equipment, farm machinery, and avionics, where the major companies assemble products delivered by a network of suppliers, productivity-enhancing innovation often comes from the suppliers. In such industries, important suppliers are often collaborators with the client company in the innovation process. Supplier innovations can strengthen the positions of growth companies or help slow the erosion of those losing global competitiveness.

J. Morris Weinberg started his company, Fibronics International, in 1977 to manufacture devices for fiber optic data transmission. To avoid competing with the giants like AT&T, Hughes, and Fujitsu, who were rushing into the fast-growing market, he staked out a niche: Today, he is the leading supplier of fiber optic links between mainframe computers, peripheral devices, telephones and security alarm controls with $13 million sales and $1 million profits in 1984. New applications for fiber optics are improving factory automation systems, among other things.[33]

Creating markets for innovations Big businesses that don't wish to make a commitment to commercial development of a proprietary technology or product developed in their labs sometimes encourage entrepreneurs to license the product from them in the hope that they will be able to pioneer a market for it. If the entrepreneur succeeds he gets rich—and the corporation profits by having a customer.

This is what happened at Du Pont in 1958 when Wilbert L. Gore quit his position as a research supervisor to go into business for himself selling products based on Gore-Tex fabric. Gore-Tex is a waterproof, breathable, Teflon-based fabric today used in running suits, camping gear, space suits, artificial arteries, and other medical products. Gore had been on one of the Du Pont teams to devise applications for Teflon. Du Pont eventually rejected the Gore-Tex fabric as a line of commercial development. But Gore, intrigued, continued working on it as a personal moonlight venture and finally as his own business. Du Pont wasn't happy to lose a scientist like Gore, but it was happy indeed to have his rapidly growing company as a customer for Teflon.[34]

Gore-Tex' beginnings weren't smooth. It finally found its first application through a sale to a struggling tentmaker. All the established tentmakers had rejected it, ostensibly because none of the chief competitors was using it. Small businesses are often more receptive to trying a little-known product and sometimes provide the important first toeholds in a market. In this way, small business serves as a secondary business market for innovations that can't crack primary markets in which they might be most efficiently applied.

Opening distribution channels Small business, by virtue of its importance in the distribution sectors of the economy, is an important conduit of innovation. This will be discussed in the next chapter.

Reallocating assets Through the winnowing process of creative destruction, small businesses reallocate assets from slow-growth to fast-growth industries, and from unsuccessful entrepreneurs into the hands of successful ones. This reward system, as author George Gilder emphasizes in his writings on entrepreneurship, tends to add momentum to the innovation process since it puts more investment capital at the disposal of those most likely to undertake successful enterprises in the future.[35]

Providing big business fast entry to new markets By being acquired, small business provides a ready means for big business to gain a leading position in promising markets. In 1983, the banner year for small high-tech companies on Wall Street, large businesses paid high price/earnings multiples to acquire 49 small venture capital-funded companies.[36] In 1984 and the first half of 1985, with high-technology stocks out of favor on Wall Street, lower stock prices have accelerated the acquisition process. Many small firms, unable to get the financing needed to market their innovations entries, have sold out at fire-sale prices.

Acquisitions also offer large corporations a quick, relatively low-cost method for plugging technical proficiency gaps in its own operations. As product life cycles shrink due to technological obsolescence in fast-changing industries, acquisition is sometimes cheaper and faster than developing a new technology internally. Even IBM, unable to develop in-house the telecommunications technology needed to grow as rapidly as it believes it must to keep up with the convergence of telecommunications and computers, has gone against ingrained corporate traditions to make several strategic acquisitions.

New Innovation Links Between Small and Big Business

In the last several years, an important new trend has emerged in the direct linkages between big and small enterprise. Rather than acquire full control of a couple of small companies, large corporations are buying noncontrolling interest in many promising firms. The new approach leaves the entrepreneur-manager in charge. This circumvents the classic problem of management controls of the large corporation, causing the founding entrepreneurs and key employees to bridle and sometimes quickly depart, often killing the entrepreneurial dynamism that had made the acquisition originally attractive and leaving the large corporations with little more than a hollow shell. For instance, Exxon can attest to the full range of problems in its failed $2 billion effort to diversify into the office equipment business through several small business acquisitions.[33]

The new strategy also allows the big business to spread its bets across several promising technological approaches concurrently. In industries with rapid product obsolescence, there often isn't time to develop a technology internally and such investments represent very inexpensive extensions of the R&D program. Having a big business patron, meanwhile, provides the small firm with financing, technical, and marketing assistance.

In effect, by this new strategy big business is institutionalizing a method to buffer the risks of the innovation process through small business. In a sense, it is a method to reduce innovation to a routine—not, however, as Schumpeter foresaw 40 years ago by obviating the entrepreneurial function, but by systematically joining it at a strategic point that complements big business' efficiency. If the new relationship proves viable, it could become a strategic component of the free-market-oriented American solution to the new economics.

In 1984, big corporations had 200 investments in small companies financed by venture capital.[38] In 1979, there were only 30.[39] About 50 corporations formalized their direct venture investment programs by 1985—a number that had doubled in three years. In the first half of the 1980s, the number of big corporations making investments through general venture capital funds, meanwhile, had increased sixfold to 150.[40]

Most of the investors are large U.S. corporations. But the trend has quickly turned global, with European corporations such as Olivetti and Siemens, and several Japanese giants forging strategic links with small U.S. firms. Small foreign firms have also received investments from multinational corporations.

The goals of these strategic alliances vary in each case. In older industries, many large corporations are looking for ways to rejuvenate their fortunes with future growth opportunities. Other strategic alliances are intended to strengthen a big corporation's technical virtuosity, or to gain access to an expertise it may lack. Some investments have the very pragmatic short-term aim of protecting a key vendor, such as IBM's $6 million investment in Sytek, which makes local area networks for the IBM PC.[41] Several major corporations enter these alliances to provide experimental alternatives or extensions to their in-house R&D.

In still other cases, it is an insurance policy intended to provide a corporation with an early warning if a breakthrough is about to be made which will make obsolete existing products. Gene Amdahl was able to obtain lavish big business financing for his ill-fated Trilogy start-up in 1980 for this reason. Amdahl, as designer of the IBM 360 and founder of Amdahl Corporation, had heavyweight credentials of success computer companies could hardly afford to ignore. Thus, he had little difficulty getting such computer giants as Sperry and Digital Equipment to pony up $40 million and $24 million for 16 and 9 percent stakes, respectively, in his venture to make a mainframe computer using large-scale integrated circuits that would be four times faster than the standard-setting IBM mainframe. By 1984 it had run into numerous technological snags. The cost of its development program was soaring. Sperry and Digital wrote off $30 million and $20 million of their investments. Neither, of course, was mortally injured by losing such unthreatening sums. The insurance policy was probably well worth the risk of becoming a me-too competitor if Trilogy had succeeded.[42]

Most of the strategic alliances include licensing rights to the investor in the event that an innovative breakthrough is made. In emerging industries where no technology has yet emerged as the industry standard, such as the robotics industry, investing in several firms is a way of hedging the risks and possibly stealing a march on competitors when a standard does emerge. Holding a significant minority stake, of course, leaves the large corporation well-positioned to acquire all of the small company should its innovation become attractive enough.

Finally, some corporations, such as Control Data, 3M, and United Technologies, make equity investments in new companies founded by former managers who are attempting to exploit technologies the large corporation has developed but doesn't want to commercialize itself. In such cases, the corporation may be effectively financing pioneers to go out and develop markets for technologies it may decide to exploit later.

The new strategic alliances between large corporations and small companies first appeared around 1980 in the high-tech fields of computers, telecommunications, and pharmaceuticals. It has since spread to industrial and service corporations hoping to exploit nontechnical growth areas.

Limits to Small Business Innovation

There are several stages in the innovation process that small business, by virtue of its economic characteristics, cannot be of great assistance in enhancing U.S. competitiveness. In these stages only big business and the government can make a major impact.

Large, high-risk or long-term R&D projects Because it lacks the financial resources, small business plays a small role in basic scientific R&D. When basic R&D is especially risky or the projects too large, even big business often shies away. In such cases, government involvement, either by financing the research or by guaranteeing markets, is often required. Long-term, expensive investments, such as the commercial development of space, or earth-sized research projects to build telecommunications networks where paybacks may take a decade, are well beyond the capacities of small business.

Product and systems standardization Rarely can small business set a commercial technological standard for an innovative product or technique. Lack of a technological standard as, say, in the competition between VHS and Beta videocassette recorder formats, creates confusion and can slow market development. It can even hurt national competitiveness. Once corporations of another nation have a common technological standard they can quickly build economies of scale production and sell to so many customers as to set standards for the nations where companies are still fighting the standardization battle at home. At that point, the competitive global battle is all but over.

In other industrialized nations, the governments often mediate to set standards in order to prevent standardization bottlenecks. In the United States, competition often makes the choice. But market competition can be inefficient, because it often slows the evolution of economies of scale. The lack of standardization problem is most acute when the market is pioneered by scores of small businesses, each with limited market clout, and when technologies are as complicated and interdependent as they are today.

In the strategic factory automation industry, for example, where this country trails Japanese corporations, highly automated and powerful machines still cannot talk to each other in an integrated system. General Motors is attempting to use its prestige and market strength to pioneer a coordinating management information system standard, MAP (manufacturing automation protocol), that would become the benchmark for manufacturing systems in the United States.

Small Business and Labor Innovation

Enhancing U.S. productivity is directly linked to finding new ways to motivate the white-collar and blue-collar work force. Although labor reform is normally associated with big business (and working condition violations are far more common at small companies),* in recent years small business has also contributed significantly to the restructuring of traditional work relationships. Big businesses are adopting some of the reforms.

Independent steel minimills have led the way with productivity-linked bonuses that can add 50 to 100 percent to managers' and workers' compensations. Minimill pioneer Nucor pays a large chunk of the cost incurred by an employee in sending his

* A recent reminder of the squalid conditions that exist at some small companies was the 1985 sentencing of three former executives of Film Recovery Systems, a silver recycling plant, to 25 years in prison for the murder of an illegal Polish immigrant who died from inhaling hazardous cyanide fumes while working at the plant.[43]

child to college. The minimills also pioneered in the application of the flexible manufacturing process techniques the Japanese have used to build their manufacturing production advantage. Management structures were always kept lean at the cost-conscious minis—even today, Nucor, a $750 million company (still a trace element by steel industry standards) has only 16 people at corporate headquarters and only three management layers—general manager, department head, and foreman—between the chairman and the shop floor.[44]

The most significant small business labor innovation has been the compensation of key employees with company equity or profit-sharing inducements. Glyn Bostick, president of $5 million Microwave Filter of East Syracuse, New York, for example, had little hope of holding his experienced engineers at a top salary of only $20,000 a year—all his cash flow would allow—while at GE their counterparts were earning $30,000. So he made up the difference with stock options and can hold the engineers he needs.

In the current fad for entrepreneurship, generous stock transfers (as well as other personal considerations, such as permitting scientist-executives to retain their academic associations) have proven so popular that big corporations in high-tech industries are regularly losing their top technicians to small, upstart firms. The trend is so pronounced in Silicon Valley that some start-ups can even lease furnishings and buy supplies by trading stock or warrants! Employee ownership participation exists in die-casting shops, steel foundries, airlines, bakeries, advertising agencies, industrial equipment suppliers, publishing companies, and radio stations.[45]

Many stock ownership plans have been extended beyond a handful of key personnel to entire company staffs. The most common form of employee ownership programs today are Employee Stock Ownership Plans, or ESOPs. Some 7,000 of them covering 8 percent of the work force have been set up through 1984 (although only 10 to 15 percent confer majority ownership on the employees and less than half of those pass through voting rights). Perhaps one-third to one-half of all ESOPs are set up by the owners of small, private companies to sell their companies. Some also use ESOPs for ulterior purposes, such as to replace a pension plan.

Captivated by the resurgence of the entrepreneurial spirit, many large corporate executives are experimenting with ways to make their bureaucracies behave more like independent small businesses. One popular scheme is intracorporate entrepreneurship, or "intrapreneurship." In one form or another "intrapreneurs" are given seed capital, increased freedom, and an incentive structure to try to grow new businesses unshackled by the usual bureaucracy. In a characteristic program, a corporation that earns $5 million from a project championed by an intrapreneur would allot him a 10 percent share, but only say, $50,000 in cash. The rest would be seed "money" he could spend on future projects within the company. Thus, he would have incentive to stay at the company to use the "capital" instead of going out on his own or bolting to a small company offering equity. 3M, GE, and IBM are among the blue-chip pioneers of intrapreneurship.

Will intrapreneurship be a passing vogue that disappears with the current fad for entrepreneurship? It is too early to say. Among the skeptics are Harold Geneen, the man who built ITT into a multibillion-dollar conglomerate. He writes, "Where, people ask, are our corporate entrepreneurs? The answer is: There are none."

Geneen thinks big business entrepreneurship schemes are a vogue. Among the obstacles Geneen sees in making big corporations truly entrepreneurial: To make it to the top of a large corporation an executive needs to make five brilliant moves, but for that he needs peer support and alliances which minimize risk-taking as much as possible; the salary structures of large corporations are very delicate and can't easily accommodate intrapreneurs; the spirit of entrepreneurship is to make careful but often big bets—big businesses can generally only do so when they are in dire straits.

Geneen believes that the true entrepreneurs will leave the big corporations once they get enough experience and cash, just as they always have. They will continue to outthink, outplan, and outhustle the corporate man on salary.[46] Intrapreneurship, although it may have salutary effects on business organization, will not be the vehicle that finally usurps the small businessman's entrepreneurial function.

Other current large corporation efforts to restructure management hierarchies toward less division of labor and toward greater integration, and to give more responsibility and pecuniary incentive to managers closer to the front lines, are inspired partly by the model of small business. Kollmorgen Corporation, for example, solved its problem competing against small, mom-and-pop-type printed circuit-board suppliers essentially by emulating them: It dissolved its unified products group into five smaller units, each with its own manager to oversee a private sales force as well as product. It made no logical sense to duplicate jobs, of course—but it worked because it speeded up communication between sales and manufacturing. It had been losing business because by the time the salesman in the field had conferred with its regional and divisional sales managers to schedule an order, the mom-and-pop competitors had frequently already made and delivered the boards.[47]

Future U.S. Innovation

The small business contribution to the innovation process has received prodigious impetus since the start of the 1980s from the substantial venture capital industry that has surged into prominence since the 1979 change liberalizing pension fund investment rules, and the two-stage lowering of the capital gains tax from 49 percent before 1978 to 20 percent in the mid-1980s, the lowest rate since 1937. Pension funds accounted for one-third of all venture capital contributed to independent U.S. venture capital funds in the seven years through 1984.

The modern venture capital industry in America is often dated to 1938 when the Rockefellers put up the funds to convert a troubled division of General Motors into Eastern Airlines with Captain Eddie Rickenbacker at the controls. VenRock also helped J. S. McDonnell get his McDonnell Aircraft Corporation off the ground. But even 20 years ago the venture-capital industry amounted to little more than a curiosity in U.S. finance.

Buoyed by such 1970s venture-capital successes as Federal Express and Apple Computer, venture capitalists, looking for three or four winners and one huge killing for every ten investments (and taking 40 to 45 percent of the stock for early stage financing) have caused venture capital to flood to sexy, high-tech, and, more recently, no-tech companies. By 1985, there were over 500 venture-capital funds with some $16 billion in committed funds, up from

$2.5 billion in 1977. Additional venture funds were being invested informally by successful businessmen.

When successfully invested, venture capital can make a powerful economic impact: A U.S. government survey of 72 firms financed partly with $209 million in venture capital, had cumulative sales in a decade of $6 billion, created 130,000 new jobs, rang up $900 million in export sales, and netted the government $450 million in tax payments.[48]

The venture-capital boom has had its destructive side, too. In retrospect, the high-tech shakeout in the mid-1980s was probably exacerbated by the flood of venture capital into high-tech start-ups. It wasted human and capital resources by financing many more me-too companies than were needed for the creative destruction winnowing process. A little less venture capital may have made surviving U.S. companies more competitive on the world market.

Gordon Moore of Intel, who has seen profitability disappear from his industry and his company, observes:

> The venture capital boom was probably a net positive. But it got way overblown. Venture capital seems to go from too little to too much. Since 1979, the amount of venture capital has far exceeded what could have efficiently exploited the new ideas. The result was that talent was spread way too thin. A lot of investments were duplicated several times over.[49]

In no other country has small business played such a prominent role in the innovation process than in the United States. One of the country's major competitive advantages in the current transition is in the design of software products, where small companies with a few creative individuals are the driving force. This is important because in software lies a key to manipulating and integrating the power of the new technologies in the most productive ways.

Innovative use of many of the new technologies requires relatively more "knowledge" and relatively less capital than in the past. This is encouraging for innovation by small business, which is chronically short of capital. For example, the spread of CAE/CAD/CAM systems seems likely to bring more power and extended reach to the small company design engineers. The trend toward market segmentation, if it continues, will provide an abundance of small niche commercial opportunities to spur still further innovation efforts.

Envious of the increased competitiveness that small business innovation has provided the United States, Western European nations and Japan have taken measures to encourage independent entrepreneurs and to stimulate the formation of venture capital.

The ability of an economic system to select the most competitive technologies from the myriad uncertain alternatives is likely, in the new economic era, to be a key to competitive success. In a national economy largely sheltered from international competition, an inferior technological choice may not be severely penalized. But in a global economy, each nation's choice—and the economic system which led to that choice—is subjected to fierce competition.

So far, European policies, which worked well in the postwar period, are struggling. The current transition may be exposing a weakness, namely, a difficulty in adapting to major change, in the successful postwar European capitalism. Although Japan's industrial policies have thus far adapted extremely well, some Japanese companies have criticized the government for narrowing the technological choices too quickly. Doing so may have involved less risk when Japan was climbing the development ladder on technologies that were already fairly well understood. In the new technologies, however, where Japanese, U.S., and European researchers are charting new knowledge at the same time, Japan has yet to prove its government-assisted approach can continue to consistently pick winners as well or better than the European or the U.S. systems.

By injecting aggressive, free market forces into the modern economy, small business permits the "invisible hand" to play an important part in selecting those innovations upon which America will compete in the new global marketplace. Future U.S. competitiveness will hinge in part on whether America's traditional free-market-oriented capitalism can produce and exploit innovations that are as good or better than those chosen by "plan-oriented" capitalist Japan and the "guided" capitalist countries of Europe.

5

Small Business
and Economic Diversity

The heyday of Cairo, Illinois, a once strategically located, thriving port on the Mississippi and Ohio rivers, belongs to a bygone era of transportation technology. There isn't much left now but a handful of stores on a dusty main thoroughfare, one company with 300 employees and a few others with a lot less, and 6,127 residents, many of whom are unemployed. Until recently it was also serviced by a couple of unprofitable freight-hauling railroad lines. Not surprisingly, when deregulatory railroad legislation made it easier for large railroads to unload unprofitable track, Conrail, the owner of the 160-mile branch line running from Mount Carmel to Cairo, put it up for sale to bidders, if there were any. Across the country, other large railroads were doing the same. It seemed a rotten deal for struggling towns like Cairo, but just as rail transportation had superseded riverboat shipping, trucks, traveling federally built, toll-free interstate highway systems, had long been winning the most profitable share of the freight shipping business from railroads.

Three men who faced immediate personal crises from Conrail's abandonment of the Cairo line were Bill Mowatt, Bill Cecil, and Dick Hockgeiger. They were railroadmen who

141

had worked on the line for most of their lifetimes. Conrail gave the men a choice—either they could be transferred to another location far away from their homes, or they could be unemployed.

Neither alternative was appealing. So instead they bought a piece of the Cairo line themselves. The story is not as unique as it sounds: In the first 12 years of deregulation, large railroads have sold about 160 freight-hauling short lines, with an average length of 28 miles each, to individual operators. About 30 had failed. But many of the others, including the Cairo Terminal Railroad, were being run at modest profits by individuals who never imagined they might one day become railroad entrepreneurs.

To try to preserve local rail service in the face of deregulation, the federal and state governments devised financial assistance programs for small businessmen who bought short lines. The Cairo trio, however, financed the purchase themselves. They took out second mortgages on their homes, and together came up with $135,000 to buy two rebuilt diesel locomotives, an old lime-colored caboose, and eight miles of worn track in Cairo. They invested another $15,000 to rehabilitate the long-neglected track. In 1982, the Cairo Terminal Railroad was in business. The very first day, one of the locomotives jumped the track. The trio had it back up and running a few hours later. But their potential customers weren't so sure that the tiny line Conrail had unloaded to three employees would be running for long.

To help persuade them to give Cairo Terminal a try, Mowatt, Cecil, and Hockgeiger set rates that were below that of local truckers. They could do so because it cost them 75 percent less than it cost Conrail to run the line. The big savings was on labor. Unlike Conrail, Cairo Terminal had no high-priced engineers to pay, no union rules to deal with, no fringe benefit costs. They had but three full-time workers—themselves—and an occasional couple of part-timers. The Cairo trio, like other independent short lines around the country, were ready to give personalized service.

This combination helped them get their first customer, Burkart Foam, Inc., a $25 million automotive and commercial parts manufacturer with 300 employees and by far Cairo's largest business. Burkart's business depended on buying scrap foam. It converted the foam into material for the underside of carpets. Then it shipped it out to customers. Shipping in sufficient quantities of scrap foam by truck, however, was too costly for Burkart to turn much of a profit. Occasionally, scrap shipments had to be made on short notice and at odd hours. The Cairo Terminal trio were happy to oblige.

Cairo Terminal's revenues its first year were $98,000, and the railroad broke even. There wasn't enough money for any of the three partners to draw salaries, and that year they lived off their savings. In 1983, another large railroad, the Illinois Central Gulf Railroad, decided to follow Conrail and drop its 17.5 mile branch out of Cairo. The three partners bid for it. The total cost was close to $1 million. The Illinois state government provided loans of $740,000, using the line's assets as security, and provided them an outright grant of $180,000 to rehabilitate the track. They borrowed another $55,000 from shippers who used the line, and who had a vested interest in keeping it operative. Along with the new short line came two paying customers. Rather than add employees they couldn't afford, the three men began working longer hours—18-hour workdays became common.

The new line presented another problem, however. Cairo Terminal's original short line was connected to the new short line by 4.5 miles of track that Illinois Central Gulf didn't want to sell. Thus, each time a Cairo Terminal train passed the 4.5 mile stretch, it had to pay a right-of-way charge to ICG. Like other short-line railroads around the country, Cairo Terminal was dependent on good relations with a larger railroad with the power, at any time, to drive it out of business. As a result, one of the Cairo trio, Mowatt, began spending a great deal of time practicing PR on ICG executives. In March 1984 Cairo Terminal obtained a lease to operate an additional 18.5 miles of track that the Missouri Pacific Railroad was planning to abandon.

The work is hard for the three partners, who between them have over 100 years of railroad experience. Although they try to rotate jobs in an egalitarian spirit, each tends to concentrate on the work he does best. Cecil, with the longest experience as an engineer, normally captains the locomotive; Hockgeiger manages the hitching and mans the switches; Mowatt is the business manager. Yet when the situation demands, all three work side by side. During a cold stretch in the winter of 1983, for example, they were all out on the line in the dead of night trying to prevent one of the locomotives and some switches from freezing by wrapping foam rubber around the pipes of the engine and pouring alcohol on the switches. Head offices for the Cairo Terminal is in the back of a florist shop in Cairo. During the week, the men live in Cairo. Friday evenings they drive 135 miles to their homes in Mount Carmel to spend the weekends with their families.

In 1984, with its additional track and additional customers, Cairo Terminal revenues reached $289,000 and the company was sufficiently in the black for the partners to pay themselves a modest salary. In 1985, they were anticipating revenues of $400,000.

The town of Cairo, and the railroad's small business customers along the line who depend on its low rates and services to protect their profitability, were pulling for them.[1]

The small business economy alone is inadequate to respond competitively to the current economic transition. Alone, small business cannot efficiently make huge R&D investments in sophisticated technologies, or provide rapid, large-scale production and global distribution. Nor, alone, can it provide the stable economic, social, and ecological environment necessary for successful management of a complex modern economic system. Yet the diversity small business provides a broad and flexible base in which the basic industrial superstructure is embedded. As such, it fulfills indispensable complementary roles with big business, government, and labor unions to enhance the U.S. economy's international competitiveness. By being so responsive to market condition changes and government economic programs, and by being a uniquely domestic resource in an economy dominated by multinationals with increasingly blurry national allegiances, it is playing a strategic role in forming the future shape of the national and regional economies.

Small Business Supplier Links

Large corporations in virtually all industries are extensively interlinked with the small business economy through a diverse network of suppliers, subcontractors, and distributors which extend and augment its efficiency. Automakers, in a tightly oligopolistic industry, for example, depend on 30,000 suppliers and nearly 25,000 auto dealers—a great number of them small—to penetrate the remotest regions of the U.S. marketplace.

The use of outside suppliers and subcontractors helps manage the problem of mass-production industries described by Andrew Carnegie by shifting some of the risk of demand fluctuations to its smaller adjuncts and thereby optimizing big industry's capacity utilization. In downturns, it cuts back orders from the outside suppliers and subcontractors, or squeezes them for price concessions—rarely so severely, however, as to jeopardize their survival: The competitive pressure they exert on prices—and their ability to produce for extra demand—are needed to optimally manage in boom times.

Outside suppliers and subcontractors also provide the large corporation with a rare opportunity to fix relatively predictable costs in its budget planning. It also alleviates some of the organizational headaches of big companies to be able to farm out tangential operations.

Reliance on dependable outside suppliers enhances large corporations maneuverability in responding to shifting international economic conditions by providing options on cost and quality. In the 1984 auto labor negotiations with GM which produced the landmark agreement, United Auto Workers' President Owen Bieber declared the elimination of "outsourcing"— the growing use of outside, often nonunion, suppliers—to be on par with job protection as the UAW's top objective. Bieber won on job protection. But he bowed to GM's demand for maintaining the flexibility outsourcing proved to compete internationally.

Large corporations also use outside suppliers to produce the specialty or high-quality parts they cannot produce as well themselves. In these instances, the outside supplier directly boosts the large company's competitiveness.

In the current economic transition, big U.S. corporations—following the trend of big foreign corporations as well—have placed greater emphasis on the importance of their supplier relationships as they experiment with strategies to improve their global competitiveness. Above all, corporations are looking to their supplier networks to improve manufacturing productivity.

Xerox now consults with its suppliers at the earliest stages of the development process to try to shorten the time it takes to get from design to production—one of America's major competitive disadvantages against the Japanese. Northrop, which used 64 million pieces of equipment or parts in 1983, has begun lending teams of its own employees at no cost to suppliers with quality problems with the caveat that they invest all labor savings in computer-controlled equipment to help them meet Northrop's specifications. This program has helped cut Northrop's component rejection rate from 3 to 2 percent for a savings of $11 million.[2]

Experiments with Japanese Just-in-Time (JIT) inventory methods rely heavily on closer supplier-producer coordination. Under JIT, components arrive from the supplier just before they are needed. This can significantly reduce inventory, and liberate capital for more productive investments. But for the system to work, the components must be delivered on time and with a very low rejection rate, lest it create production bottlenecks.

Greater use of an outside supplier network in fast-changing markets or those where high quality is essential is providing large corporations with the strategic flexibility to stay on top of the flows of the global market. General Motors' experimental Saturn car project will rely on outside suppliers for about 80 percent of its components in an effort to boost its productivity and close the huge gap with Japanese car makers. This is a significant reversal of GM manufacturing strategy, which has traditionally focused on producing most of its own parts in-house, and does so for about 70 percent of current vehicle needs.[3] Throughout industry, large corporations are able to deverticalize their in-house production system—retaining only the most profitable and secure links in the vertical chain—because there are small suppliers ready and capable of taking over the links it abandons.

In order to guarantee that its products' technological quality is up to world standards and to guarantee it maximum flexibility in rapidly obsoleting new technology markets, Ing. C. Olivetti, the international-minded Italian office machines company with whom AT&T established an international alliance in 1984 by purchasing a 25 percent equity stake, buys only up to half its components from its captive in-house suppliers—the rest the suppliers must sell competitively on the outside market. Olivetti's second-ranking executive, Elserino Piol, joint managing director for strategic planning, explains the company's supplier strategy:

We have a fully owned captive supplier of certain computer peripherals, but it is up to the inside Olivetti manager responsible for assembly to find the best parts. If it's from the inside supplier, fine. But we'll buy only up to 50 percent, to get the best price on half the supply. And the rest we'll buy outside, even at a higher price.

Vertical integration is desirable, but only up to the point it makes you inflexible. The more unstable a market is the more you want to use outside suppliers. The more stable it is, generally the more you want to do it inside. In an industry like ours which is in rapid technological and market change, the name of the game is flexibility.[4]

Whether a multinational corporation chooses to manufacture in America over a foreign location depends in part on how well small business suppliers themselves adapt to the new economics of rapid technological obsolescence and shorter periods of return on investment. U.S. suppliers must stand ready to change their mix of goods rapidly and upgrade quality if they are to hold their clients and the United States is to be attractive as a manufacturing base.

One successful supplier is Stahl Specialty Company, an aluminum foundry in Missouri, which has been run by Glenn Stahl for over 40 years. These days one-quarter of the aluminum castings market is supplied by offshore companies. The market severely contracted in the early 1980s. Yet Stahl's sales continued to grow from $24 million to $41 million by 1984, and employment reached 520 because he kept up with changing technology and the market evolution of his customers. A decade ago, most of the company's sales were unsophisticated parts for lawnmowers and barbecue grills. That business has moved offshore.

Had Stahl stayed with them, his business would have been in trouble. Instead, his main business today includes sophisticated castings for IBM storage drives, and engine parts and brake cylinders for the farm machinery and auto industry—items requiring a consistent, high quality that low-wage foreign suppliers can't match—which he turns out with the help of a dozen state-of-the-art numerically controlled machine tools, and a $400,000 CAD/CAM system.[5] Indeed, one restraint on the growth of domestic and foreign company auto production in otherwise attractive low-wage countries like South Korea and Taiwan is the absence of a developed components supply industry.

Small business suppliers foster the rapid development of future high-tech industries by rushing into fast-growing markets to fill supply niches. This helps guarantee component quality and alleviates bottlenecks that can easily result from the unevenness of rapid growth. An extensive supplier network, where components and services can be purchased as needed, reduces the cost of industry entry, confounds efforts by established companies to gain preferential access to supplies, and thus facilitates competition. In Silicon Valley and Massachusetts' Route 128, suppliers have clustered around the computer companies, making it possible for them—and new entrants—to buy inexpensively everything they need to do business except the engineering inspiration and the personal drive; plastic moldings, precision casting, or renting time on expensive machines that design microchips to be manufactured in a "silicon foundry." The same is true in biotechnology, thanks to the proliferation of independent small firms performing every function from toxicology testing to actual drug manufacturing.

Even IBM broke with its company traditions and its preferences when it turned to outside suppliers for a range of components so that it could rapidly enter the PC market. Recently, market pioneer Apple increased its ties with hardware and software suppliers in order to upgrade the technical virtuosity of its Macintosh to provide stiffer competition against the mounting dominance of IBM.

Corporations that compete in highly specialized or customized product markets often receive significant competitive advantages by relying on suppliers rather than producing themselves—above all as standardized product markets have segmented. PACCAR, Inc., a closely held $2 billion family company, has become by far the country's most profitable maker of heavy duty Class 8 trucks under its Peterbilt and Kenworth trademarks by this means. The family, which had been making railcars for many years, decided to get into the truck business in 1945. For a small company, the cheapest and fastest way in was as an assembler buying outside components. In contrast to its heavyweight competitors, which included Ford, GM, and International Harvester, which do their own manufacturing, PACCAR carved a niche in the high end of the market where customers could special order custom-built trucks. Because it was buying outside components, it always got the best of what its suppliers had available. Unlike its competitors, it could provide a myriad of options. Most important of all, it also could stop ordering during cyclic downturns without being devastated due to high fixed overhead. During the very sharp downturn at the start of the 1980s caused by the recession and trucking deregulation (which resulted in more efficient truckload usage, and hence fewer new truck orders), PACCAR came through without suffering a single quarterly loss. Meanwhile, the use of CAD/CAM has enhanced PACCAR's custom-building capabilities. In an industry in flux due to deregulation, PACCAR has gained share from its supplier-derived flexibility.[6]

Small Business Distribution Links

Small businesses, of course, have also historically played a principal role in the distribution side of the economic production-distribution equation. Big business spends billions of dollars trying to influence demand, but such expenditures would be wasteful without an efficient distribution network to deliver the goods as promised.

Economists and businessmen have grown accustomed to seeking improvements in productivity mainly on the production side of the economy. In the future, as the new epochal technologies are applied to distribution—in everything from computer catalog purchasing to electronic reading of grocery prices to speed checkout and improve accuracy—the distribution side may become an important source of productivity gains.

How? Mainly in a complementary fashion. In the technological upheaval at the end of the nineteenth century, it was the emergence of channels of mass distribution along with the new technology which helped to make mass production, and the great productivity gains that it brought, possible. Today's information technologies may provide a similar boon.

The rapid distribution of innovation has a triple benefit to U.S. productivity: (1) It allows the companies commercializing the innovation to quickly penetrate markets and maximize return on investment; (2) It quickly plants productivity advantages seeded in the innovation among customers who use it; (3) Since in many of the new information technologies knowledge compounds upon the experience of others, wide dissemination builds a momentum for further productivity-enhancing innovation.

One of this country's built-in competitive advantages is its large domestic market. Just as it helped U.S. mass-production industries build the world's most efficient economies of scale, it now provides the world's most powerful launching pad for rapidly building market share in the global competition. When Apple pioneered the first desktop PC, there was at first no distribution system to reach—and educate—the user public. The bigger computers, being big-ticket, specialized investments, had generally been sold through direct sales calls on target clients. That was economical with expensive computers, but not with PCs. The development of the PC market would have been retarded—and the competitive lead of U.S. companies may have been lost—had not an easily penetrable retail network, dominated by small businesses, sprung up as the PC explosion hit. In mid-1984, small business retailers, including franchises, represented 71.2 percent of all computer outlets.[7] The absence of such a responsive distribution network has slowed the development of the PC market in Europe.

It also, however, slowed IBM's market domination there, which has given Big Blue's European competitors some breathing space to try to catch up. Indeed, a nation may in fact receive a competitive advantage by having an efficient, small-business-dominated distribution network rather than one dominated by large companies. Why? A distribution network dominated by mass marketers opens the door to the U.S. market equally to foreign and domestic producers. It creates competitive parity where formerly the domestic producer held an advantage by virtue of his familiarity, proximity, and access to the distributors and retailers needed to successfully penetrate the market. The buffer against easy foreign penetration that small, local distributors provide has disappeared. For example, many of the foreign-made garments purchased here are sold by giants such as Sears, J. C. Penney, and K-Mart. They shop globally for their goods. In 1983, they imported a combined $5.2 billion in foreign-made goods, some of which could have been produced in this country by U.S. workers at only slightly higher cost. If they hadn't been such a magnet for foreign manufacturers due to their size and easy approachability, many of the goods they sold would have been U.S.-made. The result, as in the case of the textile industry, is fuller exposure to the global economy and often the hastened decline of older industries.

The same situation does not exist in many of the other industrialized competitor nations. In many, the continued dominance of small retailers, protected by legislation from more efficient mass retailers, insulates the market against full exposure to goods imported from abroad. The mom-and-pop shops which dominate Japan's retailing industry are protected by a law giving small stores a large degree of veto power over the expansion of competitive large retail stores. The law put an immediate halt to the rapid expansion of Japan's chain stores— and halted the progress of foreign retail imports, of which the large retailers are the main importers. Because the large retailers are limited in number and buy according to standard practices of international business, an onerous effort is not needed to sell to them. Not so small retailers. Their numbers, and cultural obstacles, make them difficult to reach. Personal ties, rather than the universals of cost efficiency, are more likely to affect their willingness to buy. Collection can be a nightmare. Thus U.S. manufacturers have a very difficult time penetrating the Japanese market, which is often left to less efficient domestic producers. As a result, U.S. trade officials and big Japanese retailers have become strange bedfellows in teaming up to petition MITI to alter the law.[8]

The small retailers in these cases, to be sure, are less efficient than the large ones. The cost of protecting them is potentially high: slower dissemination of productivity-enhancing goods through the economy, and higher inflation. Nevertheless, the phenomenon does intriguingly reveal that in a global economy an extensive small business distribution network (large franchises excluded)—especially one that is efficient by world standards—may provide a short lead time or a buffer against the sometimes abrupt and painful upheavals caused by old industries migrating to other parts of the world.

Small Business and Productivity

Much attention has been devoted to the inadequacies of the common measurements of productivity.[9] The common productivity measure, total dollar value of output divided by total work hours, fails, for instance, to register product or process modifications which may improve quality unless they are marked by real price increases. The emphasis on aggregate inputs also undervalues the importance of how these resources are utilized, and how effectively the production-distribution system is organized in determining how productive the United States truly is.

By conventional statistical measures, small business, due to its greater use of labor and less of capital almost by definition appears to produce fewer productivity gains in the economy than big business. This is accurate—to a point. Excluding small or specialized market niches in which it is the most efficient economic entity, small business enhances overall U.S. productivity in an indirect manner for which it will never receive statistical credit: It undertakes the least desirable and least efficient economic functions—yet that same entity, for the greatest total productive output from the nation's economic resources, must perform.

By filling marginal demand in an industry, supplying a low-profit component, and through its high mortality pioneering role in the innovation process, it absorbs inefficiencies and risks in the economy. This protects the big-business-managed industrial structure and thus indirectly enhances big-business productivity.

By utilizing the secondary or least attractive resources of the economy—capital and human—small business is also, in very practical, if not statistical, terms, maximizing the utility of

U.S. assets. For instance, small firms in the metal fabricating and machinery-making industries have often started by renovating existing buildings and adapting used machinery or equipment. Numerous small businesses start with used furniture. The alternative, in many cases, is not being able to afford to start up at all.

When large mining companies abandon coal mines from which they can no longer profitably use their heavy machinery to extract coal, they often lease small pits to one or two miners who dig out the remaining coal using light tools and a great deal of hard, manual labor. Their measured productivity is far below that of the machinery-driven operations of the large mining companies. But in practical terms, would it be better to leave the remaining coal unmined in the pits?

Repair services and the remanufacturing industry, overwhelmingly small company businesses, also plainly prolong the productive life of existing machines. Repair services have been especially important in the last decade of slow growth by adding life to old equipment and products.

Jobs are another example. Had small businesses produced fewer jobs in the past decade the country's measured productivity rate would have been higher. But so would its unemployment rate. This is precisely what happened in Western Europe. Yet high unemployment is hardly a desirable goal of public policy or, to plain common sense, productive.

Use of a part-time work force also often maximizes the use of human capital. Many new electronic data processing service businesses in New York City were able to start up or expand in the industry's early years by hiring fully employed specialists at night or on weekends to help them solve particular problems without taking on an onerous payroll burden.[10]

The smallest businesses usually have fewer assets per worker than large corporations, but they derive higher sales per dollar of assets in most sectors than all but the giant corporations—in other words, they get more production by better motivating or, alternatively, by sweating labor. Sweating labor may offend our social conscience. Yet, in strictly economic terms, it is merely a form of maximizing the resources of the environment under given conditions. Were economic conditions better, sweating labor would not be easily done—the employees would move on to less abusive jobs.

Overall, these small business activities may add little to the apparent productivity gains of the economy. But they do get fuller use out of human resources, and often make the difference in creating viable small enterprises which add flexibility and balance to the economy.

A significant characteristic of small business' lower manufacturing productivity in recent years is that it appears to be less due to the economies of larger production size at any single plant than to other organizational efficiencies of large-scale organization—marketing, access to cheaper capital, and buying and selling power, for example. Until plant sizes actually began to shrink in the 1970s, it had long been suggested that many industrial plants were being operated at larger than optimum size. A recent Hay Management study found that productivity in groups of under 600 workers was up to 50 percent greater than in groups of over 4,500.[11]

In comparable-sized plants, small business may be more productive than large U.S. corporations. This is due to the intangible, human motivation element and family atmosphere which pervades many small companies. Organization of people on a large scale is usually impersonal and often deters motivation. Throughout most of the mass-production management era this problem was offset by the gains of increased specialization and division of labor. Management researchers have long recognized that management attention, even if desultory, can be a boon to productivity. In the 1920s at GE's Hawthorne plant in Chicago it was discovered that the productivity of the women assembling electrical components increased simply by changing the levels of room lights—whether brighter or dimmer. At small companies, like the experience at the Robinson-Nugent machine shop, the pace and discipline of work is often more attuned to the collective rhythm of the work force. In times of tension or emergency, output may surge to meet special needs or orders. Japanese corporations have understood this psychology well in promoting human interaction between management and workers.

Small Business and Inflation

Although it has fallen from its double-digit highs with slow economic growth and out of the business page headlines, inflation remains a major destabilizing threat to the economy. The U.S. inflation rate settled at below 4 percent in the mid-1980s economic recovery. But estimates of the underlying inflation rate (that is, factoring in part of the beneficial impact on prices of 1985's $150 billion surplus in imported goods due to a strong dollar), even after the tumble in oil prices run about 5 or 6 percent. That is a historically high base for a new round of hoped-for economic growth.

Several prominent economists, such as Salomon Brothers' chief economist Henry Kaufman, warn that the slow growth–high inflation "stagflation" syndrome of the 1970s and early 1980s still underlies the economy. Some believe that the growth of the service economy in industrialized nations may have created an era of inflationary capitalism where instabilities in the economy, instead of leading to downward instability of prices as in depressions, have resulted in upward price instability leading to inflation spirals.[12] Instead of having experienced another depression in the late 1970s and early 1980s, the industrialized nations suffered acute stagflation. This could recur with future downturns.

What is small business' role in inflation? In general, it suppresses it. As individually uninfluential sources of economic power, small businesses are subject to the market forces of perfect competition. Large corporations raise their prices to reflect higher raw material, supply, or union settlement costs. Other large companies accept these higher prices and pass them on to their customers. At the end of the line are small companies. Only in rare instances can they fully pass on these higher costs to their customers. This is one reason why inflationary environments are generally harder on small companies than on large ones with more power to pass along cost hikes.

To cover inflationary cost increases, small business tends to squeeze employees for more work, cut quality or, alternatively, to give better service to justify higher prices. The tendency to do the same in large, often unionized corporations is far less strong. One noted effect of the concentration of industrial assets and the emergence of oligopolistic industries in modern American capitalism has been an inflationary tendency for corporate market leaders to raise price umbrellas within their industry. Exorbitantly inflationary price-setting, and outright gouging, is restrained partly by competition from neighboring industries with substitutable technologies, the offsetting buying power of other large corporations, and increasingly by foreign competition. In some cases, small business has imposed another effective restraint.

One of the consequences of having highly visible, centralized, large corporate, labor union, and government powers which communicate cooperative intent to other large entities in the economy through such bellwether signals as the GM-UAW labor settlement or pricing patterns established by industry market leaders, is that it can rapidly fan inflationary fires. The small business economy, due to its invisibility, on the other hand, douses inflationary expectations.

Small retailers and wholesalers sometimes restrain large corporation tendencies to raise prices on the distribution side of the economy. The $7 billion gray economy represents the intrusion of the free market, via small retailers and distributors, to undermine large corporation efforts to compel customers to accept higher prices than supply warrants.

It also is a disciplining force which limits corporations from profiting from currency exchange rate differentials around the world by selling at widely different values in different countries. Take, for example, Japanese cameras. It is believed that 20 percent of the Japanese cameras sold in the United States may be gray. U.S. discounters import the cameras from foreign distributors and dealers (outside Japan) at local prices and resell them at prices well below what the Japanese-licensed U.S. distributor-dealer network can sell them for. In the mid-1970s, most gray Japanese cameras entered from Hong Kong, but Japanese manufacturers began tracing the warranty serial numbers to their sources, where they cracked down. That, however, didn't stop the flow. It merely altered its course. Today, many of the cameras come from Eastern and Western Europe. Gray-market perfumes come via Africa. [13] There is a gray market in Mercedes automobiles and semiconductors.

In some instances, discounters offer local, instead of official manufacturer, guarantees to provide the customer with a lower—

cost alternative. This is the strategy of industrial gray marketer Dan Rife of MCI Equipment, Inc. Rife imports loaders, among other construction equipment, from the subsidiary of U.S. loader companies in France. He then writes his own warranty and sells them in the United States for $85,000—$40,000 less than what the same loader costs at a Deere & Company dealership.[14]

Small distributors who dare to undercut the pricing strategies of their large corporation suppliers often risk their own extinction. In the spring of 1984, the U.S. Supreme Court upheld a $10.5 million settlement award by Monsanto to a now-defunct Midwestern agricultural chemicals distributor, Spray-Rite Service Corporation, culminating a ten-year court battle. Monsanto had refused to renew distribution rights to Spray-Rite because it was irked at its price discounting. In court, Monsanto argued that price fixing was reasonable when attempting to assure market stability and economic efficiency. The courts, however, concluded that Monsanto was simply trying to eliminate price discounters and restrain free trade.[15] Judicial and legislative directives are meaningless guardians of price competition, however, without the disciplining influence the diverse small business economy brings to specific infringements.

Small Business and Economic Equilibrium

The diversity and aggregate size of the small business economy helps offset some of the inefficiencies and distortions of free market economics that result when big economic entities—big business, labor unions, and government—dominate the marketplace. It is especially effective in sectors of the economy where entry and survival level barriers—largely a function of capitalization requirements—are not insuperably high. In these sectors, small business, in the aggregate, ensures the "invisible hand" of the market a kind of countervailing power in the economy.

Small business erases some inefficiencies caused by groups which gain advantage from political or other influence which runs strongly counter to the voice of the marketplace. Through the political influence of taxi fleet owners, the number of medallion, or licensed, yellow taxis in New York has been frozen since 1937, with the result that there aren't enough taxis to meet demand. There is constant pressure to raise fares, which are regulated. The market price for medallions has soared to $84,000 for an independent medallion and $78,000 for a fleet medallion. Public demand for more taxis is offset by backroom political lobbying by taxi owners to create a political impasse. Small business, however, has restored equilibrium in the market. Independent car services, as well as nonlicensed independent gypsy cabs (which serve poorer neighborhoods licensed cabs ignore) have sprung up to fill the void at or slightly above taxi fare rates. Companies have caught on, and large numbers of executives now move about Manhattan in telephone-reserved car services.

As seen in the case of the powerful New York typographers' union, economic power gained through labor organization, too, can be restrained by the small business economy if it loses touch with market reality.

Small business, of course, has not hesitated to use political leverage itself to obtain competitive advantage. It has done so chiefly by exercising influence where it has always been most consequential—at the state and local level—and often obfuscated behind the banner of states' rights.

Every state but Alaska has regulated the relationship between auto manufacturers and auto dealers—almost always to the advantage of the local dealers, who are often local big shots in their towns. Most common are state rules prohibiting new dealerships within a specified radius—6 miles in Michigan, 10 miles in California, and 25 miles in Texas—and making it difficult for automakers to drop poorly performing dealers. These advantages have survived to the present day, which is a major reason why dealers everywhere are cautiously watching how GM carries through on its announced plan to establish a separate dealer network for its Saturn small-car project.[16]

On balance, however, the inefficiencies small business has succeeded in creating to its own interests are relatively inconsequential—if only because small business power has been unable to stand up to the long-term trend toward centralizing political and economic power, and the adversarial interests of big business and labor unions. Small business' legislative efforts to mitigate the power of big business, such as the chain stores and the mail-order houses, which also had power in the state capitals, in Washington and in the federal court system, for example, were notably less successful.

In all countries, socialist or capitalist, small entrepreneurs respond to the most extreme cases of economic and political failure by creating underground markets. Some, such as tax avoidance, take place within legitimate businesses; others, such as prostitution, drug trafficking, and loan sharking, operate wholly underground. Under the duress of the past decade, the U.S. underground economy exploded from an estimated $100 billion to $400 billion a year—14 percent of GNP in the early 1980s. The United States was not alone. Underground economies are booming throughout the world. It is estimated that up to one-third of all self-employment in OECD countries today depends on the underground economy.

Small business diversity establishes multilayered markets between the giant corporate buyer and the individual consumer. This permits a product line to be extended easily to new markets, thus improving returns on investment. It also offers alternative markets in case of failure in a primary target market. A diversity of markets also serves the interest of many budgets and cash flows.

Despite its declining long-term economic power, the small business economy continues to be the main decentralizing force exerting restraining power on the trend toward centralization in an economy heavily influenced by the interplay of large corporations, big labor unions, and the federal government. In theory, the 30 million owners of corporate securities represent decentralized decision-making. In practice, of course, they exercise very little. The owner-managers of the nation's 14 million small businesses, on the other hand, considered in the aggregate, do. In this way, small business again serves a democratizing political function.

One of the surprises of American capitalism in the last 50 years, given the continued centralization of economic power, has been the general tapering of industrial market concentration when U.S. markets are considerd as a whole, and a similar slowing in the concentration of industrial assets. Earlier in the century, when markets and assets were concentrating rapidly in fewer and fewer corporate hands, Adolph Berle and Gardiner

Means, in their influential book *The Modern Corporation and Private Property*, expressed a widespread concern that a few megacorporate entities would soon control such an unhealthy percentage of U.S. industrial wealth as to threaten an era of economic feudalism. While concentration remains a concern, it no longer seems overriding.

It is true that since the turn of the century concentration has risen in some industries, such as tobacco, chemicals, stone, clay, glass, and transportation equipment. Yet other important industries—food, textiles, pulp and paper, petroleum and coal products—have since become less concentrated. A study of market-share concentration among the four largest companies in any industry between 1947 and 1972 reveals a similar mixed trend.

Likewise, the trend toward concentration of manufacturing assets has eased. In the 1950s there was a burst of merger activity akin to the great merger movement at the end of the last century, followed by a great conglomerate merger wave in the 1960s. By 1971, the 100 largest manufacturing corporations owned 49 percent of all assets, a larger percentage than that held by the top 200 corporations in 1948.[17]

But during the 1970s until the mid-1980s' wave of mega-mergers that percentage had dropped slightly. Many of today's megamergers seem less menacing than in the past since they are occurring in troubled industries beset by fierce worldwide competition or in ones that are restructuring due to changes in technology and the global market. Those in industries with little foreign competition spurred by domestic deregulation are of a different sort; their implications for small business will be reviewed later.

Many factors are behind the slackening of market and asset concentration, including political restraints through antitrust campaigns beginning in the 1930s under President Franklin D. Roosevelt, more stringent (until recently) Justice Department rulings on mergers, and economic growth in new industries. The aggregate countervailing power of the small business economy has been important as well.

As industry shifted from the hands of owners to professional big business managers, a diplomatic or socialized attitude transformed the marketplace environment. In place of fierce, destabilizing competition in an effort to rule or ruin industries, the new corporate managers, through tacit consensus, often preferred to placate labor and raise price umbrellas in the industry. One effect of these umbrellas was to protect many smaller competitors. They did not eschew fierce price competition. Sometimes they stole market share. Occasionally their niches expanded with a significant innovation, improved competitive efficiency, or a favorable change in the market.

Even in their heyday, the great trusts in steel, oil, farm machinery, and others all lost significant portions of their dominant shares to aggressive small companies. Some of these small companies exploited the wedge provided by antitrust political sentiment. But mostly, they stole share by having lower costs or accepting lower profitability. In most cases, it wasn't worth the while of the large corporation to eradicate the nettlesome competitor: A giant doing significantly more volume than a smaller competitor, for example, would sacrifice so much profit on its greater volume by price cutting that even wiping out the small company would be a pyrrhic victory. Once prices were raised again, another small company was likely to take its place anyway. As long as the market was growing, and quarterly targets were being reached, the tactics of small companies could be painlessly ignored. Diplomatic-minded managers also may have liked to have smaller competitors as a propaganda shield against antitrust or other regulatory sentiment.

But the large corporations could afford to ignore successful small competitors only at their own peril. It often meant that there was a new process or market condition which the large corporation was overlooking. The most significant commercial innovation in the U.S. steel business in the last quarter century—the minimill—was introduced in a market niche and pioneered by small companies, led by Nucor Corporation. The opportunity arose when the big integrated steelmakers belatedly started to switch to basic oxygen furnaces (BOFs) after having ignored the foreign competition that had leapfrogged ahead by already having done so. The BOFs used less steel scrap than the open hearths, creating an abundance of scrap on the market. In the late 1960s, Nucor Chairman Kenneth Iverson, a man with long experience in the metalworking industry, saw an opportunity to melt the steel scrap in modern, small electric arc furnaces of the type used by the minimill operators that had sprung up in Northern Italy after World War II to produce common "merchant" bar. By using steel scrap as its basic raw material instead of pig iron, a minimill could effectively transfer the onerous overhead costs of coal and iron ore mining and of coking ovens that go into producing steel, to the big integrated steelmakers. Moreover, minimills were relatively cheap to build—under $50 million.

The integrated steelmakers sneered at the tiny minimills that began to pop up to serve local steel markets and nip into their market share in the late 1960s. But as the technical virtuosity of the minimills increased, and their innovative, productivity-bonus approach to labor improved productivity to the point where each worker was producing almost twice the steel per man hour as steelworkers in large companies, the minimills were able to turn out an even greater number of steel products at costs *below* that of the imported foreign steel that had become big steel's preoccupation. By the early 1980s, market share for the computerized and ultramodern minimills had increased to about 20 percent—almost as much as imported steel—and a few big steel companies had opened minimills of their own. The big integrated steelmakers live in constant fear that some technological development will allow the minis to produce sheet steel which is used in high volume by U.S. auto and appliance makers. In all, it took over a decade before the big steelmakers started to take the innovations of the minis seriously enough to find ways to apply them.[18] The minimill concept has also been applied to the aluminum industry, partly driven in recent years by the recycling of aluminum cans.

The growth of a small competitor, even in oligopolistic industries, is one way the free market signals future trends. As such, a small company's success may be an early warning signal of where big U.S. corporations may soon become vulnerable to foreign competitors.

Small Business and Business Cycles

The rise of mass-production industry caused swings in the business cycle to become more violent, thus heightening the danger of destabilizing shifts in demand and of a downward spiraling collapse such as occurred in the Great Depression. The aim of big business, and of much government fiscal, monetary, and tax policy, has been to soften the violence of these swings. Due to its peculiar characteristics, small business helps smooth out these swings in the natural course of pursuing profit.

The small business economy acts as a kind of elastic: It adds stretch to the economy on the downswing, and snap on the upswing. The big business economy is most prone to price and wage rigidities but has sufficient power to pass on the higher prices of this rigidity and still attain relatively secure, attractive profits. More flexibility occurs in the small business economy, in the form of lower prices, lower wages, and usually lower profits. As demand falls in a contraction, big companies use their formidable economic powers to try to maintain prices since their wage costs, kept rigid by labor union settlements, cannot easily be reduced. Yet somewhere in the economy there must be some "give" to account for the lower demand. A disproportionate amount of it comes from small businesses: Small suppliers give price concessions, while small business customers absorb the higher prices charged by their large company suppliers.

Meanwhile, small industrial sector companies which operate on the fringes of a leading core of large corporations have softened downswings through contraction, failure, switching temporarily to products for other industries, and, occasionally, through innovation. The effect of the loss of a small business' capacity is to gently strengthen demand for the capacity of the leading companies. This mitigates the urge of big companies to destructive price-cutting spirals.

Small and large corporations also maintain different but complementary schedules for capital investments in plant and equipment. While big business can carry out its investment schedule according to industry trends, and interest-rate levels, small business, which is asset poor and constantly needing to upgrade its facilities, has less flexibility in deferring expenditures to a timely moment. Rather, its priority need for working capital often dictates its capital investment schedule.

In the 1970s, both small and big business slowed their investments in new plant and equipment. Yet due to its different investment criteria, small business maintained an overall higher rate of capital investment. In 1966–68, both small and large corporations put 55 percent of their total invested funds in plant and equipment. By 1978–80, for instance, small corporations were committing 51 percent. The big corporation commitment, in a trend that has alarmed critics as to the long-term implications for U.S. productivity and overall industrial competitiveness, had fallen to 47 percent.[19] Although big business was investing proportionally less at the end of the period, the economy was still being pumped up with proportionally greater investment from secondary small business markets.

Small business also abets smoother cyclic equilibrium in the way it invests. Small business tends to spend the funds at its disposal more like consumers than like big, well-financed corporations—that is, quickly. It must. It is always trying to speed up the reinvestment of profits in order to stay ahead of subsistence. While this state of affairs is uncomfortable for the small businessman, it is a boon to the economy. The rapid recycling of money helps pump up sagging markets. Big corporation profits, and the earnings of the wealthy who live far above subsistence with the luxury to defer spending, tend to go into savings, which turn over more slowly. One cause of the Depression was that capital was too concentrated in the hands of large corporations and wealthy individuals to turn over fast enough to slow the downward momentum.

Finally, as can be recalled from the earlier chapter on employment, small business helps cushion the impact of big business layoffs in recessions by creating new employment. This is most significant for hardest-hit regions.

Small Business and Structural Change

Future U.S. competitiveness depends on the rapid shifting of assets from old to future growth industries. Small business, almost invisibly, abets the reallocation of assets between markets and regions as structural changes create new opportunities and foreclose old ones. Through rapid birth and death, small business, considered in the aggregate, shifts more quickly—if on a much smaller scale—than big companies which must carefully plan its moves to new markets.

Small business' role in creating new businesses is extremely important to regions that are hard hit by the decline of major industries. The dependency of Texas on the fortunes of the oil industry has caused that industry's problems to ripple through the state economy. Since the 1901 discovery of the great Spindletop Field gusher at Beaumont, 47 billion barrels have been pumped from Texas. The rich geologic mantle is drying up—in the unlikely event of oil prices rising to $60 a barrel, it is estimated that the remaining oil could be recovered profitably only until 1993. As a result, employment related to the oil and gas industry has fallen from 4.5 million at the end of 1981 to 3.5 million in 1984.

The fall-off in the shipping of oil has sent barge companies into bankruptcy and caused shipyards to shut down. All four major airlines that served the Jefferson County airport in the Golden Triangle, the heart of the southeast Texas Gulf Coast's refining and petrochemical industry—Delta, Eastern, Continental, and Southwest—have pulled out. In August 1985, one of the largest remaining family-owned department store chains, Sakowitz, filed for Chapter 11 of the bankruptcy code after it had aggressively expanded in expectation of continued oil industry prosperity.

A few of the unemployed have found work at Zaisan, Inc., a 1983 start-up which makes a telephone-and-computer data terminal. In its first 18 months, employment expanded from four to 170. Other small companies, such as Nautilus Environmedical Systems, which was founded in the mid-1970s to produce diving chambers for the offshore drilling industry, have switched industries. Nautilus now makes hyperbaric and flight simulation chambers for medical and military use, respectively. Sales have tripled in four and a half years to nearly $4 million.[20]

While Cleveland's population fell by 24 percent in the 1970s and the city went bankrupt in 1978 as steel, aluminum, coal, and automobile companies cut back their operations, John W. Young was expanding his pest control company, Speed Exterminating. From a one-man home-run operation in 1960, it had become a $1 million company with 22 employees by the early 1980s.[21] Alone, none of these companies are significant. But they cushion the hardship of declining regions and provide new hope for rebuilding future fortunes.

Small business participates aggressively in the ocean of perpetually churning assets which goes on deep within the American economy. Perhaps $70 billion a year goes into new start-ups alone. Most of this is invested in businesses that will soon fail and be returned to the nation's capital pool to be turned into yet new investments by other hopeful start-ups in the future. Yet a fraction of these $70 billion in assets will find its way into the surviving enterprises that are the seeds of future growth businesses. Billions more, of course, are invested by existing small businesses in current growth markets.

The inner dynamism of American capitalism is sometimes not appreciated because so much of it is invisible. Among the 500 largest industrial firms, there is more change going on than the impression left by their visible endurance—a productive reallocation of assets is often indicated by a change in market position. Among small companies, productive changes are even less visible, since they happen through extinctions and births in the marketplace, visible mainly by the rapid turnover of storefront shingles on the street and changes in local Yellow Page listings.

A high start-up and a high failure rate together is generally a sign of economic health. It means experiments are being made. Assets are constantly being reallocated between industries and from less to more capable hands to advance the process of creative destruction.

The highest birth and death rates in the United States are generally found among the fastest-growing regions of the Pacific Coast and mountain states; the lowest, in slower-growing regions. As a rule of thumb, high failure rates in fast-growing regions are healthy signals. High failure rates in slow-growth regions, however, indicate just the opposite.

U.S. failure rates leapt in the late 1970s, and through the first half of the 1980s businesses were failing at a rate only surpassed in the Great Depression. Given the economic troubles of the period, it would be ludicrous to attribute this sharp increase to health. What is healthy, however, is that would-be small businessmen have not been deterred from continuing to try new start-ups.

Small business abets the reallocation of assets process that is taking place in the form of the present wave of merger and divestitures. Large corporations generally do not wish to remain in a market where they are not among the top three competitors. Nor for the global competitiveness of the U.S. economy does it maximize general efficiency for the largest U.S.-based corporations to use their power managing assets where they cannot be strong competitors. In Japan, MITI helps rationalize industries so that it is dominated by three powerful corporations which can provide strong global competition on Japan's behalf. In this country, the rationalization process is left to market forces.

Small business fosters competitive asset reallocation both by being acquired, and by buying some of the business divisions large corporations no longer want. In 1984 large corporations sold off 900 units for $29 billion.

Many of the purchases were made by the former corporate managers of the business unit, in order to run it on their own as an independent business. Between 1982 and 1984 there were 350 management buy-outs of large corporation units—about 15 percent of all divestiture activity.

Since the purchase cost of these units is often well beyond the reach of savings from executive salaries, most of the management acquisitions are leveraged buy-outs. In a typical situation, the new owners put up about 10 percent of the acquisition price—the other 90 percent is borrowed from banks, insurance companies, and pension funds, often with no security, against projected future cash-flow projections. LBOs became so popular and individual amounts sometimes so large in 1983 and 1984, that the Federal Reserve Board, among others, publicly cautioned that the huge leverage they were building could be deleterious to the U.S. financial system. The billion-dollar LBOs abated. The smaller ones continued as aggressively as ever.

Some former corporate units have done better as independent companies. Talon, Inc. was once the U.S. zipper king. But it stagnated in the mid-1970s as part of the Textron conglomerate, and its managers watched as Japan's YKK built a plant in the United States and stole its customers. In frustration, Textron changed presidents at Talon five times. Finally, in 1981 it sold the unit, after four years of losses, to its new president and now majority owner, Sidney Merians. Merians' background was in the garment trade. Within 11 months, Talon was again profitable—and expanding.[22]

Finally, small businesses play an invisible and immeasurable but important role reallocating assets by making thousands of unrecorded takeovers of other small businesses. This is especially notable in the rescue of some of the thousands of viable small businesses which close because the owner is retiring.

Small Business and "Privatization"

The interruption in the 1970s of the long period of prosperity guided in the postwar era by the evolving social welfare state has spurred policymakers to shift emphasis back to the proven wealth generator of the past—private enterprise—to restimulate productive growth.

In the past decade, there has been a worldwide movement toward "privatization." In the United States, this has not taken the British form of selling public companies to the private sector. Instead it has taken the form of industry deregulation, and the local, state, and federal movement to contract out public services to private concerns in everything from prison to waste management.

Small business has played a disproportionately large role in virtually all privatization efforts. It has been the most responsive U.S. economic entity to the changes rendered by these government initiatives.

In deregulated industries small business has given impetus to the rush of new firm start-ups, new employment, new services, lower costs, and introduction of some innovations. Unwanted short-line regional railroads, like the Cairo line, have been sold by the major railroads and are now being run by small operators. The number of national airline carriers has surged, and as route and fare structures have been rationalized, new regional airlines have moved in either to compete or fill voids left in the marketplace. New small business competition has been especially vigorous in the trucking industry. There are hundreds of small companies now competing with the dismembered units of AT&T. There are all sorts of new regional transportation services, freight forwarders, and businesses that install, repair, and sell communications equipment.

Small businesses in deregulated industries with under 100 employees have started up twice as quickly as small businesses in the overall economy. Small firms within deregulated industries created twice as many new jobs as their proportional share in deregulated industries. Overall, nearly one-quarter of all new jobs created between 1976 and 1982 were in deregulated industries—double its one-eighth proportion of all jobs in the work force at the start of the period.

In the 1980–82 recession, small businesses of under 100 employees created four-fifths of all new jobs in deregulated industries. At the same time, their percentage of sales held steady versus a 1.8 percent decline among their counterparts in the rest of the small business economy.[23]

Due to the new competition, trucking rates have fallen by about 10 percent. Regulatory costs and barriers of entry are lower, too. The average sale price of an ICC truck operating license fell from $398,000 in 1975 to $4,900 in 1982. Today, many larger truckers are abandoning their own fleet as rates decline, and contracting out to smaller, more efficient trucking firms who have found new ways of cutting costs. For the first time in years, truckers have been forced to seek ways to optimize truckloads to survive.

The breakup of AT&T, many believe, is speeding up the exploitation of new technologies, such as satellite communications and cellular telephones. Monopoly may have been most efficient in ordinary times, but many had doubts that any monopoly, even one as efficient as AT&T, could make the best technological choices in a time of technological upheaval without the discipline of stronger competition. Small businesses that have been nibbling at AT&T's market for many years have now been turned loose to try to exploit neglected possibilities.

Fares in the airline industry are down, too, while volume has risen by 21.5 million passengers in 1975 to 46 million in 1984. The rise of airline discounters are mainly responsible. Atlanta was long excluded from the low fares because, as the hub of both Delta and Eastern, it was something of a closed shop to new airlines. But in mid-1985, as soon as People Express, the upstart discounter that with only 2.5 percent of the airline market has been able to exert widespread pressure on prices, announced a $49 one-way Atlanta-Newark fare, both Delta and Eastern immediately announced discounts from the $275 cost of their Atlanta–New York tickets.

Some of the lower airfares have come from a more efficient deployment of airplane fleets to maximize payload factors. Small regional airlines, for example, flying smaller planes, have gotten greater efficiency than major carriers using the bigger jets over short distances. For major airlines it is inefficient to maintain the many different types of aircraft that might, on a strictly payload basis, provide lower operating costs.

In industries where operating scale efficiencies are relatively low—trucking, small airlines, and local and interurban travel—small business has been most effective at finding more rational modes of operation.

Some of small business' lower costs, of course, have not come through newfound efficiencies. Cutting corners on safety regulations has yielded the competitive edge in some instances. Nearly half the highway rigs stopped in the New York, New Jersey, and Connecticut area in a mid-1985 regional crackdown had faulty brakes, defective steering, or other serious hazards. Coordination of federal and state authorities to improve inspection programs has lagged well behind the changes wrought by deregulation.[24]

Small business has also put pressure on unionized wages to gain cost advantage. In trucking and airlines, for example, the large increase in new start-ups, most nonunion, has caused industry wages to drop sharply.

New competition from deregulation, therefore, has resulted in a frontal assault on labor unions. Labor relations have grown acrimonious throughout the airline industry; there have been uncharacteristic confrontations and strikes. The response of unions in unionized companies has been to make two-tier settlements: New pilots and flight attendants receive compensation only half to three-quarters of that of the existing jobholders in order to compete with nonunionized new companies. Such settlements merely institutionalize the small business-led downward pressure on wages—in industries that are *not* under wage pressure from foreign competition.

Small business has also been a significant agent in facilitating that other main face of U.S. privatization—the trend toward contracting out more government functions to the private sector. Many of those taking on former government tasks are small businesses.

At the federal government level, where $170 billions' worth of contracts are already made annually, privatizers have identified 11,000 additional commercial activities from moviemaking to geological surveys that could be profitably switched from public to private management. The widely publicized President's Private Sector Survey on Cost Control—the Grace Commission—concluded that up to $1.1 billion a year could be saved by this means. More common estimates center at around one-fifth that amount.

One of those small companies that is already efficiently performing government tasks is D. K. Associates of Rockville, Maryland. It provides printing, graphic, administration, word processing, and other services to the Federal Aviation Administration, NASA, and the Defense Department under 14 contracts worth $4 to $5 million annually. One of its earliest projects involved audiovisual services that had been previously performed at the Lowry Air Force Base by 88 government employees. The Air Force had proposed filling the contract itself for $1.4 million. Using 35 employees, D.K. did it for $750,000—and still earned a tidy profit.[25]

Most of the privatizing of public services has been taking place at the grassroots local and state level. Here the impetus toward privatization was spurred in part by the tax revolt of the mid-1970s, most celebrated in California's Proposition 13 restricting local government's property taxing authority, which drained local treasuries and thus restricted the ability of local authorities to provide common public services.

Phoenix has been one of the cities most active in privatizing its services. The bus system, security and crowd control, trash collection, street sweepers, traffic and street light maintenance, waste disposal, municipal parking lots, and maintenance of public buildings are among the services contracted to private firms. In other parts of the country, private companies manage local airports and fire services, even, controversially, own or operate at least two dozen big prisons. In 1982, 44 percent of cities and counties in a nationwide survey had their commercial refuse collected privately, 28 percent contracted out street repairs, and 41 percent street light maintenance.

How far privatization will eventually go depends in part upon the balance struck between efficiency and the equitable delivery of basic services. Nevertheless, hard-pressed cities have the option of experimenting with such policies due to the readiness of so many small private companies to compete against one another to perform contracts.

Small Business and Industrial Policy

Many states, in the absence of a comprehensive federal industrial policy, are pushing ahead independently with industrial policies in order to cope with the impact of the international economy on its constituents. As with privatization, small businesses have been the most responsive economic entities to these initiatives.

States have taken many approaches to try to best position themselves for the changes being wrought by the economic transition. California is the leading state among those which impose a so-called unitary tax on multinational corporations operating within its borders. The unitary tax, which taxes multinationals on a percentage of their worldwide earnings, is a regional response to the frustration of trying to ascertain definitively how much a multinational earned from a given location. Intracorporate cost juggling between multinational units that trade extensively from many global locations and divergent multinational accounting rules themselves often cause large profits to be shifted to low-tax areas.

Across the country, states are bidding against one another in the forms of tax breaks, road building, and in some cases antiunion right-to-work laws to woo foreign and large U.S.-headquartered multinational corporation investments to build a base for future prosperity. Many states have promotion offices in Tokyo. Oregon and Washington have tried to take advantage of Japan's hostility to California's unitary tax by outbidding each other to redirect Japanese investments from California to themselves.

Alabama boasts it has lured in over 100 foreign companies from 19 countries to create up to 20,000 jobs. Rhode Island's catch has been 39 companies with total investments of $200 million.[26] Iowa is providing large subsidies for job training. Little-unionized Tennessee has been extremely successful in attracting Japanese firms, including carmaker Nissan, and the biggest prize of 1985, GM's Saturn plant. With the parts suppliers who will follow, that will be worth about 20,000 jobs.

Small business has also been part of efforts to add vitality to local regions. Most popular have been efforts to encourage high-tech ventures and jobs. In the first half of the 1980s, about half the 50 states had committed close to $300 million to state-run venture-capital funds intended to foster home-grown industries. While this was tiny compared to total private-venture capital, states like Massachusetts and Connecticut were each claiming to have added 1,000 jobs through their programs.[27]

Illinois, which lost 342,000 manufacturing jobs between 1979 and 1985, has launched a $1.3 billion "Build Illinois" program which includes low-interest loans to small business.[28] Arkansas ranks number 49 and 50 among the 50 states in personal income and percentage of college graduates. In the past, it has seen textile and leather plants pass through from the east en route to Asia in search of lower wages. It has embarked on a two-phase program of revitalization that starts with upgrading its educational system and follows up with a package of programs, including long-term, low-interest bond financing and private loan guarantees to back high-risk small business ventures.[29]

Texas has enticed the Microchips and Computer Corporation, the consortium of 21 computer companies uniting on their R&D efforts to meet the Japanese challenge, to set up at the University of Texas at Austin. Basic research will be done by the university, new product development by the member firms, and the intermediate stage R&D applying the basic research to new computer ideas by the consortium. Patent licenses resulting from the R&D will be available to new companies three years after they are available to members of the consortium. Texas' hope is to draw other new small companies to the state to take advantage of the R&D fruits of the program. The state has also been encouraging existing enterprises to modernize through the federal Small Business Innovation and Research program.[30]

Other universities are helping incubate small high-tech companies for their own purposes. In 1980, Rensselaer Polytechnic Institute in Troy, New York, began providing new high-tech companies workspace at low rent, low-fee business services, and consultation opportunities with its science faculty. The aim was to help small companies survive the first 12 to 24 months—and perhaps direct some R&D dollars the univeristy's way. Universities across the country have since begun imitating RPI.[31]

A high-tech industrial park outside Philadelphia on Route 202 was created out of farmland in 1977. By the mid-1980s, it was shaping up as a microcosm of Silicon Valley and Massachusetts' Route 128. Some 200 computer, biomedical, and other fledgling firms at the park were grouped around companies providing legal, accounting, and other basic services needed to enhance low-cost start-up. The park also had a day-care center, a restaurant, and a health club.

While much of the glamour is in high-tech, those industries tend to create relatively few jobs at first. Regions hardest hit by the dislocations of the economic transition cannot wait that long. They need jobs now. The Mesabi Range in Minnesota was once the richest iron ore vein the world. As recently as ten years ago, 95 1,000-foot ore ships plied their way through the Inland Waterway to supply the great steel mills. With the decline of the steel industry, and the low cost of Brazilian ore, the Mesabi Range ore industry is today a ghost of its former glory. Only 47 ore ships are still operating. Men need 20 years' seniority to get a job on board ship. Unemployment in the ore towns is double-digit, and young people have led the 5 percent of the population that has moved away. Homes that were worth $45,000 five years ago are worth only $15,000 today in many places, tying their owners to their declining towns.

In a modest effort to adjust, some of the towns have embarked on job-creating industrial projects. Most involve small companies. Perhaps the largest is the Wood Products Industrial Park in Hibbing, in the heart of the range, financed by $4 million in government and private funds. The 180-acre park will include a saw mill, a kiln-drying facility, a chopsticks manufacturer, and probably a fiberboard plant. The goal seems modest—to create 1,000 jobs—to everyone, that is, but Hibbing's unemployed.[32]

The number of small, industrial incubators has been mushrooming. By 1984, there were 120 around the country.[33]

Finally, as part of the landmark GM-UAW accord, GM will spend $100 million in cooperation with the UAW over two and a half years to start various small businesses to create new jobs for some of those thrown out of work by automation.

Small businesses have also been most responsive to policy initiatives to create opportunities for the poor. While the "enterprise zone" concept of offering incentives to businesses to set up in depressed areas was being debated in Congress throughout the Reagan administration's first term, half the states enacted enterprise zones on their own. By 1985, there were 1,281 enterprise zone programs in operation. The most common incentives were tax credits determined by the number of employees, sales tax, and real estate tax exemptions, tax breaks for capital improvements or employee training, and low-interest loans for start-up businesses.[34]

Most of those taking advantage of the state enterprise zone initiatives were small businesses. The state and local tax breaks were only about 20 percent as lucrative as those proposed by the federal government, and big business, which can afford to wait, was holding back for a federal program to get off the ground.[35] Led by small companies, enterprise zones in leading Connecticut cities had created 3,668 jobs in two years.[36]

Sometimes, enterprise zone incentives are just enough to favorably tip the balance for small businessmen inclined, for reasons of their own, such as Rafael Collado of Protocom Devices of New York's South Bronx, to locate in a poor neighborhood. Just as the pretty enclaves of Silicon Valley have become shorthand for high technology, the South Bronx has become code for the tragic cycles of slum life—poverty, crime, gutted buildings, and gutted lives. Yet not far from the rubble and boarded-up tenements is where Collado chose to make home for Protocom Devices, which with perhaps appropriate symbolism makes a product which allows incompatible computers to communicate with one another. Since October 1984, it has been located in an incubator space rented from the South Bronx Development Organization. In the spring of 1986, it will move to a new industrial park complex being built in the South Bronx by the Public Development Corporation and the Port Authority of New York and New Jersey agency. The Port Authority agency has already loaned the company $4.4 million.

Collado had opportunities to locate Protocom elsewhere. In fact, an investment banker, thinking of the impact on well-heeled investors, strongly recommended against the South Bronx location. Others suggested he'd be more at home among the high-tech firms clustered around Boston's Route 128.

But for Collado, one of Protocom's six partners, the move to the South Bronx was a homecoming. He had lived in the neighborhood while growing up. One of the fortunate few, he attended a now-defunct school for intellectually gifted but socially disadvantaged boys. A computer software engineer, Collado attended Brooklyn Polytechnic Institute before going on to several jobs in Silicon Valley and Arizona. At ITT in Scottsdale, he had his company car and his stock options. But he wasn't satisfied. In early 1983, he moved to a New Jersey manufacturer of telecommunications equipment. There he and two other engineers began work on the "pad"—an assembler/disassembler device that packages information in such a way that it allows incompatible mainframe computers made by different manufacturers to communicate with each other—that was to become Protocom's product.

The Port Authority is hoping Protocom will create 200 jobs in the coming years. Venture capitalists looking at the company think that with a successful product Protocom could achieve over $100 million in sales. Both are goals that are still a long way off. In 1984, the company had 13 employees, $1.3 million in sales, and $80,000 profit. In 1985, early indications were pointing to $7 million worth of sales, 55 employees, and a couple of million dollars profit by year's end. Its existing customer base was impressive. It included clients like Boeing Computer Systems and Citibank.

As much as making a high-tech success, Collado hopes to help lift his old neighborhood out of its endemic cycle of poverty. He has been talking to other small businesses about locating in the South Bronx. With one eye toward developing its own future executive base, the company is training minority students at Cooper Union and Manhattan College in Protocom technology. He has also donated $50,000 worth of computers to a high school for bright but socially disadvantaged youngsters designated as Protocom's unofficial charity. On a tiny scale, that is what IBM and other major computer companies do at universities and high schools to build markets for the future.

Most of all, Collado hopes that success will make him a role model for South Bronx youngsters. He hopes to replace the prevalent, highly improbable dreams of such youths of escaping the ghetto by becoming a professional athlete, with a more realistic chance of becoming a small businessman. [37]

Finally, some localities have turned to small business service firms to add equilibrium and resilience against downturns in a major local industry. In the Boston area, for example, where unemployment has been only 3 percent, policymakers have been looking to expand its economic base to defend against fluctuations in the fortunes of the high-tech companies which have led the region's revival.

Whether or not the United States will eventually formulate a broad conceptual federal industrial policy to respond to the technological and global economic changes, and what form and scope it will have if it does, in part depends on the responsiveness of the small business economy to present policy initiatives. So far its responsiveness to local programs has helped allow the U.S. economic system to respond without the kind of central government-directed economic restructuring that was necessary to adjust to the Great Depression. With the world entering a new phase of economic evolution and the new success formulas as yet undiscovered, small business is providing the country with a uniquely responsive asset for experimentation.

Simultaneously, in more traditional ways, the small business economy has been facilitating U.S. economic adjustment by acting as a fourth complementary force helping to provide an economic environment in which change can most easily occur. Its strategic role in facilitating change was not readily apparent until revealed by the extreme stresses of the present economic transition.

6

Small Business
and the Social Economy

Arnold Goldstein, fifty-eight, runs two pipe and premium cigar shops in New York with his two sons, one in midtown Manhattan, the other in an indoor Queens shopping mall. A safe, quiet, unchanging business, right? Wrong.

The tobacconist business has changed a great deal since the days Goldstein was first introduced to it through his father's cigar store, and from the time he opened his own store in the Times Square area after returning from the Korean War. Once upon a time, cigar stores were smoky places where groups of men hung out, puffing on and discussing cigars, holding bull sessions, pausing occasionally to use the spittoon—not at all like the clean, attractive stores Goldstein, a former president of the tobacconists' trade association, owns now, where women customers enter as comfortably as men.

In bridging the past and present marketplaces, Goldstein proved that even when the small businessman does nearly everything right, there are always forces beyond his control that can—and very likely will—go wrong. It is managing these forces that separates the successful from the also-rans.

To start with, the industry has always been small, and from the beginning Goldstein accepted the reality that "in retailing you can't have big eyes" for wealth. The big volume $8 billion business in cheap cigars, such as Garcia Vega and Dutch Masters, has always been a big business, supermarket, and candy store trade. Premium cigars, by comparison, even today are only a $100 million market segment. Pipes are a good deal smaller than that. Twenty-five years ago the business was big enough to support no more than 400 bona fide pipe and premium cigar stores in the whole country. Today, there are about 2,000, although most of the growth has come from existing family tobacconists adding two or three outlets in order to keep up with advancing costs.

From the start, Goldstein took only those profits he needed from the business to support his family, and plowed the rest back into building up inventory, thereby overcoming the problem of most small retailers of not retaining enough cash earnings to be able to grow. He also scrupulously followed what he says are the three basic laws of retailing: (1) Being flexible and change-oriented; (2) Working hard and working long hours; (3) Keeping overhead—notably rent, salaries, and taxes—down.

In practice, that meant 80- to 90-hour workweeks. It also meant hiring part-time retirees and young, often first-time job market entrants in order to get a blend of experience and strength with high work-hour flexibility but low wage and benefit costs. It meant doing the basic housekeeping of fresh displays and keeping the stores clean, keeping a sharp eye on competitors' windows and visiting the department stores to get display ideas. He sold cigarettes and lottery tickets to draw more customers into his store. He went to trade conventions to look for new products that might turn over more rapidly than the ones he was selling, thereby stretching the buying power of his purchasing dollar through better inventory management. And he constantly introduced new products to his store. Most didn't pan out, of course. Three that did were sunglasses, expensive lighters, and later, as consumers showed a preference for higher-cost, specialized products, fresh tobacco custom-blended in the store according to pipe smokers' personal tastes. "You can't just raise prices, so you've got to grow with the costs," says Goldstein. "You've got to offer the customer something more, like better service or new choices." By the late 1960s and early 1970s, Goldstein's store near Times Square was one of the biggest and best known in the industry.

About that time, there was a boom in suburban shopping mall construction across the country. With excess space, mall managers were offering attractive leases to retailers they believed would enhance their malls. The trend was generally deleterious to small retailers, who rarely had enough "name" appeal. But Goldstein was offered space in a new indoor mall in Queens, New York, anchored by two department stores.

He was attracted to the idea for more than expansion alone. For several years, all downtown urban areas in America had been declining with white flight from the cities to the suburbs, and he was concerned because Times Square was becoming one of the toughest evening neighborhoods in the country. Also, Goldstein's two sons, who had worked with him on weekends and vacations for many years, were reaching maturity and showing some interest in joining him in business. Goldstein moved into the mall.

The shopping mall store was an entirely different business from the urban store. About 80 percent of the business was done during 20 percent of the store hours, predominantly in the evenings and on weekends. As a result, he had to manage personnel time differently. Also, the clientele was different— women frequented the store much more than in Times Square. So the product lines were catered to appeal to the things they preferred for their husbands—more pipes, blended tobaccos, lighters—and fewer cigars. Changing consumer tastes were working to the industry's advantage as well. In the mid-1960s, the Surgeon General's warning about the cancer-causing effects of cigarette smoking had converted some men to pipes and cigars. Now, new aromatic pipe tobaccos, whose fragrance women liked having around the house, became popular. Business was going so well that Goldstein, in the late 1970s, opened a third store on the East Side of midtown Manhattan.

That's when near-disaster struck. Ironically, it came with prosperity. The fortunes of the inner city had abruptly turned around, and instead of facing a bleak, low-rent wasteland environment, urban retailers across the country were being driven out of business by soaring rents and land values. The building in which Goldstein's Times Square store had been located for 22 years was sold, and the new owners told him they had other plans for the building and would not renew his lease. At almost the same time, the lease was up at the mall in Queens and the mall managers demanded an astounding rental increase. The fortunes of the shopping mall business, too, had gone into reverse. Few malls had been built in the high interest-rate seventies. This led to a greater demand for less available space, and forced out many of the original mall shopowners.

For 18 months, Goldstein, a naturally cheerful man with seemingly indefatigable good humor, showed little of the strain to his family, as he wrestled with ways to save the simultaneous loss of his two main sources of livelihood (the third store was small, and wasn't doing especially well). He calculated what his wife and he needed to live on now that his daughter and one son were through college, and the youngest son was almost fully grown. Yet both sons continued to express an interest in joining him in the family business. One of Goldstein's sources of pleasure in those trying months was the prospect of running the business with his sons.

With that in mind, Goldstein painstakingly negotiated an acceptable deal with the Queens mall managers. His oldest son took over its daily management. His youngest son did the same in Manhattan, greatly improving its profitability. Goldstein divided his time between the two. With the family working together, prosperity began to return.

"When you go into a family business you are remarrying," he says. "You must have common goals. Ego or overpowering personality traits don't fit because they distort the common goals. When it works, it's beautiful. But like a marriage, it's a continuous growth effort."

Recently, Goldstein added a new operation to the small family empire. He purchased the pipe import business of one of his longtime suppliers, an elderly man who wanted to cut back on his daily business commitments and cash in on a lifetime's equity he'd built up. Learning the new business, Goldstein figures with a fresh excitement, will take him at least one full annual cycle. It involves travel to European suppliers, managing the novel intricacies of international trade, and some correspondence in German, a language he does not know.

And, of course, as a bonus it holds the pleasurable prospect of having a new business to share with his sons.[1]

Physical resources and technology alone are no guarantee of national economic success. Economic activity takes place within a social environment of cultural values and traditions which creates the all-important spirit of enterprise underlying each nation's economy. The social economy determines each nation's peculiar economic characteristics and tendencies. It influences the way businessmen perceive opportunity and undertake the risk to exploit it.

How successful America and its main industrial partners will be in adjusting to and competing in the new economic era depends in part on how well social economic values and ideals *motivate* productive economic activity. When these values enjoy such widespread belief as to inspire a society of individuals to work in quest of the ideals they promise, an economy is driven by a great energy that enhances its overall competitiveness. When the values can no longer inspire faith, either because they no longer seem worthy or because their ideals no longer seem attainable in reality, the nation's economic energy, and ultimately its global competitiveness, wanes.

In Europe and Japan, long feudal and homogeneous traditions have tended to perpetuate wealth and power in leading families and to institutionalize social-economic relationships by tradition. Such social economies were well suited to organizational strength, bureaucratic excellence, and top-down economic planning. Indeed, Japan and Western Europe have achieved great success by utilizing these strengths in the postwar period. They continue to shape their efforts and strategies to succeed in the current economic transition.

In the United States, social-economic ideals of opportunity and democratic individualism were built upon a tradition where positions of power were temporary and situational. Wealth and status could be won or lost within a generation through individual entrepreneurial effort. Such social-economic values were conducive to the needs of a physically huge, rapidly expanding nation built by immigrants. They remain the ideals underpinning the less planned, free-market-oriented economic system on which the country is striving to compete today even though the modern U.S. economy is vastly different from the economic environment in which these social values were formed.

While American big business may be the locus of the strictly economic realm today, small business ideals remain the core of the American social economy. As entrepreneur, the small businessman is a folk hero: His idealized virtues—individualism, energy, sense of purpose, hands-on ownership, courage to risk everything to be captain of his own destiny, resourcefulness against overwhelming odds—validate the fundamental social-economic ideals and infuse the American economy with much of its driving spirit.

Economic historian Fernand Braudel has pointed out that a certain tranquility in the social order is a prerequisite for the flourishing of capitalism and for the large corporations that constitute its modern core. Small business helps provide this tranquility by elevating conventional economic values to the level of myth and offering just enough objective reaffirming success stories to give them widespread credence.

The reality of dominant large enterprises and the complex modern industrial economy notwithstanding, small business is still the ideal image Americans see when they look in the economic mirror. It constitutes a line of delineation between U.S. free-market-oriented and other, more plan-oriented forms of industrial capitalism.

This economic self-image has been alluring enough for many businessmen, and even some economists and their models, to continue to try to act as if the laws of market economics were as applicable to modern large corporations as they are to small businesses. Such mismatch of belief and reality, of course, can become an obstacle to necessary change if sufficiently exaggerated. But kept in proportion, it is a powerful stimulant to traditional U.S.-style economic activity.

It is very hard to imagine the United States, without a tradition of bureaucratic excellence, succeeding under present conditions with a heavily plan-oriented capitalism of its own against Japan and Western Europe in the new economic environment. If such an orientation in U.S. capitalism is to evolve successfully in response to economic conditions, it must grow from America's traditionally vigorous free-market-oriented base.

Small Business and American Social Economic Ideals

It is perhaps a fitting coincidence that the Declaration of Independence and Adam Smith's *The Wealth of Nations* were both issued in 1776. The economic principles Smith espoused found a receptive audience in a country born in the cleavage in history between the fall of aristocracies where money followed inherited power and privileged birth, and the rise of commercial society where power and station were determined by the accumulation of wealth. Smith used the term "economic liberty" to describe the chief economic mechanics of the system that came to be known as capitalism. In the scheme of democratic American ideals, that economic liberty came to be equated with equality of opportunity to rise above the pack—all men were equal before the free market. Small business ownership is a principal means by which ordinary Americans exercise economic liberty to this day.

Small business today is the descendant of two main social economic traditions of economic liberty that grew up alongside each other in early America—the popular native small business tradition expressed in the Puritan ethics of work and thrift, and the ideal of the self-reliant small farmer.

Every schoolchild knows that Benjamin Franklin rose to eminence through small business. So did many of those early exploiters and innovators of Yankee ingenuity. Abraham Lincoln, for a time, was a small businessman, if an unsuccessful one. After working as a store clerk, he opened his own store with a partner who proved to be a drunkard and contracted huge debts. Lincoln earned the nickname Honest Abe, which helped his political career, by working 15 years to pay them off.

Small businessmen ran the general stores that provided the lifeline to frontier development. As with the small farmer, capital and labor are still united in the small businessman. He was likewise an upholder of the family and local community values. Throughout literature and popular media such as television and the movies, the shopkeeper has almost never been portrayed as rapacious—that role is reserved for more powerful, bigger businessmen.

Alongside the small business tradition was the agrarian ideal of the independent farmer, whom Thomas Jefferson believed to be the cornerstone of the Republic. Jefferson believed that within the small farmer lay the seed of morality and democratic virtue that distinguished America from the perceived squalor of industrial Europe. Jefferson was suspicious of business and industry. In time he came to believe that small-scale industry could be managed without corrupting America's ideals of democratic individualism—provided that the farming frontier remained open as a safety valve for people who began to be economically exploited under urban conditions.

In practice, the frontier provided less of a safety valve than Jefferson and others before and after him imagined. As a powerful symbol, it continued to shape and support American ideals of economic opportunity for a long time.[2]

It was in response to the deteriorating economic conditions caused by the Panic of 1837 that Horace Greeley of the *New York Tribune* urged "Go West, young man, go forth into the Country." When Huck Finn, the American incarnation of rough and ready individualist democracy, is threatened with "sivilization" by Aunt Sally he reckons to "light out for the Territory" ahead of the others. In 1862, Lincoln's Congress passed the Homestead Act in the ultimately frustrated hope of extending economic liberty to hundreds of thousands of new small farmers.

The safety valve myth became untenable as industrialism intruded upon the frontier. As industry became visible and farmers vanished, the small farmer was no longer a viable symbol of economic liberty. If America's democratic individualist form of economic liberty was to continue to fire the national character and economy, the calculus of those ideals needed to be transformed into new symbols.

With the closure of the frontier and the decline of the small farmer before industrialism, small business enterprise became the major symbolic vehicle of opportunity—the new safety valve. The small farmer evolved into the small businessman.

Frontier symbols were readily transferable to the independent businessman. The two types that settled the frontier—the frontiersman and the farmer—were re-clothed as businessmen. The frontiersman, who pioneered the land for settlement, was the embodiment of the rugged individualist, heroic and uncivilized. Once the land was settled, he moved on. Farmers moved in to tame the land and make it grow.

The frontiersman became the individualist entrepreneur. In the early era of industrialism, in his most outsized form, he was the self-made captain of industry, who, while widely condemned for his asocial exploitation of the environment, is treated in literature and criticism with an ambivilent awe since he succeeded on the terms available to everyone. As soon as the captain of industry gave way to the impersonal modern corporation, he was "socialized" and lost his heroic dimensions. But from this tradition, the entrepreneurial ideal still derives mystique.

The farmer became the ordinary small businessman. Although lacking the entrepreneur's verve, imagination, and egoistic drive, he possessed goodness and self-sufficiency, a kind of moral purity that came from the land, the symbol of down-home family values, the foundation of the small-town community.

Congressional rhetoric, aimed as it is at striking responsive chords in the popular American cultural imagination, offers relevant testimony to ordinary small business' enduring image. During the 1936 debate that led to the passage of the Robinson-Patman Act, which was intended to protect small business against the advantages of chain stores, the *Congressional Record* printed the following speech, plainly mixing small business and frontier imagary:

Every village, every town, every city, large and small, in the United States, was founded by a pioneer independent merchant. The first building in every one of the thousands of villages, towns and cities which dot the land, was a rude little store. Then more stores. Then from among these merchants came the men who founded little banks. They built the mills and the slaughterhouses and the little industries. They built the school systems and the water systems and the sewer systems and the light systems and the streetcar systems. They became the mayors of the towns and the civic leaders. They built the fine homes and the fine business blocks. The man who built that first little store built the fine home on the hill and the fine business block downtown, and every town and city in America is a living monument to him; and all without outside help or capital. He hewed and builded his town out of the earth. He was the foundation of the commercial structure of America. Shall he be preserved or shall he be destroyed? That is the issue.[3]

A 1978 report of a House committee on small business echoed similar sentiments 40 years later:

All the data and testimony presented . . . lead to one undeniable conclusion: the role of small business in our economy is declining at an alarming rate. As the number of small businesses in industries declines and the concentration ratios increase, the continuing viability of small firms is severely threatened. . . . A decision must be made: do the American people wish to preserve the foundations upon which our nation was built or do they wish to acquiesce to the gradual spread of a system alien to the American spirit, a system of economic oligarchy?[4]

The large corporation, despite its economic preeminence, never captured the popular imagination. It offered no alternative symbols to sustain the democratic individualist ideal of economic liberty. It offered only a feeble, elitist version of economic opportunity, once the industrialism and economic centralization it brought closed the frontier and drove the small farmer into the factory. Small business in its two guises—the individualist entrepreneur and the self-sufficient ordinary businessman—did.

Small Business and the Missing Class Struggle

Historians have been perplexed by the fact that the United States—alone among industrialized nations—never developed a politics of class struggle and never had a powerful socialist political party. Several combinations of suggestions have been put forth to explain it: America's lack of feudal class origins made the New World more democratic from the start. The ethnic heterogeneity of immigration, reinforced by skilled labor shortages, conferred value on skilled workers for what they could do regardless of family or ethnic origins. The flow of immigration into a steadily expanding economy abetted economic mobility. America's general affluence deterred the formation of economic class rigidities, as did the success of bread-and-butter-oriented labor unions in winning a middle-class share of that affluence for its rank and file by, in effect, allying themselves with, instead of opposing, the economic power of large corporations to partake of their power to earn large profits.

Small business played a contributing role, too. Upward mobility in the United States was possible. Self-employment in small business provided one main route to that end throughout the industrial period when class tensions were high.

Few may ever have risen from rags to riches, but many took a modest first step by setting up their own businesses. Furthermore, enough individuals achieved upward mobility by this means that the ideal of equality of opportunity and democratic individualism endured—perhaps even more strongly than objective success stories warranted. This blurred the lines of economic and social class division and reinforced the cultural optimism that inspired entrepreneurial risk-taking. Finally, the sizable, democratic class of independent small businessmen that did emerge provided a buffer between capital and labor to cushion such class strife as did occur.

Immigration throughout the first part of the nineteenth century brought many skilled workers from Britain, Germany, Scandinavia, and elsewhere. These immigrants were drawn by the economic opportunities of the New World, rather than being forced out by economic necessity. The capital requirements for entering business were low, and a typical pattern was for many skilled workers, such as carpenters, plumbers, draymen, and painters, to set up shop on their own after working for someone else. Many of these trained others, who, acquiring skill and capital, set up their own shops. A major study over several decades of employment in Poughkeepsie in the mid-nineteenth century found that about one-quarter of all journeymen went on to open their own shops.[5]

Around mid-century, the number of immigrant artisans who eventually opened their own shops declined, though many continued to do so. But the number of small proprietors who had been trained in business, such as sales and clerical work, increased. Skill in business, rather than craft skill, became a more promising route to prosperous self-employment in the post–Civil War era. Artisans slowly gravitated toward skilled blue-collar labor as large-scale industry grew.

Immigrants with urban business skills took up self-employment as the needs for various services grew with industrialization and urbanization. Many Jewish immigrants followed the route from peddler to pushcart owner to shopkeeper. While some

Italians were being trained in the construction trade through the padrone labor contracting system, others were setting up successful small shops in the needle and other trades. By 1910, 37.4 million immigrants had come to this country.[6] In Poughkeepsie, immigrants composed the majority of such businesses as tailoring, baking, butchering, brewing, and cigarmaking.

By and large, immigrants did best where capital requirements were modest, such as in the small groceries and retail shops off Main Street. They predominated in such marginal businesses as saloons, small hotels, and peddling. Native-born Americans predominated on Main Street, where they ran shops, such as dry goods and other businesses requiring larger amounts of capital.

In all, by 1870 there were about 500,000 nonfarm business enterprises—about equal to the number of actual corporate startups each year today. Most, of course, were very small, comprised of one or two employees working alongside the owner-proprietor.

In his famous trip through the United States in the early 1830s, Alexis de Tocqueville observed that all Americans seemed possessed of a yearning desire to rise, and all were constantly seeking property, power, or reputation. In the latter part of the nineteenth century, small business was a popular route to do so. Position of birth, or past business failure, was not an inhibiting stigma as in Europe—small business was a cultural common denominator of democratic opportunity. .

Frequently, the new small business entrepreneur learned his trade and drew confidence by working alongside or in close contact with his boss, whom he soon saw to be of human dimensions like himself. But with industrialism and modern management, the boss disappeared from the larger factories and large shops and was replaced by an impersonal foreman or manager. The division between capital and labor became physically apparent. In 1883, a brass worker related the change in the state of affairs.

"Well, I remember that fourteen years ago the workmen and the foremen and the boss were all as one happy family; it was just as easy and as free to speak to the boss as anyone else, but now the boss is superior, and the men all go to the foremen; but we would not think of looking the foremen in the face now any more than we would the boss."[7]

The leaders of the large enterprises that grew in this period were different from those of the small, independent businessmen in two important ways. First, organizational expertise, not the assumption of capitalist risk, was their route to success. Second, a very high percentage came from comfortable backgrounds and were well educated.

One study of 185 business leaders in the first decade of the twentieth century showed that 47 percent reached their positions through the bureaucratic route and another 12 percent through the professions, chiefly law. Only 14 percent were self-made entrepreneurs; 27 percent rose through existing family businesses. An earlier study of 303 business leaders in the textile, railroad, and steel industries in the 1870s revealed that the overwhelming majority were born in the United States to American-born parents. Some 90 percent were raised in a middle or upper-class family. About one-third had graduated from college. Fully half hadn't gone to work before age nineteen and less than one-quarter had worked before the age of sixteen.[8]

Success through the large business enterprise, in other words, was restricted, as by and large it is today, to an elite class drawn from those with advantaged backgrounds. In this situation were present the outlines of class society and class struggle.

Yet small business continued to offer opportunity for the less-advantaged American. To be sure, most small businessmen, as today, were also likely to come from fairly comfortable circumstances. But in small businesses, the boss continued to be an everyday presence and a familial atmosphere frequently prevailed. Small business, as today, hired and trained the less educated and the less desirable in general; advancement came through performance. And in a small but significant proportion of cases, small business continued to be enough of a corridor between the classes to give sufficient credence to the cultural ideal of equality of opportunity and democratic individualism to help deflect impetus toward class conflict.

Indeed, a post–World War II study revealed just how much the self-employment small business ideal continued to appeal to blue-collar industrial workers who would objectively seem to have little hope of achieving it. The study of automobile workers found that the idea of someday going into business for themselves remained a powerful aspiration, if not a goal, for many men on the assembly line.[9]

Today the small business entrepreneurial ideal has been a strong, formative force in the U. S. free-market-oriented response to the economic transition. By and large, the lack of a politics of class struggle, coupled with the continued strength of ideals of American democratic individualism, has contributed to this country's minor emphasis on planning and on social welfare programs.

In contrast, the European class politics married socialist tendencies for planning with aristocratic noblesse oblige (and the disdain both traditions held for business ownership) to contribute to the European social democratic response to past and current economic problems with a more bureaucratically guided, welfare-oriented capitalism. Japan managed through its period of industrial labor conflict in the post–World War II period by grafting its traditional family and clan values of duty and obligation onto a modern labor-management structure, and onto the general plan-oriented economic structure. It has helped it attain great economic equality and, thus far, international competitive success.

Self-Employment

Despite small business' second-class position in an economy dominated by large industrial corporations, its vigor is periodically forceful enough to be the locomotive of growth. Bursts of entrepreneurship in the late nineteenth century and in the 1920s helped shape the way new technologies and new business organizational methods were applied to the economy. Contemplating the demobilization of 10 million men after World War II, the Office of Mobilization and Reconversion predicted there would be 8 million unemployed by spring 1946. Postwar unemployment, however, reached only 2.7 million. Pent-up wartime demand was met, in part, by an unexpected burst of entrepreneurship, which corrected the sharp fall-off in self-employment caused by the war. The unanticipated rush of start-ups, notably in contract construction, manufacturing, and transportation, eased a difficult transition. Likewise, today's burst of entrepreneurship indicates that small business still has sufficient critical mass to drive the economy in transitional periods.

The current burst comes after a long period of slight interest in business self-employment. The surge in new business started immediately after World War II even though, by the late 1940s, *Fortune* observed about the new young generation, "The role of the entrepreneur is not coveted. . . . The class of 1949 wants to work for somebody else—preferably somebody big."[10] Likewise, novelists like John Marquand found little love of nonconformity and risk-taking in the psyche of the postwar generation which had grown up in the uncertain times of Depression and war. In the prosperity of the 1960s, the interest of Americans born during or after the war was directed more toward social justice than business entrepreneurship.

Yet since the mid-1970s, the entrepreneurial ideal has been resurgent. Thousands of business students and middle-management executives dream of running a fast-growing, innovative small firm, notwithstanding the fact that this ideal of the new entrepreneurship is a magnification of a statistically tiny fraction of the small business universe.

In 1967, only ten universities offered courses in entrepreneurship. By 1985, it had mushroomed to 340, with some schools offering majors in the subject.[11] A Babson College survey of its six to ten years alumni reported that 86 percent of those working for someone else wished to own their own businesses. A survey of 3,300 Michigan high school seniors over five years consistently found the order of preference for a professional career to be self-employment, employment at a small business, followed by employment in big business, government, and social services.[12]

A recent Roper poll of the general population found that 43 percent of Americans have a highly favorable view of small business versus only 17 percent for large corporations.

The circulation and advertising revenues of magazines that chronicle the small galaxy of glamorous, small-growth firms are booming: Prior to 1979, *Inc.* and *Venture* magazines didn't even exist. Today, their combined paid circulations are about one million; *Inc.*'s ad revenue in 1985 was 37th among all U.S. magazines, while *Venture's* was 84th.[13] Entrenched big business magazines such as *Business Week, Forbes,* and *Fortune* have extended their traditional coverage to include smaller companies. The *Wall Street Journal,* which now carries a weekly column on small business, found the topic so popular that in 1985 it dedicated its first of a new series of special subject reports—112 pages, including a rich assortment of advertisements—to small business.[14]

In recent years, with slow growth among their main Fortune 500 corporation client bases, many Big Eight accounting firms and major urban banks have set up special small business units to offer services which include cash management, account reconciliation, and bill and loan payment scheduling.

One of the major trends in American history has been the decline of self-employment. Although the figures are approximate, and not directly comparable between periods, in 1880 about 37 percent of Americans in the total work force were self-employed. That number decreased steadily until today it is about 10.5 percent.[15]

Yet the self-employed nonagricultural business population, despite fluctuations, has been remarkably *constant* over the entire period at about 9 percent. Throughout the century in which corporate wealth and economic output concentrated into fewer and bigger economic entities, the absolute number of independent firms has kept pace with population growth. The work force has become increasingly employee-based over the years, but that has been a result of an ongoing exodus from small farming to factory or service employment. In 1880, for example, 28 percent of the 37 percent self-employed were farmers. Today, less than 1.5 percent of the 10.5 percent full-time self-employed earn their income from the land. Since World War II, business self-employment has risen sharply in services and to a lesser extent in construction, while declining modestly in manufacturing and somewhat more sharply in the retail sector.

Since the mid-1970s, there has been a much-heralded statistical increase in the number of self-employed—today, about 10 million Americans make a full-time living from self-owned business enterprises. This does not include the large self-employed population in the underground economy.

To what extent does this increase in self-employment indicate a fundamental, long-term shift toward more entrepreneurship and new economics favoring smaller business units? Or is it merely a temporary shift due to a period of economic transition and the demographic effect of the baby boom? It is too early to say. However, the demographic increase in the thirty-five to forty-five-year-old prime-age population—those most likely to start businesses—favors a continuation of the resurgence of entrepreneurship in the near future. In 1975, 16.7 million Americans were in the prime-age category; by 1995, 34 million will be.

What are the factors behind the resurgence of the *ideal* of self-employment? Some of the impetus to create new businesses comes from the sluggishness and decline of the basic American industries that were the main engines of so much past prosperity. Demographics are at work, too. As corporate managers of the baby-boom generation find their upward mobility slowed by the sluggish growth of their companies and increasingly intense competition from peers, many are finding in small business an alternative for their ambitions.

Intriguingly, self-employment has so far provided an appealing avenue of opportunity among those who have enjoyed high levels of affluence and education and whose world-view values were shaped in the social upheaval of the 1960s. Capitalism's chief historic value has been its great ability to create wealth. But at a certain level of affluence, working to increase already high levels of material affluence becomes pointless. As the desire and ability to accumulate and to consume more material goods diminishes, so may some of the drive and willingness to endure the material sacrifices integral to starting a business.

Yet so far the taste for self-employment among the Woodstock generation, raised in the long postwar period of prosperity, supported by a working spouse and perhaps believing that the worst consequence of entrepreneurial failure is to return to regular employment, or at absolute worst, to fall back temporarily upon the social welfare net built since the Depression, seems as strong as ever. This is not due to a desire for wealth: Studies reveal that the drive to make money has fallen as a motivational factor. In the late 1960s, a majority of entrepreneurs cited the desire to make money as the primary reason they went into business; ten years later, 56 percent—double the 1960s figure—said that their principal motivation was that they didn't like working for someone else.[16]

The main impetus, rather, appears to be social. For the generally affluent and educated, small business self-employment has so far provided an attractive and economically productive means to channel personal energies to structure an independently chosen life-style. For many, the quality of life has replaced further material affluence as a major motivation.

Large corporations have experienced the change in social values as well. It has been widely noted, for instance, that young corporate executives today are less willing than in the past to sacrifice personal activities for their corporations. One impulse behind the current corporate trend for management teams and the deemphasis of organizational hierarchies is to find a better way to motivate these highly educated, affluent young corporate executives by getting them to understand and identify with the purpose of their work. Educated people, above all, resent being managed from the top down. A similar trend is evident in other industrialized nations as well. A survey found that job security was the principal concern of nine of ten Frenchmen in 1950; today, only three in ten. Today, even with high unemployment, Frenchmen cited personal expression as the most important factor in their work.[17]

Self-employment in small business has been an appealing route to satisfy the desire for an independence and self-fulfillment outside the mainstream channels of corporate or professional employment. This covers a wide range of personalities and personal ambitions. Ken Williams, the founder of $12 million computer software company Sierra On-Line, for example, married an ambitious, $4.1 million venture-capital-financed high-tech project with a love of nature sports by locating his corporate offices just outside Yosemite National Park in California, where whitewater rafting, mountain climbing, skiing, and hiking were just minutes away.[18] David Unowsky and his wife, Rolla, by contrast, run the Hungry Mind bookstore near the Macalester College campus in St. Paul, Minnesota. One of the 738 outlets of the B. Dalton book chain is only a five-minute drive away, but Unowsky has survived for 14 years with marginal profitability by selling high-brow titles and textbooks.[19]

Small business self-employment has been a principal route by which women have been able to fulfill the desire expressed by the feminist movement for greater participation in parts of the economy traditionally reserved for men. Indeed, women have been the driving impetus behind the self-employment boom. Self-employment among women has been increasing three times faster than total self-employment growth. By the early 1980s, women represented about one-third of all self-employed, up from one-quarter in 1975.[20]

Some of women's new businesses, of course, are part-time, and reflect the trend toward work for women with children. The telecommunications capabilities of the computer are creating expanded opportunities for businesses that can be run from the home. Many, however, are full-time. Some are prominent among the 6 million American women who earn more than their husbands.

Lillian Katz, founder and owner of the Lillian Vernon mail-order catalog, is one of those who started from a part-time, home-based operation to build a thriving full-time enterprise. Katz started her business in 1951 when she was a twenty-three-year-old housewife, pregnant with her first child. Her first products were an inexpensive matching leather handbag and belt she had designed and her father, who was in the handbag business, manufactured. They were sold by mail. Her first ad was in the September 1951 issue of *Seventeen* magazine. It drew $1,500 worth of orders within six weeks, which kept Katz busy typing, packing, and shipping orders. Other products and advertisements in other magazines like *Redbook* and *Vogue* followed. By 1956, five years after starting, Lillian Vernon shipped orders worth $198,000.

The first Lillian Vernon catalog was published in 1960, an eight-page pamphlet with black-and-white photos of the merchandise it offered. It wasn't as profitable as the advertisements—and wouldn't be until the 1970s. Nevertheless, she turned down advice to fold it. By 1983, she had stopped advertising in magazines altogether. Consumer tastes had changed. The ads just didn't pull anymore; her customers no longer were interested in seeing only single items at a time. The catalog, meanwhile, had grown to 150 pages.

By 1969, the year Katz and her husband were divorced after twenty years of marriage, the mail-order business had grown to $1 million a year. Throughout the 1970s, Katz built her business, adding and pruning products from her highly varied, seasonal catalogs containing gifts, housewares, and small specialty items. By the 1980s, the company's product list had reached 2,500 items, and its customers list passed 5 million—96 percent of them women. Up to one-half of the products were being custom-tailored for Katz, whose staff today includes several product designers and artists.

In 1981, Katz hired a direct-marketing consultant to devise a growth strategy for Lillian Vernon, then growing at a robust 18 percent annually. The consultant came up with three options: (1) Expand the product line; (2) Mail catalogs more often; (3) Send larger catalogs to a wider audience.

Katz' decision was to do all three things. In 1982, the company grew 40 percent. By 1984, sales had reached $113 million. In a $70 billion industry dominated by big names like Sears, J. C. Penney, and, until it folded its 113-year-old, 1,000-page catalog recently, Montgomery Ward, that doesn't count for much. But Lillian Vernon's profitability is reportedly on a par with such successful direct mail sellers as L. L. Bean and Spiegel, way at the top of the 6,500 different mail-order catalogs sent out to Americans each year in the mid-1980s. Profits from her catalog have made Katz a millionaire, and bought her a Mercedes and a large house in affluent Greenwich, Connecticut.

It has also made the business far too big for her to manage all of it. A chief operating officer, with management experience at large corporations Amerada Hess and IBM, was hired. The future? Katz says she has one more dream: to crown the achievement of growing a humble part-time business started by a young mother from her home in a time prior to the current trend for female entrepreneurship, by selling shares of Lillian Vernon on the public stock market.[21]

There is also a darker side to the increase in self-employment in the last decade. In times of economic trouble, self-employment in small business has historically been a last refuge against unemployment and inadequate income. Laid-off workers have turned to self-employment when unemployment benefits end and until regular employment opportunities reemerge. In the Depression, unemployed cigar workers became self-employed cigar makers called "buckeyes"; laid-off workers in the Paterson broad silk industry opened their own "cockroach" shops.

Although this is often overlooked in the euphoria of today's entrepreneurship boom, a large number of today's new entrepreneurs have become self-employed from necessity, not preference. Between 1979 and 1983, part-time self-employment among people already employed increased a staggering 468 percent—at a time when real income was falling.[22] In Illinois, where wage and salary employment fell 3.8 percent in the recession at the start of the 1980s, nonfarm self-employment grew 5.3 percent. A similar pattern can be seen in other states.[23] In a healthy economy of growing wealth, wages, and jobs, these marginal self-employed would happily disappear into the better-paid ranks of employees.

On occasion, those thrown unwillingly into self-employment find in it an unexpected boon. Such is the case of Paul Stewart, who was laid off from his $16,000-a-year assembly-line job at Chrysler in 1979. To make ends meet, he began driving authors and celebrities to news interviews in the Detroit area. Today, his Media Escort Service chauffeurs clients, helps prepare them for the interviews, and critiques them afterward. From this small business, Stewart earned more than $40,000 in 1984.[24]

Cases like Stewart's, of course, are rare. Most often, the worker who is compelled to do for his own account the type of work he'd done for a steady employer manages at best a subsistence living until improved economic conditions bring back his old job. Some make ends meet as one of the thousands of street vendors, selling cut-rate goods without a license and paying no taxes, who have appeared in recent years on big city streets across America.

Who are the self-employed small businessmen? The myth is that they come from deprived backgrounds and that rising from poverty is what drives them. Celebrated exceptions notwithstanding, this is balderdash.

For most small businessmen hard work alone is not enough. Surveys show that small businessmen tend to come from comparatively comfortable middle-class circumstances. They are far more likely to have been to college than their counterparts in the general population. They are almost three times more likely than members of the work force at large to have had self-employed parents. Whether notably successful or not, a self-employed parent provides an important role model for continued self-employment among their children.[25]

Consistent with findings early in the century, however, small businessmen today continue to come from less privileged backgrounds than the leaders of large corporations. Although their backgrounds were by and large comfortable, small businessmen are not likely to be polished children of the elite.

Comparisons between postwar studies indicate that small businessmen are about twice as likely to have had fathers who
were unskilled or skilled blue-collar workers than corporate
business leaders. Big business leaders are far more likely to
have had corporate managers for fathers, and somewhat less
likely to have had self-employed fathers than small business
entrepreneurs.

In comparing the backgrounds of small businessmen, it is
useful to distinguish between fast-growth company entrepreneurs and the mass of more ordinary small businessmen. In 1985,
the Gallup organization conducted a survey for the *Wall Street
Journal* comparing the backgrounds and habits of Fortune 500
executives, small business executives, and a category called
entrepreneurs, whose ranks were drawn from the *Inc.* magazine
list of the 500 fastest-growing smaller private companies—85
percent of whom had doubled sales in the previous five years.
Small business executives qualified for the survey provided
their company had 20 employees and did under $50 million a
year in sales. Of this group, 7 percent could boast that their
company's sales had doubled in the previous five years. By
limiting the survey to small businesses with at least 20 employees, the survey is heavily skewed toward *successful* small businessmen, and excludes a sizable chunk of the small business
universe. Nevertheless, the results of the survey for small businessmen, while hardly average, are indicative of (if somewhat
more glamorous than) more common small businessmen in
general.

Fortune 500 executives, unsurprisingly, were far more
likely to have college degrees, to have had better grades, to have
attended more prestigious colleges, and to have participated in
stereotypical all-American activities than either the Gallup entrepreneurs or the small businessmen. They were less likely to
have changed jobs, took more vacations, and were far more
likely to belong to a country club than the others.

In most respects, the small business executives were less
privileged, less mainstream versions of the Fortune 500 executives. About the same percentage, roughly two-thirds, of the
small businessmen as Fortune 500 executives had white Anglo-
Saxon Protestant origins; their religious profiles are almost
identical; they were almost equally as likely to belong to a local

civic organization; they were just as likely to have operated a business in high school or college; and, like Fortune executives, they had an overwhelming preference for American-made cars.

At the same time, they were only half as likely as the Fortune executives to have a college degree (but, with 47 percent having degrees, were far more likely to have college degrees than the less than 20 percent of the population at large with degrees). They did less well academically; they were about half as likely to belong to a country club; took less vacation; they were about half as likely to belong to a political group or a cultural organization; and somewhat less likely to be driving the large American cars they preferred.

The entrepreneurs were of an altogether different sort. Fitting the psychological stereotype, they can best be characterized as high-achievement and recognition-oriented, driven and restless, social misfits. A high percentage, 76 percent (but not nearly as high as the 94 percent of Fortune 500 executives) had college degrees. High-tech entrepreneurs, as usual among the small business population, are exceptions: Nearly all have at least an undergraduate degree; many have graduate degrees as well.

The entrepreneurs were more like the ordinary small businessmen in having attended less prestigious schools, in having achieved lower grades, and in participating less in all-American activities like varsity sports, fraternity or sorority membership, and school government. They were about twice as likely as the Fortune or small business executives to have been expelled or suspended from school. They were also far more likely to have worked at four or more companies—and, at 31 percent, more than three times as likely to have been fired from a job.

In comparison with the others, they are less likely to join civic clubs, take fewer vacations, and were much more likely to have operated a business in high school or college. Over half drive foreign cars.

Their ethnic and religious profile is different, too. Less than half of the entrepreneurs—versus two-thirds for the Fortune or small business executives—came from other than white Anglo-Saxon Protestant backgrounds. They were twice as likely to be Jewish or have no religious preference. Their psychological profiles, which will be examined in the next chapter, are markedly different as well.[26]

It has been widely noted that immigrants and their children are far more likely to be self-employed businessmen than an average drawn from the population at large. Indeed, one Michigan study found immigrants were three times, and their children two times, more likely to be self-employed than average. By contrast, immigrant large corporate executives constitute only their proportional representation among the general population.[27]

The high incidence of small business entrepreneurship among immigrants is often cited as evidence that economic hardship motivates the self-employed. Indeed, throughout American history immigrants have brought skills and energy to entrepreneurial new businesses which have added formative dynamism to America's free-market-oriented economy and reinforced the ideals of opportunity and democratic individualism which propel it. This remains so today. The United States, with 5 percent of the world's population, today takes in 50 percent of the world's nonrefugee population—this immigrant resource continues to be one of its competitive strengths.*

Many of the immigrants admitted to America may be poor, and overcoming economic hardship is very likely one major motivation that drives them to start small businesses. But they are not a representative sampling of the poor of their native lands, or of the poor in the United States.

They are an *elite* among the poor. The fact that they are capable of raising themselves above their hard lives, to make the sacrifices and endure the risks and uncertainties of relocating in a foreign land indicates this. Atypical of the poor, their values are future-oriented, that is, they defer present gratification in the optimistic faith that such sacrifices will yield greater gratification in the future—just like the middle or upper-middle classes who constitute the mainstream of self-employment.[28]

---

*In all, about one million immigrants come annually to the United States, half a million legally, and perhaps another half-million illegally. About half of these eventually leave the country. Only one-third of legal immigrants are men; men dominate immigration only from Africa and the Middle East, and, it is believed, compose the main body of illegal immigration.

That they have endured the travails of immigration makes them better prepared than the average native American to work the long hours at difficult, dirty work and to be more mobile in relocating wherever necessary to find promising opportunities for upward mobility.

A dramatic example can be seen by comparing the two waves of immigration from Southeast Asia after the Vietnam War. The first wave of 125,000, which arrived in 1975 to escape political retribution and to find new economic opportunity just like many immigrants of the past, was overendowed with those most likely to succeed in any environment. There were lots of lawyers, army officers, and bureaucrats. Within four years, their incomes were above the American median. A decade later, their unemployment rate was below the United States as a whole.

The second wave of 600,000, who began arriving in 1979, represented a much more random sampling of the poor of Southeast Asia, including Hmong tribesmen, lowland Lao, and Cambodians. They were forced out by the spread of war and economic devastation in their homelands which followed the American withdrawal from the region. They came less of their own volition and more of dire necessity than the first group. Four years after arriving, at a time when the 1975 immigrants were already self-sufficient, nearly half the Southeast Asians of 1979–80 were on some sort of welfare. Their unemployment rate was 14.6 percent—double the U.S. average—with many doing black-market piecework in the semiconductor and garment industries below minimum wage. Three-quarters of those in the San Diego area were living below the poverty line versus an overall U.S. poverty rate of 11 percent (and 20 percent for San Diego blacks and Hispanics).[29]

Immigrants traditionally build small businesses in fields that are easiest to enter. In cities, immigrants tend to go into unskilled, labor-intensive businesses which can absorb many family workers and which have low capital requirements. In New York, Koreans have bought groceries, Greeks coffee shops, and Indians, Pakistanis, and Bangladeshi newsstands.

Low capital start-up costs and a ready immigrant Indian work force were the major attributes which attracted Bhawnesh and Suresh Kapor to the New York newsstand business. The Kapors, who emigrated here from New Delhi in the mid-1970s, bought their first newsstand in 1978, on Wall Street. Since then, they have expanded rapidly, adding modern newsstands to a newsstand chain that totaled 212 throughout the New York area by the mid-1980s.

Many of the newsstands are open from 5:00 A.M. to 1:00 A.M. Most are manned by other Indian immigrants—35 of their 54 employees are freshly arrived fellow countrymen—willing to work 12 hours a day and earn an average of only $250 a week. They're willing to do so because they know that after three or four years, if they jealously husband their savings, they, too, will be able to afford the $30,000 required to buy a newsstand of their own.

New York City, among other cities in the country, is having its urban economic landscape transformed by new waves of immigrants. As in immigrant waves of the past, the new immigrants rely on networks of fellow countrymen and relatives already established for direction and financing to set up in many businesses eschewed by native-born Americans because of the initial low pay and grueling hours. Through years of self-denial and hard work, some build thriving businesses that bring to fruition yet another cycle in the American dream.

That dream is already coming true for the Kapors. In 1981, they borrowed $90,000 from the Small Business Administration and from Indian immigrant friends to make the down payment on a huge contract they won from New York's Metropolitan Transit Authority to operate 143 subway newsstands and a ten-year license to operate all the newsstands at stations of the suburban Long Island Railroad. To win the contract the Kapors promised to invest $1.2 million to transform 75 of the dingiest subway newsstands into models of the modern newsstands they planted around New York. By the mid-1980s, the Kapors' rapidly expanding newsstand empire was grossing about $20 million in sales each year.[30]

Highly skilled immigrants are still important sources of machine tool shop start-ups. Typically, those in the small machine shop business have no college but at least five years of shop floor experience working for others.

Small business self-employment offers an attractive route to upward mobility for people who, for one reason or another, don't fit into the professional or corporate mainstream. As such, it is a very valuable social-economic channel for making fuller productive use of human resources in society. This includes would-be empire builders, immigrants, creative oddballs, different drummers, laid-off senior corporate executives unable to return to the corporate world, social misfits, and those who simply prefer independence and business challenge.

There is one large exception in the nonunderground economy self-employment picture: racial—particularly black and Hispanic—minorities. While small business entrepreneurship among minorities has increased in recent years, minority entrepreneurs equal less than one-third the proportional representation of minorities in the U.S. population. Minorities control an even tinier proportional percentage than that of business assets. Minority businesses are much more likely to be sole proprietorships than white-owned businesses; only 2 percent of minority-owned firms are corporations versus 19 percent for the entire business population.[31] Not surprisingly, therefore, income from minority businesses is significantly lower than from white-owned ones. The two largest black-owned businesses, Johnson Publishing and Motown, both had just under $140 million in sales in 1984. The tenth largest, Applied Science Corporation, did under $50 million.

The Family Business

The overwhelming majority of American businesses are family affairs. In all but a few exceptional cases, the American family business, like that of tobacconist Arnold Goldstein, is small business. The family business adds a personal character to the social economy, especially to the social economies of towns and of ethnic neighborhoods in urban environments. In many towns, the family retail shops dotting Main Street are the last modern links to the mom-and-pop general store epoch of Americana. The general merchandise general store selling limited quantities of dry goods, hardware, housewares, and the other basics has been disappearing for many decades. In 1967, there were 27,000 general stores with under 25 employees; by 1982, less than half that number remained.

Small family businesses, of course, have endured with their traditional tenacity with varying success in all broad sectors of retail, services, and industry. As ever, the life of the small family business is likely to be a hard one. Subsistence incomes earned from long hours and unpaid help from family members is more the rule than the exception. As noted by Goldstein, the business operation reflects the relations among family members, normal family ego problems, and family affections. If a son or daughter wishes to make a career of the family business in adulthood, how the parent shares decision-making authority with him—especially the attendant problems of succession—and how well the son or daughter adapts to caretaking a business started by someone else, is likewise an intensely personal affair.

The dynamics of the continuity of the U. S. family business, however, is different from many other industrialized nations. In continental Europe, for example, social traditions and limited economic opportunity have combined to make it more likely for children to follow their parents in the family business. In America, the trajectory of cultural tradition has generally propelled sons and daughters to eschew the family business and make their own fortunes. Even in the mid-nineteenth century, the Poughkeepsie study found that sons only rarely succeeded fathers in the father's business.

America's democratic individualist tradition encourages children to make their own mark in the world. Often, the children wish to find alternatives to the long, hard hours the parent often puts into the family business. These tendencies are often encouraged by the parent's own wish to see his son and daughter have a better life than he did. One version of the American dream is to achieve familial upward mobility through the next generation, working to send a son through college and to a white-collar desk job in the professions or perhaps manager in a large corporation.

Immigration has traditionally provided an important source of replenishment for American family businesses. Of course, new generations of native-born American entrepreneurs sometimes carry on their family's businesses.

This may be changing. With the corporate fast track slowed by the sluggish economic growth of the last decade and by competition from baby-boom-aged managers, more young MBAs have been finding their family's businesses an attractive alternative means to wielding management power and fulfilling business ambitions. A large number of these businesses were founded in the entrepreneurial boom after World War II, and their founders are conveniently approaching retirement age. As a further attraction, many young sons and daughters believe that their family businesses are more accommodating to their personal life-style preferences than they would find at a large corporation. Several universities now offer courses in family business.

Nevertheless, the new family businessmen must overcome the grim facts of transfer of family businesses between generations. Only about 30 percent of family businesses are handed down from the founder to his family heirs and only 15 percent make it to the third generation. Most fail. Others are sold or liquidated. Not a few are ruined or sold due to family squabbles over control upon the death of a founder who has not provided a clear line of succession beforehand. Others are done in or diluted by estate taxes: The Wrigley chewing gum family had to sell the Chicago Cubs baseball team, and the Coors beer family had to sell shares to the public, to meet their tax obligations.

Finally, surviving is not thriving. One study of the history of 200 family businesses over a 60-year period found that only 26 survived as private family businesses. Of those, only six—a mere 3 percent of the original group—grew and prospered.[32]

Small Business and Social Welfare

Social welfare is mainly a large corporation, not small business, ethic and practice. Big corporations have the best record in adhering to pollution control, workplace health and other government set standards, and in maintaining good labor practices. The enlightened self-interest of a large corporation with ongoing economic interests causes it to practice a variety of social goodwill gestures. In the 1930s, chain stores responded to the clamor small retailers and state politicians raised against them by encouraging branch managers to join civic associations and identify in other ways with their local communities. Today many corporations, including Citicorp and 3M, have executives one of whose defined responsibilities is to follow local community politics so that relations with the corporation will remain favorable. Large corporation coffers fund many worthy philanthropic causes from the arts to public television and research foundations. In 1983, corporations gave $3 billion to various charities, led by IBM's $105 million contribution. Several corporations give prestigious awards for a variety of causes. Westinghouse Electric, for example, has given cash prizes to top high school science students since 1942.

Small businessmen, whose interests represent the profit motive in its purest form and whose ability to practice social amenities even if they wished to do so is constrained by their limited profits, typically lead the lists of pollution, workplace health, and labor practice offenders.

Yet small business does contribute to the social welfare in ancillary ways. Large corporate philanthropy tends to be directed toward mainstream or status quo–oriented organizations. The small number of highly successful small businessmen who personally make charitable contributions are bound by no such stricture. Their contributions are as diverse—and sometimes bizarre—as their interests. This serves the interest of political and cultural diversity.

Small businessmen serve the social welfare in nonpecuniary ways through commitments to local community activities and through political lobbying action on behalf of local interests, even if often their own. Small businessmen are notably active in local Chambers of Commerce and Rotary Clubs. The local auto dealer, who is often the largest businessman in town, the local banker, and others have strong commitments to—as well as self-interested personal and business incentives to foster—the long-term development of the local community. They are active in civic activities as well as economic ones. They serve on hospital building committees and as trustees of local colleges. State legislators and national politicians often rise from the ranks of successful small businessmen. The millionaires' club known as the U.S. Senate has a large representation of former small business owners. Together, they constitute an important layer of influence that reinforces representative democracy in the U.S. political system.

Small Business and Small Town

Since the days when the frontier general store was the main source of supplies, often the only source of credit, and the social gathering place for reading and conversation, small business has been a vital part of rural and small-town economy and life. The more remote the area, the less effectively big business' economies of size penetrate the region and the greater the dependence on small business. Even in towns big enough to have a K-Mart or a J.C. Penney or a Sears, these branches of big business exist alongside a diverse range of hardware shops, pharmacies, grocers, coffee shops, lumber operations, auto dealers, bars, and other small businesses which, in the aggregate, are often more integral to the health of the local economy and community.

Wooing a big company to put down roots locally may provide a sudden economic boon to a community at one stroke. Yet the introduction of a big corporation immediately exposes the small town to the shifting fortunes of that big corporation in the international economy. The local economy may feel the indirect impact of events occurring thousands of miles away on the other side of the globe. Small firms that produce a limited quantity of goods for a limited, regional market, on the other hand, tend to insulate the town from twists in the global economy. Moreover, they are far more likely than big business to create new local entrepreneurs and spin off new businesses than the operation of a big corporation. Some localities, hurt by dependence on a single declining large company in the past, have been consciously trying to recruit a diverse base of smaller enterprises instead.

Small businesses tend to buy locally, thus reinforcing the economic base. While media attention is focused on big Madison Avenue advertising agencies, which normally turn up their noses at clients that don't spend more than $250,000 a year, local advertising in the United States amounts to $27 billion a year. That's about half the U.S. total, excluding direct mail. Much of the local advertising is placed in local newspapers, and created not by professional ad agencies but by the newspapers themselves.[33] That local ad revenue finances America's hundreds of local newspapers, which are mainstays of community affairs. The unique heritage of thousands of small-town community banks has reinforced local investment by recycling local deposits for local business loans.

Small business diversity is also the mainstay of many regional traits and customs that would be lost in an economy where only larger economic entities existed. Regional and ethnic foods, for example, such as gumbo, lutefish and lefsa, kielbasa, catfish, and Rocky Mountain oysters are served only by small businesses. A national chain like McDonald's depends on the common denominator of national menus for much of its efficiency.

Finally, small businesses often preserve living traces of Americana. In Sutter Creek, California, 100 miles east of San Francisco in the gold-mine country of the foothills of the Sierra Nevada mountains, Carl Borgh and a couple of employees work the oldest cast-iron foundry in California and the water-powered machine shop, perhaps the oldest in the United States, which adjoins it. The foundry was built in 1873 by Samuel Knight, who invented a high-powered water turbine, the Knight Water Wheel, which revolutionized the local mining industry in its time. Borgh, a former aeronautical engineer with McDonnell-Douglas and an independent designer, bought the foundry in 1970 from the owner's widow at a bid that included a promise to keep it as it was. Today, the foundry business does custom work. Big contracts have come from pouring all the iron work and cast-iron filigree work for restoring the California state capitol building, and for a similar project restoring a historic county courthouse.[34]

A strong small business economy depends on an economic environment which, if not encouraging to small business formation and growth, at minimum is able to sustain a critical mass of small business activity. Studies show that existing small businesses are by far the most important breeding ground of new entrepreneurs. In an effort to quantify just how prolific existing small businesses are, one study found that small businesses were ten times more likely to produce entrepreneurs than big ones. Studies also show that small divisions of large corporations are more likely to produce independent entrepreneurs than large divisions. Nowhere is this hothouse breeding effect more evident than in Silicon Valley. The champion high-tech breeding stud is Fairchild Semiconductor, whose family tree since the mid-1950s boasts some 100 offspring, including such important companies as Intel and National Semiconductor.[35]

Small business entities endow several qualities of entrepreneurship that larger business entities cannot. By virtue of its size, it familiarizes employees with all aspects of the broader business operation, and imparts some generalist skills through everyday operations. It permits, even compels, important employees to take greater individual decision-making responsibility, since there are few, if any, management layers between decision and enactment, and no approval committees other than the boss. In contrast to the narrow perspectives to which specialists within a larger corporate division are prone, the small business employee generally gains a broad view of the business market which permits him to go beyond a conceptual understanding of general trends to see specific opportunities within those trends which may become the basis for a new business. Finally, the small business owner, by virtue of his entrepreneurial constitution and his ongoing interaction with his employees, serves as an important role model for prospective entrepreneurs, just as he does even more strongly for his son or daughter. Maintenance of a viable entrepreneurial environment for small business is related to another vital issue of the social economy—the form of future economic freedom of expression. A future global economy dominated by centralized economic entities may foster admirable ideals of social equity, but bigness can also suffocate opportunities for individual enterprise that are at the core of the American concept of liberty. The evolution of the economy may in time reveal a path to viable balance between more central planning and individual initiative that satisfies the peculiarly American version of economic liberty. If self-employment in small business loses its economic viability to such an extent as to discourage entrepreneurs before that should occur, however, the cultural values that provide the spirit for current American enterprise may lose some inspiration and vigor as well.

7

Small Business Profitability

In 1978, small businessman Allen E. Paulson took the gamble of a lifetime by purchasing the general aviation subsidiary of the billion-dollar defense contractor Grumman Corporation. Paulson, a former TWA mechanic who had gone on to build a $35 million business converting surplus passenger aircraft into cargo planes, knew the aircraft business. Gut instinct told him that underexploited among the Grumman subsidiary's line of lackluster light aircraft, and the parent executive management's main preoccupation with Defense Department contracts, was one unpolished gem, the Cadillac of business jets, the Gulfstream. The hands-on, single-minded attention of a technically proficient small businessman could make it shine.

In 1983, at the peak of the boom in the Initial Public Offerings market, Paulson, after several years of polishing, took Gulfstream Aerospace public. His reward: $85 million in cash and stock worth $551 million—about ten times what he had paid for the Grumman subsidiary only five years before. That year, Gulfstream's total stock market value was four-fifths the entire value Wall Street assigned for *all* of the four times larger Grumman. In 1985, Paulson sold his remaining 71 percent to

Chrysler, which intended to run Gulfstream Aerospace as an independent subsidiary with Paulson at its head.

The Gulfstream had been at the core of Grumman's largest profit-margin subsidiary. It had also represented its major diversification outside its huge military aircraft business, which had been tainted by foreign order payoff scandals. How did Grumman come to give it up to Paulson and, with only five years' hindsight, so cheaply?

The answer lies in a combination of the occasional near-sightedness and the different risk/reward considerations of a large corporation. It also includes a parable why small business and big business rarely make compatible bedfellows.

The story's origin began in 1973, when Grumman's new chairman, John C. Bierwirth, bought a small, money-losing Ohio maker of light, inexpensive aircraft and combined it in a new subsidiary with its own Gulfstream jet. Bierwirth says the suggestion to do so came to him in a folder left behind by Grumman's late chairman, who'd died suddenly. On the surface, there seemed to be two attractions to the Ohio company—an $11.2 million tax loss carry-forward, and an apparent opportunity to grow in the then promising general aviation business. The price tag, however, also included new partners who got 20 percent of the new subsidiary, and an operating executive for the division.

Almost immediately conflicts developed between the independent-minded operating executive, who had been chief executive officer of the light aircraft manufacturer, and Grumman corporate headquarters, which insisted that it have final say over all significant decisions. In a short time, the subsidiary's chief executive left to become chairman of Cessna (which he ran successfully for over a decade before General Dynamics bought it in 1985).

The minority shareholders, led by a group of three wealthy and strong-minded businessmen, Cleveland Browns football team owner Arthur Modell, David S. Ingalls, Jr., and Duane Stranahan, Jr., of the Champion Spark Plug family, were upset when Grumman inserted one of its own loyal managers as a replacement. To protect their investment, they wanted some say in how the subsidiary was run—or they wanted out. The price of their shares, they informed Grumman, was $20 million;

Grumman executives informed them they would only pay $10 million.

The standoff—with Grumman running the subsidiary on its own terms—lasted over three years. During that period the minority shareholders' frustration had been aggravated by the perception that Grumman had kept them poorly informed on the Securities and Exchange Commission investigation in 1976 of Grumman's overseas payments to win sales orders, which included the Gulfstream.

The bad feelings turned to anger—and then suspicion—when the development costs for the Grumman III aircraft doubled over original estimates to $150 million (the design was ultimately scrapped). At that point they demanded that they be allowed to bring in outside bidders on the expensive development program, or at least an independent consulting firm to guarantee that Grumman wasn't bilking the subsidiary through exorbitant charges for its engineering work. Showdown time had come.

In February 1978, the two sides met at the Waldorf-Astoria hotel in New York in the middle of a raging blizzard. The minority shareholders repeated their insistence that Grumman buy them out—reducing their demand to $17 million—or that steps be taken to make the subsidiary more independent with more outside directors and an independent audit committee. If nothing was done, they said they were prepared to sue. Grumman executives capitulated. They agreed to make the subsidiary more independent.

In July, however, while steps were being taken to make the subsidiary more independent as pledged, Grumman suddenly announced it was selling its 80 percent to Paulson. Modell, Ingalls, and Stranahan were stunned. Feeling they had little alternative they sold, too, for $12 million.

Grumman sold not only because of the problems it was having with the minority shareholders and the development of the G-III, but because its cash flow had been severely strained by the acquisition of a bus company, Flxible, several months earlier, which it hoped would supply its long-sought diversification. (Flxible ultimately proved disappointing; many of the 845 that were sold to New York developed mechanical problems and became the object of a $324 million lawsuit against Grumman).

Allen Paulson had always made the best of his opportunities. The Gulfstream would be no exception. Growing up as an Iowa farmboy in the Depression, Paulson had helped make ends meet by selling newspapers and cleaning hotel bathrooms. After high school at age nineteen he got a job for 30¢ an hour as a TWA mechanic. He also moonlighted in an auto repair garage. He learned aviation by taking apart airplane engines, and then by flying jets himself. Later, he sold surplus airplane parts. Finally, in 1951, then in his twenties, he began converting surplus passenger aircraft into cargo planes in his own business which a quarter-century later had grown strong enough to be the vehicle for the takeover of Gulfstream. In a few short years, by improving quality, cutting costs, and shortening delivery times, Paulson transformed the Gulfstream into a world leader in the highly competitive corporate jet market with commensurate profits: In 1983, it ranked on two of *Forbes'* 500 Yardsticks— for greatest profitability and highest cash flow.

Paulson was not shy about enjoying the fortune it made him. A year after cashing in through the public market, he was building himself a huge antebellum mansion near Savannah, Georgia, replete with extensive porches, two man-made lakes, a nine-hole golf course, a tennis court, a boat dock, and a landing pad for his helicopter, which he uses for short business trips and to go to his Hilton Head property. Around the country he had four other homes. Not everything about his celebrity and wealth was pleasurable, however, especially when it led to an attempted kidnapping of his son.

Why did Paulson sell to Chrysler at age sixty-two instead of running the company as its boss? One reason appears to be to cover losses on a bad investment gamble on the U.S. steel industry. Paulson had bought 34 percent of Wheeling-Pittsburgh Steel in the belief that the U.S. steel industry would eventually rebound. He learned the hard way that talent in one business doesn't automatically guarantee savvy in another when Wheeling subsequently filed for bankruptcy.[1]

One enduring appeal of small business entrepreneurship is that it offers a concrete route for the simultaneous realization of two fundamental American ideals: the desire for independence, and the desire to rise economically.

Unique in history, the "nobility" in the United States was comprised of self-made men, often humbly born, most starting as small businessmen. Unlike Europe, with its inherited feudal social class traditions, their exalted status in America perpetually hinged on their continued proficiency in business and bumping aside upstarts who tried to displace them—not on fortuitous accidents of birth.

In 1848 the richest man in America was fur trader and real estate speculator John Jacob Astor. His $20 million fortune, adjusted for inflation, would have been worth $233 million in 1984. At his death in 1877, railroad operator Cornelius Vanderbilt, the richest man of his day, left $100 million—in 1984 dollars, that was worth $947 million. The richest man 60 years later, J. D. Rockefeller, the oil man, left his heirs $1 billion—worth $7 billion today.[2]

The fortunes amassed by these barons, and some others almost as wealthy, were sometimes so vast that their heirs generations later still figure among the richest people in the country. Yet new self-made individuals were always pushing in. On the *Forbes* "Rich List" of 1985, 165 of the 400 richest individuals in the United States—those with a net worth of at least $150 million—possessed mostly self-made fortunes. Some 4 percent were immigrants. They included the richest individual in the country, Sam Moore Walton, who started selling shirts for J. C. Penney after college and went on to amass a net worth of $2.8 billion from his Wal-Mart discount drugstore chain concentrated in Sunbelt towns of fewer than 25,000 people. Third was Hewlett-Packard founder David Packard, worth over $1.5 billion. There was "potato king" J. R. Simplot, who quit school in the eighth grade and made a fortune in excess of $550 million partly by selling 700 million pounds of French fries to McDonald's and Burger King each year. The youngest self-made member of the list was thirty-seven-year-old James Jaeger. He amassed his $175 million fortune after quitting a $19,000-a-year job as an electrical engineer and developing a radar detector to protect speeding motorists from the police. Then, of course, there was Gulfstream entrepreneur Allen Paulson.[3]

Only an elite fraction of small businessmen ever taste such superwealth, of course. By the time they do, they remain "small business entrepreneurs" only in the widest possible sense of the term.

Well below the tiny circle of superwealthy is a more common circle of economic success—the millionaires' club. In 1880 there were but 100 millionaires in the country. By 1916, 40,000.[4] Today there are perhaps one million millionaires in the United States. *Forbes* estimates that 80 percent are self-made. Many are doctors, lawyers, and Fortune 500 executives. But for a very substantial number—according to one decade-long study, most of them—wealth and independence have been achieved through the arduous hours and thrift of small business.

To be sure, $1 million today is not what it once was. Just in the past decade, the ranks of millionaires have swelled due to double-digit inflation and the speculative, soaring value of real estate. Adjusted for inflation, $1 million in 1985 was worth only $500,000 in 1974 dollars. Many of today's millionaires cannot afford the luxuries traditionally associated with such wealth. For instance, the fully taxed investment income on $1 million cash is about $75,000—insufficient to support a yacht and nowhere near the cost of buying one.[5]

Many of the millionaires never enjoy their cool million because most of it is tied up in their businesses or in their homes. To fully enjoy it, they would have to sell out, like Michael Berolzheimer, the founder of Duraflame, Inc. Berolzheimer started by salvaging wood chips from saw mills to package into fireplace logs with $35,000 of his own money; in 1978, he sold his company to Clorox for over $9 million. He now invests and participates in other people's businesses. For every Berolzheimer there is someone who doesn't want to sell, however, because doing so often means giving up a business that has grown to be part of himself, that may add pleasure to life, and for some fulfills a psychological necessity.

Small Business Profits

Only a small percentage of self-employed Americans ever achieve millionaire status. Those that do are drawn from the 15 percent of small businesses with growth characteristics. For the other 85 percent the economic reality is far different, the goal more basic—survival.

The income data on small business is inadequate. The inference is that small business does poorly. The two indicators of general small business profitability—aggregate income data and data on business failure—undoubtedly mask thousands of important success stories. Most full-time small businessmen, however, would probably earn more money as employees than working for themselves.

Roughly three-quarters of U.S. businesses transact less than $100,000 in total business volume. Less than 5 percent do over $1 million in revenue. How profitable are these companies?

In 1981, sole proprietorships with under $50,000 in annual sales averaged $10,500 in sales and reported an average of only $2,150 in net income. Active partnerships with under $100,000 turnover, and the corporations transacting less than $500,000, each had cumulative losses. As a result, three-fourths of America's businesses (perhaps two-thirds of them part-time) net losses or very marginal incomes for their owners.

What of the rest? For companies above the 75th percentile, but excluding the top 10 percent of American companies, the average reported net profit was below $15,000 a year—less than a steelworker or a white-color middle manager.

Only the reported income of the elite top 10 percent of U.S. businesses fulfills the stereotypical picture of successful entrepreneurship: Sole proprietors doing over $100,000 a year, and averaging $300,000 in revenues, in 1981 netted $25,000 in profits. Corporations with over $1 million in revenue—but excluding the largest 3,000 corporations—averaged about $6.5 million in revenues and $150,000 in net income. Finally came the elite partnerships, highly weighted with lawyers and financial firms, recording more than $500,000 and averaging $2.2 million in revenue, with an average net income that year of $193,000.[6]

An indicator of the profitability of the absolute elite of small companies is *Inc.* magazine's list of the fastest-growing small companies. In 1983, the median company on the *Inc.* 100 (which measures the fastest-growing publicly held companies that had under $25 million in sales in 1975–79) had $27.2 million in sales and $2.6 million in net income. In 1984, probably due to the shakeout in the computer industry, that fell to $20.2 million and $1.2 million.[7]

There are important caveats that may add some cheer to this sober portrait of U.S. small business profits: Not included in the reported income filings is compensation the small businessman may have taken from his company as salary or as dividends. It doesn't include the perquisites he may give himself. In larger small businesses, the typical owner drives an expensive car provided by the company, receives life and other insurance from the company, and has at least one club membership written off on the company's books. Nor does it count the personal expenses he may charge to his business for tax advantage. Nor the huge and growing amount of outright profit skimming that goes on throughout small businesses. In 1984, it was estimated that the government loss on unreported income by small businesses totaled about $27 billion—a sum equal to 13 percent of the federal deficit that year.[8]

In general, the larger the small business the more profitable it is likely to be. Corporate data shows that asset size and profitability run in tandem.

The profit squeeze is greatest on the smallest companies. For those with under five employees, more often than not the wage bill is a weekly worry. Survival and success, if it is to come at all, generally comes through economic tenacity and sweating labor.

The failure-rate data, the second main indicator of small business profitability, sustains the relatively bleak portrait of small business profitability.[9] Standard estimates are that about half to two-thirds of all small businesses never reach their fifth birthday. By the tenth year, 80 percent are gone. Firms that are more than ten years old account for about only 20 percent of all failures.

Small business accounts for over 99 percent of all business failure. In most studies survival probability increases progressively with size, capitalization levels, and age of the firm.[10] About one-quarter of firms with under ten employees fail to survive their first year. After the fourth year, about three-fifths of firms with under 20 employees will have shut their doors.

Failures are most common in retailing, followed by services and construction. Restaurants and bookstores have notoriously high failure rates. Evidence seems to indicate that franchising increases the chances of survival: Perhaps one in three franchisees fails within the first two years, although failure rates tend to level off after that, probably as a franchise establishes itself. Companies that start in one of the industrial incubators popping up around the country also seem to have better early changes of survival. One Small Business Administration study has found that about three-quarters of them survive at least three years versus one-third for similar firms that set up independently.[11]

Longevity, though an indicator of higher future survival probability, is not a sign of profitability, however. Of every ten business closures, nine are voluntary. The most common reason is the retirement of the owner. In most such cases, the marginal profitability of the business fails to attract a buyer or an heir.

Small business' uninspiring aggregate profitability is not surprising given its generally inferior position to large business in the private economy. By and large, small businesses are forced toward the lowest and least secure profit zones of the economy as more powerful big businesses command the markets that yield handsome and, above a certain minimum level, the most secure profits.

Attributes of Success

Few businesses seem like promising ventures at the start. Yet a few succeed, while most don't. Why?

On the surface, there seems to be little pattern for predicting profitability. In 1946, William Moore, then twenty-nine, was one of tens of thousands of demobilized World War II veterans looking to go into business for himself. Demobilization had triggered a boom in housing, as young men and women set up families in record numbers. Houses needed to be painted— and it was the paint business that caught Moore's attention. He knew little about it, but he knew William Kelly, then sixty-eight, who had recently retired from the paint business. He convinced Kelly to unretire. For their market niche they targeted painting contractors on the West Coast. The national paint brands, they believed, were looking past the professional contractor end of the business to the much larger do-it-yourself consumer market.

Forty years after starting out, Kelly-Moore Paint Company is still a regional Western company, but it is also the most profitable competitor in the industry. While bigger national corporations like Sherwin-Williams and Glidden net about 2.5 percent on sales, Kelly-Moore usually nets over 10 percent. In 1984, net profits were over $11 million on sales of $136 million.

Kelly-Moore's marketing strategy is built around the needs of painting contractors. Since painting contractors generally work from their homes, they buy their high quality paint as needed for each job. By maintaining stores that are two and a half times larger than the industry average, Kelly-Moore is sure to have enough stock in all colors on hand whenever they drop in. Having its stores, in effect, double as its customers' warehouses enables it to keep track of clients' inventories and likely needs. This helps Kelly-Moore inventory turn over 12 times a year. That is five times the industry average—and a major reason why its net margins are almost five times higher as well.

Kelly-Moore has parlayed its strength with painting contractors into an increasingly strong position among consumers. This has served it especially well in the past troubled decade when economy-minded consumers have been doing more of their own painting. How has it done so? Amazingly simple: Professional painters usually leave partly used cans behind when they finish a job. Consumers find the Kelly-Moore label, and a product sample, right in their own homes to help them decide which paint to buy when it comes time to repaint. Today, just about the age Kelly was when they started in 1946, Moore, who owns 97 percent of the company, rides to work in a Rolls-Royce.[12]

For the Eisenstadt family of Brooklyn, New York, which started its packaging business, Cumberland Packing Corporation after World War II, and were the first to market sugar in small paper envelopes for table-top use, real success didn't come until 1958 when it started packaging sugar-substitute saccharin in the now familiar pink envelopes and named it Sweet 'n Low after one of their favorite songs. They survived Food and Drug Administration publicity about saccharin's carcinogenic potential. But they now face a probably overwhelming challenge from G. D. Searle's aspartame-based sugar substitute, NutraSweet.[13]

Other small businesses in fields as diverse as roller skates, wood stoves, and diet chocolate fudge soda have enjoyed sudden, short-lived surges in business as their products caught the

American consumers' notoriously faddish tastes. Yet thousands of other small businessmen who never make the limelight—and indeed shun it for fear of attracting unwanted competition—log steady, high-profit margins in niches in all sectors of the American economy.

While exceptions are indeed part of the rule in small business profitability, there are dominant patterns among the successful firms that go beyond merely choosing a good product in a good market. Successful small business entrepreneurs, like Allen Paulson, usually had long experience in their fields before venturing into business on their own, often in another small business. Even in Silicon Valley, where popular reputation boasts stories of inexperienced young geniuses becoming overnight successes, the average entrepreneur had been a manager for ten years before founding his own business.[14] Finally, there seems to be some correlation between educational attainment and levels of small business income.

The personal constitution of the small businessman must be hardy enough to endure the rough early months and years to make what wouldn't seem an especially promising venture into one that turns a profit. Workweeks of 70 hours or more are normal fare at the beginning for both successful and unsuccessful entrepreneurs. These long hours often accompany paying oneself little or no salary, depending on the help of spouse, family, and friends, working in makeshift offices, perpetually struggling to generate internal, or obtain external, financing, and, of course, living with constant self-doubt.

Such demands were almost too much for the five young Silicon Valley men who founded the $4 million, 35-employee Hunter & Ready, which makes an operating system to regulate microprocessor chips used in automobiles, medical devices, and elevators. Their small office was located above a camera shop in downtown Menlo Park, California. One suffered a severe prolonged depression; another a broken marriage. At the start, only one of the five owners, the design engineer, received a salary, and the other four chipped in to pay him. They charmed journalists at computer trade shows to get their product written up in the trade journals. Those write-ups helped attract venture capital, for which they traded 45 percent of their equity. Even then, 80-hour workweeks were the routine. The finished product was launched in a recession and initial sales were poor. This led to shouting matches among the partners, and aggravated their personal problems. "We were living every day in fear we would have nothing to show [for our efforts]," one of the founders reported. The first profitable month finally came in January 1984, two years after starting the business.[15]

Even in profitable, maturer businesses entrepreneurs often put in 60-hour workweeks and endure the anxieties, sometimes acute, of ill fortunes in the business environment. Writing about his experience in the severe depression of 1893, J. D. Rockefeller noted:

[I wondered] how we came through them. You know how often I had not an unbroken night's sleep, worrying about how it was all coming out. All the fortune I have made has not served to compensate for the anxiety of the period. Work by day and worry by night, week in and week out, month after month.[16]

Many small businessmen are propelled to entrepreneurship by an unforeseen external event. Sometimes this is propitious, as in the case of getting a guaranteed first customer or, to a lesser extent, an important supplier. Good fortune took a hand in the case of Wilton H. Jones, the founder of Multimate International Corporation, which produces a popular word processing program. In 1982, Jones ran a two-man consulting firm. A client, Connecticut Mutual Life Insurance Company, which had ordered 1,000 IBM PCs for its insurance agents, wanted a software program for them akin to that of its existing Wang system. Jones was a mainframe expert. But he needed work, so he made a low bid for the development project. He won it with no idea whether he could make it or not.

A friend bootlegged a copy of IBM's still unpublished PC manual, and Jones hired computer programmers, some of whom used vacation time from their existing jobs, from around the eastern part of the United States. Within 30 days, he knew the word processing project would succeed. More important, he also realized that other companies with Wang systems would need similar programs. He arranged to buy the marketing rights to the word processing system from Connecticut Mutual, which took a 5 percent stake in his new company, Multimate. He also repaid the insurance giant's $500,000 program development investment out of Multimate's early sales. With Multimate revenues accruing at a rate of $30 million a year in 1985, and with 20 percent pretax margins, Jones cashed in by selling Multimate to competitor Ashton-Tate for $19 million.[17]

The propelling event in the life of Chicago-born entrepreneur Lenny Mattioli was far more disagreeable—the death, in 1969, of his older brother. Mattioli, who'd been working as a mechanical engineer for Eastman Kodak in Rochester, New York, went to Madison, Wisconsin, to liquidate his brother's struggling TV sales and service shop and pay off some of the six-figure debt he'd left behind. Mattioli discovered he liked selling TV sets. Even more, he liked the direct risks and rewards of being in business for himself. At Kodak, he and the other engineers pretty much got the same raise regardless of how good they were or how hard they worked. He quit Kodak. He began building American TV & Appliance of Madison, Inc. By 1984, it was a $160 million company with 850 employees and several football-field-sized stores selling TVs, cameras, computers, stereo equipment, appliances, and furniture. Mattioli's marketing strategy was based on a system almost the antithesis of what he experienced at Kodak. There were no prices in his stores; consumers negotiated the best prices they could with salespeople whose compensations were tied to the net profit garnered on each sale.[18]

Finally, for Hank Heeber, owner of four tire and auto repair shops, three shoe stores, and a cattle ranch, the propelling event was nothing more than a paltry raise of $50 from his former tire store employer. "I looked at it [the $50] and said, 'This isn't a raise, it's an insult.' Then I left," said Heeber, who promptly went into competition.[19]

Much has been written about the psychology and background of highly successful entrepreneurs. A common finding is that the psychological profits of self-employment seem to be as important a motivational factor as the ultimate pecuniary reward.

Highly successful entrepreneurs often have an extreme need for recognition, power, independence, and the satisfaction of creating something wholly their own. Most are highly competitive and see only two places to finish—first or last. Many draw no distinction between work and play. They are often colorful, eccentric, and sometimes rebellious personalities that have trouble with authority figures of all sorts. Often they are loners, and—before finding success in business—drifters. The 1985 *Wall Street Journal* survey of small business found that entrepreneurs on *Inc.*'s list of fastest-growing private companies were three times more likely to have been fired from a previous job than the Fortune 500 executives, and twice as likely to have worked at four or more jobs. Yet they were six times more likely to be under forty-five years old. They were also found to be two and a half times more likely than the *Fortune* executives or the sampling of small businessmen to need to be recognized as a leader in their fields.[20]

Although some are analytical, business instinct strongly influences in the entrepreneur's decisions. They tend to see incompetence everywhere, and feel (often with justification) that no one can do the work as well as they can. Often, they are highly suspicious of a wide range of individuals, including former employers, employees, and customers. Sometimes they act upon it. Once, when a customer kept postponing payment for his tires to Hank Heeber, Heeber and a colleague visited the customer's car late at night and removed the tires; Don Muller, president of Jukeboxes Unlimited in Van Nuys, California, once made a "service call" at a delinquent customer and removed a key part from the jukebox.[21] Finally, once they are successful, they tend to grow bored quickly. Like entrepreneur Wilson Harrell, who took on and beat Procter & Gamble, they often then seek fresh challenges through new business ventures.

In pragmatic terms, the psychological attributes of entrepreneurs increase the odds of business success. The high need to achieve translates into a single-minded devotion to work and a restless drive that is willing to endure great hardship. If they suffer high levels of stress, the fear of failure motivates, rather than paralyzes, them.

Trends in Small Business Profitability

Depending chiefly on the secondary resources of the economy, small business depends above all else on a fundamentally good economic environment to earn satisfactory profits. Profits are severely squeezed in recessions and during the downswing of industry cycles. Owners commonly are forced to make fresh capital contributions to the company and often lay off employees during these difficult periods to survive until better times return. If the downturns are too severe, small businessmen shut their doors. This is common in highly cyclical industries, such as the oil business.

In the 1960s, cheap foreign oil drove nearly half of the small wildcatters out of business. Many returned in the 1970s to enjoy the boom set off by the OPEC oil embargo and the soaring oil prices. In 1981 alone, banks and drilling funds funneled $22 billion into the oil industry. In the oil slump and world recession that followed, all that money dried up. Between 1981 and 1985 one-fourth of the nation's 20,000 independent oil companies went out of business.[22]

The decade of the 1970s, when America began exhibiting the difficulties associated with the current economic transformation, generally impinged on small business profitability more than it did that of large corporations whose woes became regular newspaper and magazine features. Small companies had less margin to sustain downturns—and it showed. Between 1966 and 1980, liabilities piled up faster than assets for both small and large corporations. But the net worth (the difference between assets and liabilities) of large corporations was less severely squeezed than for small ones. The pattern was the same for overall sales growth, with small corporation sales growth lagging behind that of large corporations.[23] This is reflective of the continuing trend to bigness in nearly all industries.

With profits insufficient to finance more growth internally, small and big corporations turned to the debt market. However, due to the uncertainty of high inflation and high interest rates—the real (inflation-adjusted) prime interest rate nearly tripled in the period from 2.1 to 5.7 percent—large corporate financial officers reversed historic patterns and bypassed long-term debt in favor of small business' traditional short-term debt markets. The trend has continued right through the recession and the recovery in the 1980s. In 1984, two-thirds of all corporate debt financing was short-term—bringing the short-term share of total corporate debt up to 51 versus 30 percent in 1960.

The effect of big business crowding into the short-term debt market was to drive up already high short-term interest rates. In combination with the slowdown in economic growth, this was crushing to small business: In 1967–69, interest charges represented 15 percent of small corporations' use of funds; ten years later it was 19 percent, and in 1980, as the prime rate soared, small businesses were using 34 percent of their funds to meet interest expenses![24]

This contributed to a severe cash-flow squeeze that continued through the early 1980s. To keep going small businessmen dug into their own pockets for additional financing. Net shareholder loans to their small corporations normally show huge leaps in recession years to compensate for sharp decreases in funding from other sources. This is normally made up in the subsequent recovery periods, when profits and funding from external sources are more readily obtainable. In the recession years 1970 and 1975, drops in funding caused net shareholder loans to increase by $1.4 billion and $2.2 billion respectively. In 1980, small corporation owners added $5 billion in fresh capital to their businesses. Yet in the nonrecession years between 1975 and 1980, small business funding never really recovered—as small businessmen found it necessary to keep up a historically high level of personal funding to their corporations.[25]

For those tens of thousands of small businessmen unable to make fresh capital contributions, or those whose personal wealth was finally drained in financing their companies' cash-flow deficits, the outcome has been a *tripling* of the business failure rate. In 1983, the failure rate was 110 per 10,000 firms—four-fifths of the failure rate of the Great Depression. Moreover, they were leaving behind much higher average current liabilities than in the past. Some 60,000 to 70,000 companies a year, nearly all small, were filing for bankruptcy.

Small business' economic accomplishments in the past decade, in other words, have been achieved from a base of eroding profits. They are testimony to small business' economic tenacity and resourcefulness in the face of adversity—not to its economic renaissance. Between 1958 and 1977, only large companies with over 500 employees gained sales share. Nearly all the gain came at the expense of the smallest companies with under 20 employees.

Most of the sales growth among larger corporations, however, took place before the mid-1970s. Under the duress of economic transition, their share of sales growth has risen more slowly since then. Their share of employment growth—in an effort to maintain profit margins—has fallen.

The best small business performers in this generally difficult economic environment went to small businesses with over 100 but under 500 employees. They increased their relative sales share by 2 percent between 1976 and 1982. The relative sales gain did not necessarily translate into greater profitability, however. Much of the sales gain was offset by their increasing share of employment and escalating financing and other business costs. The biggest small business losers continued to be the smallest companies with under 20 employees.[26]

For healthy profit levels, small business is generally dependent on a growing economic pie. When times are tough, as they've been since the early 1970s, small business' *sales* may be better maintained relative to big business—*but its profits aren't.* Small business' often low and insecure profits diminish first; the profits of big business, which has greater economic means at its disposal to maintain the level and security of its profit flow, tend to fall only afterward.

What has happened since the 1970s is that small business' profits have been sacrificed to protect the profitability of big business, whose health is of such primary importance to the stability of the economy. Big business has retrenched in the period to the most profitable cores of each industry. Thus it has shown little sales gain. Small business, by comparison, has dug for profits by trying to expand at the less profitable margins. Propelled by the entrepreneurial boom, it has managed to pump up economic output (and sometimes to innovate)—but with tremendously high mortality and low reward of profits.

John Maynard Keynes once commented that business entrepreneurs are motivated more by an irrational optimism and an ambition for achievement than any reasonable calculation of business profits. If they were motivated by nothing but a mathematical expectation of profits, he noted, enterprise would fade and die.

To be dynamic, free-enterprise capitalism in the long run must offer sufficient inducements of pecuniary and psychological profits to those with an urge for entrepreneurship. In coldly rational terms, the likelihood of achieving significant pecuniary profits from independent business is not cheering. Much depends, therefore, on the motivation of psychological profits, which are born of the marriage between the ego needs of entrepreneurial personalities and social-economic values.

The United States offers advanced industrial capitalism's most favorable social-economic environment for ambitious, independent entrepreneurial activity. For example, unlike in Europe or Japan, entrepreneurial failure in America is often regarded not as a disgrace but as experience gained toward future success. Celebrated case histories reinforce this. R. H. Macy failed several times in small towns before discovering that his department store retailing concept was best suited to large cities. P. T. Barnum, before turning to circuses, also did poorly in retailing ventures.[27] Even Henry Ford experienced business failure before creating the modern auto industry. To the present day, stories like these inspire entrepreneurs to the optimistic, and irrational, faith that they will be among the fraction that achieve great economic success through business enterprise.

Occasionally, they succeed grandly—and the economy gets a powerful shot in the arm. As George Bernard Shaw amusingly put it in a different vein: "The reasonable man adapts himself to the world, the unreasonable one persists in trying to adapt the world to himself. Therefore all progress depends on the unreasonable man."[28]

For small business to continue to invigorate the U.S. social economy and continue to inspire entrepreneurial dreamers to undertake the irrational risks of independent enterprise, however, small businessmen, even unreasonable ones, must also have tangible long-term prospects of earning attractive profits. Those prospects, in turn, rest on satisfactory management of the profound long-term problems that have eroded its past profitability—as well as those likely to arise from the new competitive balances accompanying the evolution of a global, information technology-driven economy.

8

Problems
of Small Business

It is lunchtime in the small Kansas town of Marysville, a former Pony Express way station with a population of 3,500. Polo-shirted John C. Schmidt leaves the keys in the ignition of his Chevy pickup and enters June's Bar and Grill. He greets a few of June's patrons by their first names, and orders his usual cheeseburger and iced tea. This casual lunch routine has been repeated hundreds of times before, but lately, wherever Schmidt enters, his presence raises a subtle tension.

Schmidt, in his mid-forties, is president of Marysville's dominant bank, the Exchange Bank of Schmidt & Koester. The bank was founded by his great-grandfather shortly after the Civil War to service the local farm economy. Schmidt himself did almost every job in the bank before becoming president, from sweeping up, sorting the mail, starting the trust department, and introducing computers. But now, faced with the mounting U.S. farm crisis, Schmidt must do something he has never done before: He must tell lifelong clients, many of whom he used to play football with in high school, that they must sell some of their land or machinery and change the way they've been running their farms or businesses for years, lest he be compelled to force them into bankruptcy. Through the first half of 1985, Schmidt had only forced one customer into bankruptcy—out of 20 that a harder-nosed, or nonlocal community, banker might have exacted. But he had acquired 4,444 acres of farmland and a grain elevator through loan defaults in the prior two years. Previously, his bank owned no land.

Schmidt is one of the nation's luckier small bankers. His bank is still profitable. Scores of other small banks with significant exposure to the huge unserviceable portion of the $200 billion debt held by the nation's farmers have been failing at rates last experienced in the Great Depression. Between 1983 and mid-1985, the number of problem "farm" banks has quintupled.

Schmidt's Exchange Bank is a typical small-town bank. It has assets of about $75 million and 34 employees. It has been an aggressive lender in northeastern Kansas, where the main farm crops are milo, wheat, and soybeans. About half its loans are made directly to farmers. Another 25 percent or more goes to businesses which are indirectly dependent on the income of the farm economy, such as Bergren Motors and Marvin's Barber Shop.

Although Schmidt's bank earned about $1.5 million on gross income of about $8 million in 1984, it also absorbed losses of $500,000 on sour loans. Schmidt was expecting at least similar levels of losses in 1985 and 1986. In mid-1985 no interest was being paid on about 12 percent of all bank loans. About 1 percent were delinquent or past due by a month or more. Another 10 percent had been renegotiated in some way.

Schmidt recognized that he needed to raise lending rates due to the squeeze. But he has had to forgo doing so since he also recognized that clients simply couldn't pay any more. Schmidt's crisis strategy, like that of other small-town farm bankers loath to repossess the property of lifelong clients and friends, has been to renegotiate longer repayment periods, reduce interest rate burdens, help farmers get fresh financing from the Farmers Home Administration (a federal agency whose loans already carry a 30 percent delinquency rate; by contrast, private bank Continental Illinois had to be saved when its bad loan rate reached 7 percent), and, most of all, to pray for a federal government bail-out.

If the nation's farmers were a single company, they would be seeking protection from their creditors under the nation's bankruptcy codes. Their cumulative debt of $200 billion is equal to that of the Third World's two leading debtor nations, Mexico and Brazil, combined. Indeed, the sector is so large, affecting the fortunes not only of small family farmers but of farm machinery corporations, small-town bankers, and small-town businesses, and so much a nerve center of the U.S. social economy, that irresistible political pressure has mounted on the federal government to facilitate a rescue above and beyond the routine lavish subsidies it hands out. In 1983, the value of those subsidies was $20 billion, equal to 10 percent of the federal government deficit. Various subsidy programs cover half of all farm output.

John Schmidt and other farm bankers are being compelled to restructure the way they do business because of the farm crisis. Federal regulators have been demanding much stricter compliance with existing rules. Schmidt and other fellow rural bankers have always based lending decisions on the strength of assets such as farmland machinery and receivables—and on personal acquaintance. Now they are being forced by regulators to base further lending on cash flow and profitability. That requires doing cash-flow workups that have never been done before—and often taking a much sterner position with long-standing friends and clients. Whatever federal programs are enacted to help farm bankers and their clients manage through the current farm liquidity crisis are bound to bring stricter regulations with them.

Schmidt has already begun to diversify the Exchange Bank's operations to reduce his dependence on loan income into fields that his great-grandfather would find quite foreign to the rudimentary banking operations of the bank's early days. He has expanded into fee-earning services in farm management and discount brokerage, and plans to move into insurance. He is also studying real estate brokerage and the fast-growing industry of performing accounting and payroll work for small local businesses.

Sadly, Schmidt expects he will soon be forced to end one friendly long-standing bank tradition of charging all its borrowers the same interest rate, 13 percent in mid-1985. This tradition reflected Marysville's highly personal, almost familial small-town community. Any difference in interest charges, whether or not justified on strictly individual business considerations, would quickly become known in Marysville and draw complaints from those paying more.

Now, however, survival through the farm crisis requires putting certain friendly traditions aside. If doing so enables Schmidt to avoid or delay foreclosing on farms and businesses—and of course to keep his own bank in the black while others around him fail—it will have a sad, but satisfactory trade-off.[1]

As the profit data and the historical, slow decline of small business' share of GNP and private sales indicate, small business suffers from fundamental long-term competitiveness problems. Today, it confronts new problems of relating to the transition to a "postindustrial" information technology-based global economy. Small business' future depends on how these problems evolve and are met.

Basic Problems

In addition to the lack of economies of size, small business entrepreneurs' three major weaknesses are: (1) Unsound or too little analysis in choosing an initial field of business; (2) Inadequate capitalization; and (3) Poor management skills. As a result, the majority of small businessmen set up their particular businesses based on ease of entry into the field rather than on any study of maximum profit opportunity.

Small business' chronic shortage of capital handicaps the small businessman from the start. It prevents him from making the capital investment in labor-substituting machinery that leads to increased productivity and satisfactory profitability. It hampers efforts to staff expert and formidable business organizations. It makes it more difficult for small businessmen to meet whatever costs may be soaring in the business environment in any given period—today, for instance, liability insurance, a decade ago, energy. It is a principal reason why small businesses are commonly plagued with short life spans.

Small business' precarious capitalization means that its investment time horizons are short—returns must come rapidly if a venture is to survive. In the majority of cases, such short-term investment requirements invariably hinder the inherent profit potential of an enterprise. Those who accuse big business of forsaking long-term investment for short-term, quarterly earnings growth—and those who often feel an accompanying alarm when these tendencies are juxtaposed to the markedly long-term strategies of Japanese companies—cannot be assuaged by looking at small companies whose investment horizons are almost always shorter still.

Low profitability gives the small businessman a low rate of retained earnings. Without reinvesting retained earnings at a high level a small business cannot grow. It remains trapped in its undercapitalization/diseconomical small size conundrum.

Insufficient funds commonly drive small businessmen to set up in low rental sites. Rents may be low, however, because the location is poor—perhaps off a main street or in a poor or low-density neighborhood—or the space is too constricted to conduct a profitable, growing business. This is a particularly common problem among retailers. A small space hurts retailers who try to sell fast-moving, low-profit-margin items such as TVs, videocassette recorders, and low-cost consumer electronics products. Limited inventory space restricts the overall volume of business a small retailer—even one with several outlets—can do, compelling him to try to price his merchandise to yield a higher profit margin. But huge electronic superstores, buying in sufficient volume to obtain purchase price discounts from the supplier, and selling low to entice customers, undercut him.

Even where the economies of volume purchasing do not come into play, the retailer whose success relies on breadth of product line runs into competitive problems if his space is too small. Such is the case among many videocassette stores. Although a small storefront in a good metropolitan location in early 1985 could have been opened for under $100,000, the space was too small to stock enough old titles and to keep up with the 2,000 new titles being issued each year. Customers looking for diversity of choice instead flocked to the big stores which had the space to maintain an inventory of one or two copies of a far broader selection of tapes. To open such a large store, however, costs at least $200,000.

Today's surging rentals in reviving urban areas may have been good for urban renewal, but it has swept away many of the longtime retailers who struggled to keep the faith during the neighborhood's bad times just as rewarding profits were in view.

The problem of inadequate capitalization is often accompanied by a lack of business savvy in choosing which business to enter. Sometimes the small businessman enters a business that puts him into competition with a large company. Far more often, however, small businessmen enter fields where there are too many others like himself—that is, those who have chosen it mainly because the entry barriers were low—for anyone to earn rewarding profits. Like thousands of others, Stanley Wilson got wind of the video craze and in 1984 became the seventeenth video store to open in Grand Junction, Colorado. Sales were a profitable $1,500 a week almost from the start. Within a year, however, the number of competitors had soared to 80. Rental prices plunged from $3 a day to 69¢. So did profits.[2]

The small businessman's problems are frequently compounded by his lack of sophistication and management skills. Inventory management, for example, is an art: Fast turnover of a broad range of merchandise is a key to profitability. Yet commonly the small businessman turns over most of his inventory far too slowly. In effect, he is tying up scarce capital in the form of stock. This compels him to earn higher profit margins than may be competitive in the marketplace on the merchandise which does turn over quickly. Tobacconist Arnold Goldstein constantly reviews his inventory and searches for substitute products at trade shows, as well as experimenting with new display formats, to increase turnover rates across his product line.

Small businessmen are notoriously bad at bookkeeping. In a very small business, company and personal funds are often intermingled. Poor bookkeeping prevents the small businessman from getting a clear picture of, and thus devising solutions to, the problems of business. It also makes it difficult for him to work up the kind of financial information a bank officer wants to see before granting the loan which might keep him going. Part of this problem is being met by a rapidly increasing number of companies, which are contracting their payroll and other bookkeeping work out to firms springing up to handle small companies' paperwork, much like the new accounting service Marysville banker John Schmidt may offer as part of his diversification plans.

Problems of Growth Companies

Even a company fortunate enough to overcome the early obstacles to become one of the fastest-growing companies, often stumbles. Of the 100 top companies on *Forbes'* "Up and Comer" list of 1979, only one-third of the 75 that had remained independent were still on the list five years later.[3]

Quite often, the owner of a small-growth company is afflicted by the same paucity of business management skill as his counterpart in a small company that is going nowhere. But his management inadequacies are magnified by rapid growth. The best business prospect in the world cannot be exploited without a good business organization. It was good organization that helped the great industrialists a century ago grow large while their entrepreneurial competitors died or remained small.

Every growth firm undergoes a progression of changes, from a single-product, single-location operation directly managed by the owner, to a multiproduct, multilocation and, ultimately, multidivisional company in which the owner's involvement becomes more managerial and remote at every stage of growth. Depending on the type of business, it is common that at 25 to 30 employees the owner can no longer personally oversee every operation and appoints supervisory surrogates. By the time the company reaches 250 employees, the supervisors may have surrogates and the owner is two steps from direct control. Additional management-layer thresholds lie ahead, until the owner's entrepreneurial instinct has lost most of its importance to his management ability.

Few businessmen, however, are both good entrepreneurs and good managers. The blind spots and instinctive decision-making that may have supplied entrepreneurial conviction while the company was being started, become liabilities to organized growth later on. That is why so few founders of exceptional growth companies remain in charge once the small business becomes large. In 1985, for example, Apple Computer founder Steven Jobs relinquished operational direction of his company to a former Pepsico executive (before eventually leaving the company altogether). Venture capitalist Don Valentine, a principal investor in Apple among other major successful ventures, notes:

After having made investments in perhaps 150 companies, we are inclined to believe that there is one set of management skills needed to start a company and another set needed to manage a bigger company. They are rarely resident in the same person.[4]

Thomas Watson, Sr., used to say that companies don't get in trouble in hard times, but during prosperity. Overexpansion or simple lack of control can add operational flab and threaten years of counting pennies and struggling to make it.

Poor record keeping and inventory control in the face of sales growth from $5 million a year to $100 million between 1982 and 1984 caused losses of at least $6 million in parts—10 percent of total inventory—at Kaypro, the maker of the highly popular inexpensive Kaypro II portable computer. Growth so far outstripped the family's ability to manage it that parts were stockpiled in trucks, in bags on the lawn, and under a circus tent on a bluff overlooking the Pacific Ocean. Defective parts were never entered on the company's books.[5]

Very fast-growing companies must be efficiently managed in order to obtain the often enormous additional financing needed to meet the demands of the expanding market—and thus prevent new competitors from stealing a march on them. In the new economics of rapidly changing technology and shorter periods to garner profitable returns on investment, the importance of obtaining such financing is paramount.

Few fast-growing companies can finance their growth out of retained earnings. Many experience severe negative cash positions even though accrual-basis profits may be quite healthy. Iomega Corporation is a producer of high-storage-capacity computer disks. Even though it had a gross profit margin of 35 percent in the first quarter of 1985, and annual sales which had grown from $7 million to $51 million in a single year, it had a negative cash flow (based on actual bank balances) of $13.3 million. This was because collections of accounts receivable lagged behind its explosive growth. As a result, it went to the capital markets for additional financing. But the capital markets are sometimes capricious. Iomega, a public company, was forced to sell more equity—diluting the value of stockowners' shares—instead of raising debt as it originally wanted.[6]

Some hot companies quickly fade because their markets are too small and quickly saturated, or can easily be invaded by large corporations.

Few know this as well as the innovative and persistent Robert Taylor, founder of Minnetonka, Inc. One of these years, the combination is bound to pay off for him. When he was twenty-six, Taylor left his sales job at Johnson & Johnson. He had noticed that hand-rolled soap from Europe was a popular item in gift shops, and felt sure he could produce an equally attractive, but lower cost, locally made soap himself. The "cold process" soap he needed was obsolete, but he was able to go to the library and dig up the lost formula. To get into business, he went to the troubled Rath Packing meat-packing company of Waterloo, Iowa. One by-product of meat packing is the tallow used in making soap. Rath Packing's hard-pressed executives agreed to cook the tallow into soap for him. Kicking around the Rath facilities, Taylor found an obsolete sausage-casing machine that could be used to extrude the 60-pound blocks Rath was making into small lumps that could be rolled by hand.

In short order, Taylor's Village Bath products were in gift shops and later in department stores. For nine straight years sales more than doubled annually. When Taylor took Minnetonka public in 1972, the price soared to 40 times earnings.

Not all the publicity was good, however. Minnetonka's hand-rolled soap success attracted the attention of Gillette and Clairol. They launched similar products in huge volumes at lower prices in drugstores and supermarkets instead of gift shops. Overnight, $8 million Minnetonka was destroyed. Its once lofty shares were available to anyone for two bits; half its equity vanished.

By 1978 Taylor, after husbanding his equity, was back test-marketing a new product, Softsoap, a pump-dispensed liquid soap. This time, Taylor decided to take the fight right to the big corporations. He put Softsoap in the supermarket right next to the bar soaps. To launch the product nationwide, he bet the company, spending $6 million.

For a short time, Taylor looked like a genius. Earnings increased nearly fourfold to $5.5 million in 1980. Once again the stock soared. But Taylor had repeated his mistake. Inventiveness was not enough. The product was easily imitatable—not too costly or technically difficult to make—and the market was desirable enough to attract large corporate competition. The big promotion campaign for Taylor's pump-dispensed liquid soap opened the market for heavyweight competitors like Jergens to step in with me-too mass-market products at lower prices. Once again, Minnetonka's earnings turned to losses.

Taylor, however, is nothing if not indefatigable. In the mid-1980s he was back again. But this time he was joint-venturing with West Germany's $3.3 billion chemical and consumer products Henkel KGaA to supply staying power. Their product: a pump toothpaste called Check-Up. Colgate was already on the market with a knock-off product priced well below that of Taylor and his German ally. But Taylor was optimistic that this time the German alliance was the right formula to help him to withstand the bulldozer marketing tactics of his large U.S. competitors—and finally provide his big payoff.[7]

In technologically innovative products, small business profits are normally earned at the earliest stages of a product's life cycle before economies of scale become important. At this period market shares are volatile and the rates of entry and failure are high.

In backing a new venture, venture capitalists commonly want to see a stage in its market where potential big business competitors are too unsure of the eventual size and technological standards of the market to be enticed to enter. Of course, some prospective high-profit markets disappoint their early investors because the lack of technological standard inhibits customers from buying too soon. Real profitability may await the entry of a big economic entity—as a producer or as a customer—to set the industry standard.

Finally, many young growth companies disappoint because they remain a single-product company for too long. Any single-product company is vulnerable to an eventual downturn. The first step is to make product add-ons. The second, and most difficult, step is to find a new growth product. Few entrepreneurs are so gifted as to be able to repeat their initial success. This generally must be made while the profit trajectory of the first product is positive.

Relations with Big Business

The history of small business has largely been one of trying to avoid direct competition with big business. Although the fact that in many industries large corporations are operating an enormously increased number of smaller plants may indicate that big business' celebrated economies of production-scale advantages may have diminished over the years, this has been offset by other organizational efficiencies of size: efficiencies in marketing, specialized management, price leverage in purchasing and selling, and financing.

As commerce and industry became national and global, there has also been a tendency for large economic entities, governmental or corporate, to prefer to deal with other large economic entities. Although large corporations are relying increasingly on outside suppliers and subcontractors in decentralized locations around the globe, this trend has been accompanied by an extension of central administrative organization from national to global settings. As industries globalize, fewer larger economic entities will probably arise as the major forces on worldwide markets as they have in national market settings in the past. The likely result is a continued centralization of economic power that is deleterious to small business.

Small business' health lies in economic decentralization, diversity, and product differentiation. A small retailer whose products are the same as those of the department store is in dire trouble, just as a small manufacturer cannot often compete head to head with a larger competitor, as Robert Taylor of Minnetonka learned more than once. When consumer tastes are homogeneous, and business strategies uniformly similar, small business has difficulty. But where mass markets fragment into smaller, specialized markets, as today, or where changing technology creates a diversity of product or service options and strategies, small businesses have more opportunity to find market niches in which to survive, grow, and have maximum beneficial effects on the economy.

Yet even where small businesses succeed in finding market niches of the type outlined in the second chapter—such as specialized, small, or unstable secondary markets or those that are labor-intensive or where technology hasn't favored large size—the presence of an economy dominated by large economic entities applies pressure that circumscribe small business' economic well-being.

Due to its general position of inferior economic leverage in the economy, small business is highly vulnerable to shifts of conditions in the big business economy. Large corporations have a far wider array of options to deflect the impact of a negative economic development—including shifting it to the small business economy. Small business normally has little such option but to accept it. Throughout nearly every sector of the economy, a small businessman runs into the superior, if often indirectly wielded, influence of larger enterprises. Somewhere along the business chain there is a large supplier, middleman, or buyer with the economic power to get the most advantageous price for himself at the expense of his smaller clients' profits.

Indirect pressure is felt in the competition for skilled employees. As knowledge skill becomes an increasing competitive advantage in the transition to an information technology-driven economy, the competition for skilled employees becomes more important. Due to its lower profits, small businesses are at a competitive disadvantage in offering attractive salaries and benefits. Few insurance industry health plans are organized to offer cost effective coverage for smaller groups. ERISA (Employment Retirement Income Security Act) pension-plan legislation of the mid-1970s has been a boon to retirement security in the United States, but its beneficial impact falls mainly on plans offered by large corporations. Because the administrative costs of setting up a pension plan are more or less the same regardless of the number of individuals covered, the burden is relatively greater for small companies to set one up. One study found that it cost a small firm $1,080 per employee to set up a pension plan—about double what it cost for a large business.[8]

Indirect competition for financing puts greater pressure on small economic entities, which are normally served last by the financial markets. On average, small companies these days pay 3 percent more on loans—when they can get them—than large corporations. This means that already pressed small companies must earn 3 percent more on their invested debt capital than their large competitors just to stay even.

Big suppliers or customers dictate payment terms to small companies. They can, and do, squeeze small firms' cash flow by demanding rapid payments as suppliers and stretching accounts payable as customers.

The constant pressure on small business cash flow makes small firms heavily dependent on expensive trade credit. It also sometimes makes them, in effect, prisoners of their clients. This can hurt if a big supplier's prices or quality may not be the best available or if a big customer is beset with problems of his own.

Small businesses that are dependent on a single customer or supplier for a sizable percentage of their business are independent in name only. In reality, they are satellites vulnerable to devastation by a shift in the fortunes or strategies of their clients and ostensible masters.

When giant pharmaceutical company Searle, which holds key licenses on an amino acid essential to the manufacture of the popular new sweetener Nutrasweet, decided in 1985 to build a plant to produce the amino acid itself, it caused a bloodbath among its suppliers. The suppliers were given short notice of Searle's intentions. One supplier, Genex, a biotech start-up, had just invested $25 million in a production facility to produce the amino acid for Searle. Beyond Searle, the market for the amino acid is tiny. Genex now faced the prospects one of its former suppliers, Cell Products, had experienced the previous year when Genex dropped *its* contract for the amino acid (accounting for nearly all Cell's sales) upon deciding to invest the $25 million to produce it itself. In the end, Searle retained only one supplier—the Japanese giant Ajinomoto, which it needs to help set up its production facilities and to help market the product worldwide.[9]

Large corporations often consolidate their distribution systems as they grow and as market conditions change. When they do, small distributors dependent upon them for much of their supply are often pushed to the wall. Sanyo reorganized its distribution network to provide exclusive territories to a smaller number of bigger distributors in 1984. The strategy appeared to pay off, as Sanyo's sales grew three and a half times faster than the consumer electronics industry as a whole. One who didn't share Sanyo's satisfaction, however, was Robert L. Molstad of Sioux City, Iowa, a 12-year Sanyo distributor cut out in the reorganization. In 1983, Sanyo accounted for 40 percent of $1.5 million Molstad Distributing's turnover. To save his business, Molstad fired two of his six salesmen. [10]

Because large corporations generally prefer to deal with large entities rather than a myriad small ones, they tend to create economic conditions which generate larger clients. This adds impetus to the trend to larger minimum economic size for profitability. This is the effect Sanyo's reorganization had on its distributors.

In February 1985, K-Mart dealt a crushing blow to scores of its regional and local suppliers of earth products, such as peat and topsoil, when it granted an exclusive national contract to one of them, Hyponex. For K-Mart, the move to a single line relieved an organizational supply headache, and simplified advertising promotion. Obligingly, Hyponex began a national TV and radio ad campaign in the spring. The impact on the former suppliers, many of whom lost 25 percent of their business, was cutthroat price competition to try to fend off Hyponex–K-Mart and to fight among one another to make up their lost sales shares. Some of the smaller suppliers began talking about pooling their resources for marketing and advertising against Hyponex. [11]

The effort of K-Mart's former earth products suppliers to organize compensating economies of size is a familiar chapter in the history of U.S. small business. In response to the superior economies and inroads of chain stores over many years, small businesses have tried to organize countervailing economies of purchasing, wholesaling, and marketing by forming cooperative and voluntary chains of their own and, more recently, franchises. In response to the expansion of general merchandise mail-order companies Sears and Montgomery Ward to retailing store operations starting in the 1920s, individual department stores formed "ownership groups". These centralized chains, such as Federated Department Stores and Associated Dry Goods, which left supervision with the founding family but provided increasing central direction, improved access to financing and some joint merchandising. Cooperative and voluntary chains have been most effective in the grocery and supermarket business—in the mid-1970s, 57 percent of U.S. supermarkets were operated by members of cooperative and voluntary chains—and also in hardware, pharmacies, auto supply, and general merchandise.[12]

Franchising, which today accounts for one-third of all retailing—and over two-fifths of all eating places—is expanding rapidly in all kinds of services. With the imminence of interstate banking, some small banks, facing direct competition from the big money center banks such as Citibank, Chase, and Manufacturer's Hanover, have begun to organize in franchises, among other organizational schemes to unite.

Each countervailing organizational format small business has tried has involved trading off some business autonomy for protection under the united umbrella. In time, some small retailers became puppets within the larger organization—hardly independent small businesses at all.

Franchising poses still other dangers, such as exorbitant franchise fees and outright franchisor scams. Each year thousands of individuals lose an estimated $500 million in franchise and business opportunity frauds.[13] Bad franchise contracts are another trap for the unwary new franchisee: Among common contract problems are lack of geographical exclusivity, excessive service and royalty fees, term leases, and giving too much leverage to the franchisor by permitting him to be landlord as well as exclusive supplier. In a dramatic example of the latter case, between 1976 and 1984 the number of franchised gas service stations fell from 226,000 to 130,000 as the large oil companies, which both supplied gasoline and collected rent, killed off gas station franchise owners they no longer wanted by rationing their supply (which determined profit levels) and being strict about timely rent payments.

With improved communication and transportation technology, the chain stores continue penetrating more small business markets—most recently, Sears and K-Mart have been preparing plans to launch expansions in the small business heartland of towns under 10,000 inhabitants.

Other popular and more recent ways independent small businessmen have attempted to compensate for big business' organizational economies include participation in the ware-housing order houses which sell $4 billion worth of goods a year to small businesses at wholesale discounts, and in the 500 or so barter exchanges which swap excess inventory for services, that have sprung up in the past decade. Also springing up are informal "networking" roundtable groups of a dozen or so dues-paying small business executives in noncompeting fields to help overcome the small businessman's isolation to provide disinterested evaluations of his company's problems. With the spread of computers, there are also a growing number of data-bank companies to provide, for a fee, customer or service leads that at a large corporation would be handled by the middle-level organizational bureaucracy.

Farming

Farming is a special kind of small business. Today, it is in the throes of a severe crisis that in one form is a continuation of the historical shakeout resulting from large gains in farm pro-ductivity. It will end as it always has—with the migration of still more small farmers from the land to more productive employment in service and industry.

The immediate cause of the current crisis is a boom-and-bust cycle that started in the 1970s. In the 1970s, farmers re-sponded to a surge in grain prices caused by foreign crop failures (which led the Russians, among others, to buy enor-mous amounts of grain) and a serious decline in world fish catches, by buying and planting more acreage. The purchases, and the inflationary environment, set off a speculative surge in land prices.

Federally subsidized loans encouraged farmers to add 62 million acres, much of it marginal land, to their holdings. In the process, the average price of land quintupled, and farmers' debt quadrupled. But because most of their windfall earnings gains went to finance their loans, farmers reaped very little net tangi-ble income benefit.

Then, in the early 1980s, came the bust. Other nations, notably Brazil and Australia, encouraged by the artificial price floor U.S. government minimum price supports for farmers built into the world market, had vigorously expanded their farm output in the 1970s. Meanwhile the green revolution in some former large Third World agricultural importers, and recovery among foreign farmers, caused competition in export grain markets to intensify. The strong dollar in the 1980s further priced U.S. farmers out of the competition.

Farmers again drew heavily on federal farm support prices. But even with the price supports, the income of about 300,000 farmers was insufficient to service the high-cost debt they'd incurred in land expansion in the 1970s. Desperate farmers sold land. Land prices collapsed. The orders of farm machinery makers dried up. The number of farms sold at auction soared, and the current farmers' liquidity crisis reached proportions that compelled the Reagan administration to shelve its desire to phase out farm subsidies and consider bail-out plans to stave off the threat to general economic stability.

Tens of thousands of small family farmers will be driven from the land in the current crisis. In time, with or without government subsidies, tens of thousands more will follow. The U.S. farm population has declined steadily as farm productivity has increased. In 1935 there were 6.8 million farmers; in the mid-1980s, under 3 million. Over the last two decades, American farm output has increased at an annual average rate of 2.5 percent due to advances in farm machinery, fertilizers, and other capital-intensive farming methods. Labor was half the cost of farming before 1940. By the mid-1980s, it was but 13 percent.

The genetic engineering revolution all but assures that such growth will continue. Yet while more farm products are produced with less effort, the markets for those additional goods are not expanding as rapidly. The ultimate economic result will be that the less productive farmers must leave the land for more economically productive pursuits.

This is already happening: Some 300,000 farmers with holdings that average 500 acres currently produce two-thirds of the value of U.S. farm goods. Some half all U.S. farmers earn two-thirds their income from second jobs they hold outside farming.

Financing

Small business must have access to readily available sources of reasonably priced financing if it is to exert its salutary effects on the economy. Minimum start-up and working capital requirements for competitive operations have increased throughout American business. As markets grow and become crowded with more efficient competitors, entry barrier costs rise.

Between 1984 and 1985, the estimated cost of starting a sufficiently large video rental store in a metropolitan area rose from $140,000 to $200,000. In high-tech industries, second-generation products must be more sophisticated than the pioneering products, and marketing efforts must from the start thoroughly blanket a far wider customer audience to make a profitable impact. Both these factors translate into sharply increasing capitalization requirements as markets develop. By the time the markets are dominated by a few corporations, of course, only other large corporations, or a truy innovative small business pioneer, possess the wherewithal to overcome the entry barriers to apply competitive pressure.

There are three fundamentals that govern small business finance: (1) Banks want to lend only to those who don't need the money; (2) Even the most attractive growth companies look like a bad credit risk at some point in their lives; and (3) Small business is always the last to be served by the credit market.

The first hurdle faced by the small businessman, therefore, is simply gaining access to credit of any kind. This poses a significant difficulty to prospective entrepreneurs who lack a previous track record.

Borrowing is less difficult for existing businesses. Profitable existing small companies do not have a debt capital access problem in the United States. Their major concern is the cost of borrowed funds. The administrative costs to a bank of making a small or a large loan are equivalent. Yet the total return rises with the size of the loan, so banks prefer making large loans. Because small company loans tend to be for relatively small amounts—and because small businesses are perceived (rightly) to be large credit risks—small business loans carry higher interest charges than loans to large enterprises and are predominantly shorter term than loans available to large corporations.

Small business financing differs from that of big corporations in another important respect. The sources of small business funds are drawn overwhelmingly from individual personal savings. Big business is funded mainly by institutional capital—pension funds, insurance money, and banks. In the last 20 years, the pool of institutional capital has grown astronomically—it is one of the notable phenomena of capitalist economic evolution, and is a driving force behind the globalization of the world's capital markets. Personal savings growth has been much more modest.

Individual personal savings (including money lent by friends and family, and especially any rich uncles) directly finance over two-thirds of small business start-ups. Although most of the other third comes from lending institutions, it is almost always lent against some sort of personal collateral, such as the equity vested in a home. To obtain these personal funds, prospective small businessmen, with high or low incomes (although obviously far less painfully for those with higher incomes), have been assiduous savers, trading momentary comforts for future-oriented ambitions.

In some cases small businessmen can start the venture while retaining a steady job to see if it becomes viable. That's what Henry Garcia did before opening his PC repair service, Microaide, in Iselin, New York. Garcia, formerly a senior engineer at Consolidated Edison in New York, began moonlighting in the now $1 billion personal computer repair business with $20,000 in spare parts and $5,000 in diagnostic equipment. When his client base grew big enough in 1984, he left Con Ed and set up shop on his own, with two repairmen and a secretary.[14]

The principal source of institutional capital for small businessmen is the nation's small banks. The United States has the most decentralized banking system in the industrialized world. There are about 15,000 commercial banks—ten times as many as in any other wealthy country. The overwhelming number are small. The 100 largest bank-holding companies control over half U.S. banking assets; the smallest 10,000 control 10 percent. Many of these small banks are single-office operations, often located in towns.[15]

These small banks, like that of John Schmidt, are run by a family or a group of families, which are frequently prominent in the local economy's main businesses. They personally know, or know of, the prospective small businessmen who approach them for business loans. Being local, they can knowledgeably evaluate the merits of such proposals.

Controlling a bank, of course, is a source of power in a local economy. While this is often a source of abuse through insider loans to the businesses of directors or of favored clients,* the small-town banker has several incentives to be sympathetic to the loan proposals of those who wish to do business in town: Improving general local prosperity is good for business; power not exercised reduces the small banker's influence; and finally, in turning down loan requests there is always the danger of the small businessmen finding a warmer reception at another nearby bank looking to expand its influence.

The sheer fragmentation of competing banks has made small business lending an inefficient market. At any given time in recent years, interest charges on comparable small business loans have varied by as much as 6 percent. Thus some small businessmen have been able to shop around to obtain loans at rates commonly paid by larger companies.

Since the pension fund investment rules were altered in 1979, venture capital has become an increasingly significant source of institutional capital funding for small business. It is, however, restricted to an elite of high-growth potential, and high-capital-absorbing small businesses—no more than perhaps 1,000 firms a year. It started with high-tech, but has since spread to low-tech and no-tech businesses. As institutional money has become more prominent and growth industries have grown more crowded, the average investment was $2.3 million, generally spread between three or four venture-capital funds contributing $500,000 to $800,000 apiece and dividing about two-fifths the company equity. Being partnerships of perhaps eight to ten years' duration, most venture-capital deals are oriented toward companies with the capacity to grow to $25 to $50 million within five years so they can quickly be cashed in on by going public whenever a window on the fickle Wall Street IPO (Initial Public Offering) market opens.

High-growth companies are the very few small businesses with significant access to the public equity market. Because the

*According to the Federal Deposit Insurance Corporation, nearly half the banks that failed in the first part of the 1980s had insider loans that went bad.

outstanding public equity floats for the 40,000 often closely held public companies are so tiny and trading opportunities so rare, institutional investors, whose minimum investments must be large and easily liquidated, avoid them.

Many potentially attractive small companies with an inclination to tap the public market for equity financing are dissuaded from doing so by the costly fees involved. Typical fees for printing, lawyers, accountants, and Securities and Exchange Commission registration filings run about $250,000; investment banker underwriting commissions are an additional 8 to 10 percent of the public offering value. As a result, the offering has to be fairly large—usually too large for a small corporation—to justify the expense involved. To facilitate broader use of the public equity markets, SEC filing registrations have been simplified for small corporations in recent years. But small companies continue to have very limited practical access to public equity capital.

The Small Business Administration provides direct loans and loan guarantees, among its various programs, to encourage small business lending. In 1985, the SBA underwrote $2.3 billion in loan guarantees for 15,422 companies and made 1,419 direct loans worth $83.6 million.

In general, SBA loan programs are used by small businessmen who have been denied credit from other sources. The bad-loan rate is very high. In recent years, Reagan budget-cutters' efforts to trim, and even dismantle, the SBA has reduced its credit activities in real dollar terms. Federal loan activity to small business was sharply cut from its peak of 31,700 loans for $3.9 billion in 1980.[16]

Small Business Investment Companies (SBICs) and Minority Enterprise Small Business Investment Companies (MESBICs) are privately owned investment companies licensed and partly funded by the SBA to encourage venture-capital-type financing of small and small minority firms. Neither program is very large. In all there are about 350 SBICs, many run by banks. In 1984, SBICs invested $425 million in 2,750 small companies. MESBICs, of which there are almost 150, invested $89 million in 1,087 small minority businesses.

In addition to federal government small business programs, individual states spend about $20 billion on various programs, 90 percent raised through Industrial Revenue Bonds, to help fund small businesses.

Small business' likelihood to be undercapitalized from the start tends to make it heavily dependent on high-cost financing sources that stretch its operating cash flow. Many struggling restaurants are carried along by their butchers and landlords; publishers may stretch out bill payments, with interest penalties accruing, to their printers. Leasing and factoring of receivables and other assets are used extensively as well. The difficulty with them all is that the high-interest premiums they entail burden profitability.

Given small business' difficulty in obtaining capital, and the high cost it must pay for it when it does, there has been a great deal of agitation to make small business financing easier. After all, without competitive access to financing, there is no way small business can compete effectively in the marketplace in a global economy increasingly dominated by large economic entities.

Much of the clamor has been for easier bank debt financing. But should bank debt financing be made easier for small business? Probably not.

Small business' high mortality rate and its low profitability suggest that lending to small business *is* a high-risk proposition. It is a risk commercial banks, whose essential business and importance in providing an environment of financial stability dictate conservatism, cannot prudently increase through easier credit terms. More appropriate for high-risk small businesses than easier commercial bank debt financing are better equity finance mechanisms. Ideally, such mechanisms could be structured to overcome the small businessman's traditional reluctance to share equity.

At the moment, there appear to be two significant gaps in the way financial markets currently finance small business. The first is a dearth of funds for start-ups requiring perhaps $150,000 or less. In part, the reason is the high risk inherent in the smallest new businesses. But part of the cause is the institutional trend toward larger financial and business entities—as the scale of operations increase, big entities find it increasingly less efficient to deal with smaller ones and smaller sums.

Yet among the smallest businessmen are tomorrow's fast-growth entrepreneurs. Personal individual wealth is the bedrock of small business finance and, therefore, a vital ingredient in maintaining a healthy entrepreneurial environment.

The second significant gap is among small-growth companies foundering on the swings of stock-market and venture-capital cycles. When small-growth companies need large infusions of capital to continue to grow, they commonly look to sell shares on the public equity market. Yet Wall Street's receptivity is erratic: Sometimes small-growth companies are in favor; sometimes they have a hard time raising anything at all.

In the peak year of Wall Street's romance with small-growth companies, 1983, 888 IPOs (Initial Public Offerings) raised $12.6 billion. This compared with 121 IPOs and $459 million in 1979. But the boom faded in 1984 and 529 IPOs raised only $3.8 billion. Receptivity warmed again in 1985. Small-growth companies looked to secondary sources for "bridge" financing until it became easier to sell public equity again. But the traditional secondary sources of finance, including venture capital, family groups, and large institutional investors, also dried up. They, too, are oriented to the stock market. As a result, the sudden absence of funds caused many growth companies to scale back their expansion plans. Deserving start-ups were denied funding as well by venture capitalists keyed to the initial public offerings market, just as undeserving ones were overfunded in the exuberance of the 1983 boom to aggravate the shakeout in the computer industry.

As a result, some promising small-growth companies that could have boosted America's international market position and provided stiffer competition to the industry giants financed by steadier sources have been irrevocably damaged. These cyclical swings may eventually ease as this important financing mechanism matures, but until they do, the country's general competitiveness may be dangerously harmed by tying small-growth companies' financial lifeline so closely to such erratic sources of capital.

As the disparity between the funds available for investment controlled by institutions and individuals increases, there is a danger that the small business economy, denied a proportionate share of total financing, will shrink relative to the big business economy. The eventual resolution depends in part on what new institutional sources of finance may evolve from the country's highly innovative capital markets to serve a wider universe of small businesses. The unforeseen rapid boom in the venture capital and initial public equity offerings markets encourages some hope that new sources may eventually develop. But it is not yet clear how or when.

In the past several years, following deregulation of interest-rate ceilings on deposits, larger small companies have been increasingly solicited by large banks, which have lost large corporate clients able to borrow less expensively from the Euro-bond market and other emerging sources of the global capital market. This trend underlines the fact that small business is the last served by the capital market. When the priority borrowers have filled their needs, what's left trickles down to small business. When capital is tight, the trickle stops. In all cases, the last money lent carries the highest interest charges.

Being a second-choice client, small business depends, above all, on a prosperous or at least stable banking environment. It lacks big business' options of issuing public securities; it is limited to financing opportunities in the United States. A survey in the third quarter 1984 revealed that the average small business was paying 14.7 percent on its bank borrowings—10 percent above inflation. A 10 percent real interest rate meant that a company had to earn a 10 percent profit on the investment from that capital just to break even. With financing burdens like that, an unexpected economic slump would bring a bloodbath of bankruptcies.

The mounting debt burden—corporate, farm, Third World, federal government, and consumer—is especially threatening to small businesses, both for the financial havoc it could cause and its potential to crowd out small business borrowers from the attractive credit opportunities. Financial market deregulations have disrupted time-tested techniques, maximally efficient or not, for policing the world's financial system. Alarmed, the world's central bank governors at the Bank of International Settlements (BIS) in Basel, Switzerland, have cautioned that the rapidity and disorderliness of deregulation have caused new stresses in the world financial and banking system which could touch off financial panic. Meanwhile, the advent of interstate banking and new competition from other large banklike institutions will almost certainly eliminate thousands of small banks and alter the traditional structure of small business financing.

Deregulation

The United States is making two financial system transitions simultaneously—one to a national capital market and one to a global capital market. Banking regulations have made this country unique among major industrial nations in delaying the evolution to a consolidated national banking system. But technology and economic developments have made it inevitable that the United States banking structure must change. Today, financial markets are electronic and do business 24 hours a day from interconnected locations all over the globe.

Banking deregulation involves the elimination of the state barriers that have traditionally limited commercial bank operations to the confines of a single state, and a liberalization of rules governing the nation's banking and financial system established in the aftermath of the Depression. In practice, the rules have been cracking and systematic changes have been occurring in bits and pieces for a long time. The nation's biggest banks have found loopholes to operate in roundabout ways outside their home states and in other nations. Giant retailers and security brokerages have begun to offer the financial services of banks, but free from their regulatory apparatus. In the global arena, the barriers between commercial and investment banking have been eroding.

The lifting of interstate banking barriers will set off a free-for-all competition and shakeout. To give the smaller banks a chance to consolidate competitively and to make the transition somewhat more orderly, Federal Reserve Board Chairman Paul Volcker in 1985 recommended Congressional legislation for a three-year transition period before the full implementation of interstate banking. It is generally believed that banks with under $100 million in assets—80 percent of the total bank population—suffer diseconomies of scale that greatly reduce their chances of survival.

Bank failures have been running at record rates and increasing annually. Some 150 banks, all of them small, with average assets of $40 million, are expected to fail in 1986. In addition, the Federal Deposit Insurance Corporation's (FDIC) list of problem banks has increased nearly sevenfold since 1981 to 1,300 in 1986. The emergence of electronic and global capital markets has transformed finance into a fast-moving, sophisticated industry. Many small bankers who grew up in sleepier times simply lack the cunning to survive in the new environment.

Interstate banking will mark the end of a tradition of decentralized independent banking that has its roots in the early Federalist-Republican debates to delineate federal and state powers. State-chartered banking, the protective umbrella of small banking, won the decisive victory in the 1830s when Andrew Jackson failed to renew the charter of the Second Bank of the United States. From then on, the number of banks operating increased enormously. The vast majority were single-office operations capitalized by individuals or groups of businessmen and serving local, often small communities, like the bank John Schmidt's great-grandfather established in Marysville, Kansas, in 1870.

Given the rudimentary communications technology and the great continental expanse with variable and fluid local conditions—and mostly small businesses—to be served, the local banking system was probably an efficient means of financing America's extensive growth in the nineteenth century. Throughout the rise of large industrial enterprises, small banking continued to flourish. Between 1900 and 1920, the number of American banks increased from 12,000 to 30,000.[17]

Bank failures during the Depression trimmed the banking population. Since then, improvements in communication and transportation technology, urbanization, and the increasing capital requirements of larger enterprises, have gradually swung the competitive balance in favor of large banks. Were it not for banking rules established in an earlier era, it is doubtful how many of the country's 15,000 commercial banks would be in existence today.

The final impact of interstate banking on small business depends on the number of banks that survive and the type of banking functions they perform. The likely demise of small banks will have a deleterious effect on small business financing. Arguments that interstate banking will make bank financing more efficient (that is, less costly to the most efficient, best-risk producers) are little consolation to the vast majority of small businesses. On an individual company basis the most efficient enterprises in the modern economy, and the best risk from the perspective of a large banking institution, are large ones.

The small banker is an independent small businessman with a self-interest in and knowledge of his local economy. He is likely to have personal knowledge of the small businessmen in the community, and shares many of their same concerns. He is likely to understand through close experience the problems of running a small business. Unlike an independent banker such as John Schmidt of the Exchange Bank of Schmidt & Koester who may bend the rules to help a troubled client gain more time, or to finance a start-up based heavily on personal character, a big bank with numerous branches must rely on strict lending formulas in order to maintain organizational order. Branch lending officers may have some discretion, but they do not undertake entrepreneurial risks.

Unlike small banks whose future is tied to the fortunes of the local economy, big banks have vested interests in other U.S. communities—and in other communities around the world. They will likely be inclined to use local deposits to finance activity far away from the local community as more profitable opportunities arise. Just as international corporations shop for supplies around the world, so, too, will international banks eventually finance foreign competitors of local small businesses whose activities helped to generate the local deposits for the financing. This will increase the exposure of local U.S. economies to global competition. Likewise, big banks will be more prone to panic at signs of local small business distress and choke off financing when it is needed most, just as they sometimes have in rushing to bail out of foreign debtor countries at early signs of trouble.

Drastically fewer small banks could harm small business by diminishing the current diversity of competition among lenders. In England, where banking is highly centralized, as it is in most of Europe, the small businessman must plead his case to a loan officer at one of the big London clearinghouse banks. If he's denied—as often he is—he's all but dead.

It is not clear the extent to which small independent banking anchors a small business economy. Cultural traditions are important, too. It may be coincidental that the country's small business economy is comparatively robust and the United States has so many more independent small banks than Europe. A European exception is Italy, which also has both a plethora of small regional banks and a dynamic small business population.

The fact that major banks such as Continental Illinois are not permitted to fail puts small banks at a further, government-created, competitive disadvantage. The failure of a major financial institution would create world financial panic and possibly set off a crash. Everyone knows it, and reassured by those bail-outs that do occur, they act on the assumption that there is a federal guarantee behind the major institutions. This puts pressure on small banks, which, lacking such a guarantee, must offer higher interest rates in order to attract bigger depositors. But to be able to offer higher rates, they must make riskier investments with higher potential returns—and a greater likelihood of eventual problems.

Salomon Brothers' chief economist, Henry Kaufman, argues that without the discipline of failure, free-market competition via deregulation is a sham. It favors large institutions and tempts general recklessness on the part of the privileged institutions. In the end, it may lead to problems that will result in the imposition of broader regulatory machinery. Kaufman has written: "There cannot be a true 'level playing field' among financial institutions in our system. The financial system would look more like a zoo with the bars let down, with all of the attendant adverse consequences."[18]

The distortion of a nonlevel playing field created by government bail-outs is not limited to major financial institutions. Government bail-outs of Chrysler, Lockheed, Penn Central, and others also distort the basic government of a free market economy. In a global, highly integrated economy, government intervention in the fates of individual economic entities, and in markets, is becoming increasingly inevitable. The priority of governments will be to protect larger institutions whose disruption could have wider adverse ramifications for the national and international economy. Small business increasingly will suffer the competitive disadvantages of starting on the down-slope of this nonlevel playing field by being judged a relatively still greater credit risk by lenders, suppliers, and customers.

Just as banking deregulation is likely to increase concentration in banking, so it may in other deregulated industries. On the eve of airline deregulation in 1978, former TWA Chairman Charlie Tillinghast predicted that deregulation would result in several years of increased competition followed by a return to concentration and higher prices.[19]

By the mid-1980s, Wall Street analysts were in fact predicting that six huge airlines would come to dominate the industry, shaking out or acquiring all but a few strong regionals and local airlines. In the first nine months of 1984, five major carriers controlled 47.7 percent of the traffic—the same as before deregulation—and accounted for 94 percent of industry profits. Many small competitors had gone belly up. Wall Street, many times burned, had lost its appetite for financing new start-ups. Alfred Kahn, the Carter administration chairman of the Civil Aeronautics Board who led the fight for deregulation, was confessing his concern and recommending stronger enforcement of antitrust laws.

The return of the free market via deregulation simply substitutes the advantages held through regulation with the natural advantages of market competition. Where the market favors economies of size, small companies will be shaken out and the less competitive oligopolistic structure will emerge as it would have earlier had not regulation prevented it. Only in industries such as trucking, with relatively low-entry barriers and levels of operating efficiency, may deregulation enhance small business' chances.

Government

Any time power flows away from decentralized localities to states and the federal government, small business loses political influence, and as a consequence, economic power. The rise of interstate commerce in the 1870s foreshadowed the increasing intervention of federal authority in state economic affairs in order to help govern the emergence of large economic entities

with interstate interests. Today, increasing coordination between sovereign governments is intended to govern their international engagements.

There is a paradoxical aspect to small business' relationship
with the U.S. federal government: Small business *needs* the
government to restrain the economic activities of big business.
Unregulated, capitalism rapidly leads to economic concentration
and the liquidation of small business, or its reduction to subservience. Today, small business needs the government to maintain
an artificial approximation of a neo-classical free market level
playing field that leaves ample latitude for small enterprise.

This presents an ongoing danger, since the general activities of government favor big business. One irony of the
modern American economy is that big business, which already
enjoys competitive advantages over small business, gets on balance a further edge through the intervention of government—
thus exaggerating, rather than leveling, the tilt of the business
playing field. Much macroeconomic policy, as often applied,
favors large corporations. There is nothing sinister in this. The
actions are often best for the general economy, which is to say its
main economic entities, big business. When a large business has
a major need, government usually responds strongly. This in
part is due to the organizational relationships between business
and the state in the modern U.S. economy. John Kenneth Galbraith has written:

> As the individual member of the market system cannot typically
> influence his customers, so he cannot influence the state. The presi-
> dent of General Motors has a prescriptive right, on visiting Wash-
> ington, to see the President of the United States. The president of
> General Electric has a right to see the Secretary of Defense and the
> president of General Dynamics to see any general. The individual
> farmer has no similar access to the Secretary of Agriculture; the
> individual retailer has no entrée to the Secretary of Commerce. It
> would be of little value to them if they did. The public bureaucracy
> . . . can be effectively and durably influenced only by another
> organization.[20]

Big business is the preferred customer of government at no
time more so than when government's power is at its peak in
wartime. War, by creating urgent mass-market demand, has

hastened the growth and dominance of large enterprises since the Civil War, when the need for uniforms turned the ready-made clothing industry into a large-scale industry overnight. The same was true of the meat-packing and canned-meat industries. The unprecedented military need for iron plate for warships and iron rails for tracks cut short the era of the small-scale metalworking shops.[21]

When World War II started, the demand for dried foods, spurred by massive orders by the U.S. Army, took off. One beneficiary was entrepreneur J. R. Simplot, who won orders to supply dried potatoes. The huge demand enabled Simplot to expand his production at a prodigious rate until he soon enjoyed economies of scale and a market position that no small competitor could hope to match. After enduring the shock withdrawal of the postwar period, Simplot used his position to build a $1 billion company (including, as mentioned earlier, supplying frozen French fries to McDonald's starting in the mid-1960s) and became known as the potato king.[22]

Government procurement since World War II has reinforced the growth of large-scale enterprise. The defense industry, which in 1983 spent 80 percent of the government's $170 billion procurement budget, is dominated by billion-dollar, nominally private corporate satellites of the Pentagon whose government contracts reinforce their competitive advantages in related, nonmilitary commercial fields. Only a fraction of the major Pentagon contracts are even open to competitive bidding. In many of the rest, small business is dissuaded from participating due to the huge administrative costs involved in preparing complex and bureaucratically governed bids.

In all, small businesses received 29 percent of total government procurement dollars even though the small business economy accounted for 38 percent of GNP. Small business' share of contracts worth $10,000 or more has been declining for several years.[23] As government projects, such as for space or defense, become larger in size, companies that are simply too small to handle them are eliminated from contract consideration.

Small business' share of R&D procurement dollars has also been falling. In view of small business' prominent high-tech role, the federal government has initiated several programs to increase funds for innovative R&D at small companies. The

Small Business Innovation Research program (SBIR), passed in 1982, was intended to stem small business' diminishing, paltry 3 percent share of federal research funding. It requires 12 federal agencies with total R&D budgets of $50 billion annually, to earmark at least 1.25 percent of their research money for small business.[24]

Finally, compliance with most government regulations, such as those governing safety, health, pollution, and drugs, falls proportionately harder on small businesses (those who obey them) with less wherewithal to absorb the expense. The FDA cycle for testing and approval of a new drug—a necessity for protecting the social welfare—is so long and expensive that it represents a protective barrier for big business.

Occasionally small business wins judicial battles against big business. But court battles are normally prohibitively expensive for small companies to wage. Sometimes when they win, as in the case of the small distributor against Monsanto, the victory comes too late to save the business.

Financial limitations also restrict small business' political leverage. Although small business political interests have successfully lobbied for recent legislation intended to redress some of small business' low share of federal procurement dollars and other federal government-created disadvantages, its political influence in Washington remains relatively weak. The small business committees in both houses are well-known as weak committees to which few Congressmen actively seek assignment.

Few of small business' legislative victories over the years have had major lasting impacts. Rarely in the battle for federal legislation has small business found allies in labor or big business, which is one reason for small business' generally weak influence. Small businessmen were significant forces behind the passage of the Sherman Anti-Trust Act of 1890 and the Clayton Anti-Trust Act of 1914.[25] Two other notable small-business-inspired pieces of legislation were the Robinson-Patman Act of 1936 and Miller-Tydings Act of 1937, both targeting the growing strength of chain stores. Neither law had more than a minor effect on the marketplace. When Miller-Tydings was repealed in 1976, it received scant notice outside the trade press.[26]

Despite the creation of the Smaller War Plants Corporation to help mobilize small business resources, small manufacturers complained during World War II about receiving less than a proportionate share of federal procurement dollars. Indeed, they came out of the war with a relatively weakened status.[27] After the war, the lending authority of the Smaller War Plants Corporation was transferred to the big-business-oriented Reconstruction Finance Corporation, the giant agency created in 1932 to help lift the nation from Depression. With the Korean War, small business got renewed assistance through the Small Defense Plants Administration. Then, in 1953 the Small Business Administration was created.

The activities of the SBA have grown over the years. Its major functions have been to provide loan guarantees, direct loans, and physical disaster loans to small business, management assistance, and to represent small business interests in Washington as an independent agency. Since 1976 it has been building a data base on small business that eventually will provide a major statistical source for analyzing and assessing small business' status in the United States.

Over the years, the SBA has been a favorite target of budget cutters. During its 1985 budget-cutting drive, the Reagan administration, following a critical report by the conservative Heritage Foundation think tank, proposed abolishing the SBA altogether along with most of its programs, claiming first-year savings of $1.2 billion. But the Washington "Iron Triangle" of program beneficiaries, Congressional overseers, and program administrators rallied enough support to save it. In 1986, the administration tried again. While small business interest groups are generally cool to its management assistance and lending programs, they value its advocacy activities.

The government does help create a level playing field for small business in several instances. For example, to help small businesses build retained earnings for growth, and simply to help small businessmen to survive, business tax rates are graduated starting at 15 percent for incomes below $100,000, at which point all companies are taxed at a flat 46 percent. Small business interests have been lobbying hard to retain a graduated table in the debate over tax reform.

A truly simplified tax structure, as with simplified regulations in general, would help create a more level playing environment for small business. More complex laws are a comparative advantage for large business because only it can afford batteries of lawyers, tax specialists, and special interest lobbyists to negotiate optimum, if esoteric, individual case solutions. Moreover, many legislated tax breaks are intended to stimulate a particular category of economic activity; in practice most benefit those best able to make their needs understood in government—large business.

Many government projects that would ostensibly apply universally to all citizens would, in practice, help level the playing field for small business in the marketplace. A national health program, for instance, would offset some of small business' current disadvantage in soliciting desirable employees due to its less competitive health benefits.

Maintenance of universal flat rates for fundamental and efficiently dispensed public or quasi-public services, such as electricity, water, and until recently, telephone, helps small business' relative competitive position. Discounts for volume users helps big business.

Overhaul of America's decaying infrastructure—roads, bridges, sewers and, above all, the public education system—could significantly improve the economic environment for small business. High-quality public infrastructure may offset the advantage of special roads and other services big businesses frequently negotiate as the price of locating in a local community, or the special infrastructure big business builds for itself.

Good infrastructure is essential for small firms to gain competitive economies and shared skills through clustering, which may become an important means by which small businesses compete successfully in the future economy.

Exporting

The growth of U.S. involvement in world trade has been a major economic trend of the postwar economy. In the future, successful business will depend increasingly on selling to markets all over the globe.

This poses a major problem to small business, which participates proportionately far less in the international than in the domestic economy. U.S. exporting is dominated by big business. The top 250 exporting firms account for 85 percent of the value of all U.S. exports.[28]

There are many obstacles to small business exporting. All ultimately relate to the need to have high minimum business volume before the large expenses and complexities involved in exporting becomes profitable. Exporting involves a large initial commitment of travel and research of foreign markets. Pricing calculations must take into account the cost of various tariffs (there are well over a dozen different tariff classifications systems in use by major trading nations), surcharges, licenses and freight charges and limits imposed by nontariff protectionist trade barriers such as quotas. International financing requires a knowledge of how to best use international letters of credit and various bank export financing. Small hometown banks often are ignorant of the workings of international trade finance. Currency risks must be assessed. Finally, there are language obstacles, local business customs to master, metric measurement conversions for packaging and calculating costs, and the difficulty and expense of building distribution and after-sales service networks. An export manager's salary plus travel, communication, and administrative expenses probably surpasses $100,000 a year—meaning that a company with a 10 percent profit margin must export at least $1 million worth of goods to make the export proposition economically enticing.

Nevertheless, the Government Accounting Office believes there are at least 11,000 small U.S. firms that could be successful exporters, but don't try to export. There have been various initiatives to try to encourage U.S. exporting in general, and small business exporting in particular.[29]

Recent legislation intended to encourage small business exporting gives antitrust immunity to export trading companies. These ETCs provide market research, transportation, warehousing, trade financing, and other exporting functions to client exporters. Starting in 1984, the Eximbank, otherwise known as "Boeing's bank" for its trade finance support for the aircraft manufacturer, began setting aside a certain percentage of its trade financing subsidies for small business exporters.

Ultimately 10 percent of the Eximbank's subsidies will be earmarked for small business—in 1984 dollars, that would have amounted to $450 million in direct loans and $1.1 billion in loan guarantees and insurance. Some states have authorized export finance agencies, although their actual activities so far are inconsequential.

Export trading companies have operated in Europe and Japan, where they conduct over 50 percent of that nation's international trade, for a long time. The early indication is that greater incentives will be required before they become operational in this country. One problem is that the export trading companies that have been set up, many by banks, aren't interested in small transactions which cost as much to do as big ones.

To launch products globally requires far more financing and higher degrees of business organization than small business possesses. Even large corporations have formed international strategic alliances and joint ventures with large Japanese and European corporations to muscle up to meet the demands of marketing in the new global economy. Few small businesses can compete against these alliances of international corporations.

The internationalization of advertising is one disadvantage. International ad agencies are handling larger volumes of the world's $160 billion spent on advertising. International corporations such as Revlon with its Flex shampoo and Bank of America with its travelers' checks are attempting to decimate local competitors by blanketing the globe with uniform product ad campaigns as consumer tastes homogenize among markets. The spread of self-service retailing favors the products of these large corporations since there is little other recommendation of a product than ad promotion. With the need for rapid penetration of markets, big distributors will tend to be increasingly preferred by multinational producers.

The emergence of global goods and capital markets initially favors big business, which has the expertise and the vast networks to shop globally for the best terms. Small U.S. suppliers have been pitted against foreign parts supplies in areas of the world they may never have heard of through the intermediation of the big corporations, which roam the globe looking for the most attractive supplies. Every time a major U.S. corporation switches to overseas manufacturing or buys supplies from abroad, hundreds of U.S.-based suppliers lose contracts, and their employees lose jobs. Big business' leverage over small suppliers is likely to increase as global sourcing becomes more sophisticated and local suppliers are goaded into competing fiercely against one another for an international corporation's favor.

Finally, recognizing that U.S. industries are far less concentrated when viewed in the context of a global market, U.S. antitrust policy has been shifting to allow greater concentration in U.S. markets. This may improve the competitiveness of large U.S. companies, but it will likely have a chilling effect on small businesses that must contend with these large companies domestically.

9

Foreign
Small Business

For many years, the Veneto region of northeastern Italy was one of that nation's economic backwaters. Tourists passed briefly through Verona and Padua en route to Venice. Poor Italians from the south migrating north in search of jobs in the large industrial projects left its residents, farmers, and regional craftsmen undisturbed as they passed by. In the last two or three decades, however, the Veneto has been transformed from one of the poorer to one of the richer regions of Italy.

It has done so through small manufacturing. Today, three-fifths of the 30,000 mostly family-run manufacturing firms employ under 100 workers. The clusters of small manufacturers built their businesses upon local craft traditions, which includes Venetian glass, Visentine jewelry, fancy shoemaking in Brenta, and furniture from Verona, and the extensive work-at-home subcontracting networks of increasingly skilled peasants who moved down to the villages from the hillside farms. Over time, the small businessmen applied their craft skills to more sophisticated tools, and ultimately to reprogrammable computer-driven machines. This has enabled them to stay ahead of competition from lower-wage regions around the world.

Some of the subcontractors developed internationally known trademarks, and organized for export. Being small and gaining strength from the clustering of local craft skills, the firms have been able to maintain their decentralized local roots. The combined population of Padua, Verona, Vicenza, and Treviso is less than one million, but each town has kept its own newspaper. What has happened in the Veneto has happened in other rural provinces of Italy. It is one possible vision of small manufacturing's future in the industrialized world.

The best-known manufacturing firm in the Veneto is Benetton, the $330 million sales, $17.5 million net profits, manufacturer of popular, colorful wool garments. It is located in a 350-year-old restored villa in the tiny town of Ponzano, 13 miles north of Venice. The company was started in 1965 by three brothers and a sister (who designed the original sweaters). Lacking capital to purchase machinery, the Benetton family relied on a regional craft tradition to make the first sweaters: The wool was pounded with a wooden pole in a tub of water until soft.

Today, Benetton is a vision of ultramodernity. It has more computer technicians on its payroll than seamstresses. CAD terminals are used to design shirts and sweaters. Two central computers—one for wool and one for cotton—keep track of the distribution of a garment from the day it is ordered to the time it is sold in one of the 3,000 franchised Benetton stores around the world. Most of the cash registers in its European stores are point-of-sale terminals, which immediately relay information about how many of each kind of garment have been sold each day—and how many more each store needs to order—to Benetton headquarters.

Once the information is processed in Benetton's central computers, rollers in the cutting room spread the appropriate number of layers of raw cloth for cutting. Dye machines produce small batches of precisely the number of each color needed. Benetton produces a dozen different styles in 30 different colors. But because of the computer distribution tracking system and because of the cost efficiency of computerized small-batch production, it maintains only a bare-minimum inventory. Its warehouse is manned by $20 million worth of robots and two human overseers. Benetton, however, does not do everything itself or by computer. Most of the weaving and cutting is still farmed out to the local support network of sub-contractors. These, in turn, pass the work on to entire families, many of whom work at home on a low-cost piecework basis.

Benetton garments are sold in stores throughout America, Japan and, of course, Europe. In Italy, Benetton sells through seven different-named chains aimed at different images, although each are Benetton franchises and stock essentially the same garments. Having seven different storefronts not only allows Benetton to target different clienteles, but it permits much deeper market saturation of each city. Franchisees, the Benetton family has found, are also more aggressive sellers when they know the store across the street is carrying the same garments.

Because of its relative lack of smokestack industry, the Veneto, and other regions of Italy like it which have followed a similar evolution, has hardly felt the pain of industrial rationalization that has marked the transition to the new global economy. In the clusters of small, flexible craft-based technology manufacturers of the Veneto, the new economy has already arrived. Benetton represents the apex of what many others hope soon to attain themselves.[1]

In foreign nations, small business has evolved under different economic and social-economic conditions from the United States. Although the fundamental roles served by small business are similar in kind to those in this country, in no leading nation of the world has small business had such a dynamic impact on the ongoing process of economic change—and on the adjustment to the current economic transition in particular—as in the United States. In much of Europe and Japan, the social-economic environment produced a tradition of public bureaucratic excellence which attracted the most talented individuals to manage their more planning-oriented economic systems. Spurred by the creative spark that small, particularly high-tech, U.S. companies have added to America's economic transformation, most European nations and Japan have launched efforts to produce similar results. Many nations in the communist and developing worlds have also embarked on small business strategies to help them achieve their economic agendas.

Western Europe

Although capitalism was born in Europe, it was in the United States that it found the economic and social conditions which permitted it to reach its fullest vigor. In the cramped markets and hierarchical social relationships of Western Europe, economic development went forward with a stunted small business economy—not so much in sheer size as in vitality and competitive spirit. It never enjoyed the kind of economic environment to develop into the powerful complementary force that it did in the United States.

Nevertheless, from the ruins of the war Western Europe in the 1940s and 1950s turned in the strongest economic growth in its history. Rates of per capita growth doubled and tripled over its pre–World War I performance—and far exceeded growth in the United States. By the 1970s, Western Europe's living standards had largely caught up with those in America. European industry posed tough international competition for U.S. corporations.

This impressive achievement was the result of a "guided" capitalism—the cooperation of government, large industry, and labor leaders in planning and executing economic growth. In most of Western Europe small business played a very minor role in this process.

The system worked well during the long period of postwar growth while Europe was catching up and the path to industrial growth could be charted by following developments in this country. But as in the United States, the period of slow growth and economic transition that began in the 1970s caused economic strains. Basic heavy industries had to be rationalized, and new industrial winners had to be picked.

As in this country, the large economic entities of industry, government, and labor adapted slowly. In the United States, small business emerged spontaneously to facilitate change and ease the economic strains. In most of Western Europe, the small business economy remained relatively moribund.

While small business helped produce some 20 million jobs in America between the early 1970s and early 1980s, Western Europe created no net new jobs. By mid-1985, in the maturity of an economic recovery, unemployment in the European Economic Community (EEC) was stuck at 19 million, or 11 percent of the work force. Unemployment among youths under twenty-five was double and triple that in some countries. Silicon Valley, Boston's Route 128, and other places spontaneously came alive with hundreds of small innovative high-tech companies to spark the boom which made the United States a world leader in producing and applying the information technologies that will lead the next cycle of economic growth. In Europe—very little.

A fatalistic sense that Europe will be unable to close, or even maintain, the perceived technology gap with the United States and Japan, was generating "Europessimism" through much of Europe in the mid-1980s. European leaders were deeply concerned about the loss of world market share in the semiconductor and other information technology industries, and by the fact that America and Japan were selling three times and five times respectively more computer equipment and electrical goods to EEC countries than they were buying in return. They were openly worrying that they would be left behind in the growth boom anticipated in the wake of the current economic transition, just as they were in the last boom at the turn of the century.[2]

The lack of jobs provided a picture of what the U.S. situation could have been like had it not created so many new jobs and new companies. High unemployment was generating severe political pressure to preserve rather than trim old unprofitable industries in the face of competition from newly industrializing countries. It was creating deep hostility against technological innovation. Technology was seen, in a cruel zero sum game, not as the future generator but as the present destroyer of prosperous livelihoods. As a result, Europe has been slow to shift assets from yesterday's to tomorrow's growth industries. The social-democratic compact between capital and labor which has provided the modus operandi of postwar prosperity is under pressure.

Why has small business been less dynamic in Europe than in this country? Here the big markets which permitted full exploitation of mass production economies of scale, an encouraging social-economic environment, as well as decentralized political influences and credit sources were conducive to a rapidly expanding economy which gave ample latitude to small business entrepreneurs. In Europe, slower growth, smaller and cartelized markets, a forbidding social-economic environment, centralized banking sources, cooperative relations between existing large enterprise and political leaderships, and the perpetuation of social class bias, have tended to restrict entrepreneurial small business initiative.

Economic power concentrated more rapidly in Europe than in the developing expanse of the United States. Small markets—often circumscribed by the borders of each nation—limited economies of production scale. National corporations producing smaller volumes operated in a high-cost, high-profit margin environment which rewarded unaggressive business strategies rather than entrepreneurial risks.

In Europe, capitalism was built upon a feudal base. This built-in the class conflict bred by that system, ultimately in the form of a division between "capital" and "labor." While in the New World individuals from the poorer classes looked to capitalist enterprise to fulfill their democratic and individualistic ambitions to rise, in the social-economic environment of Europe they put their hopes instead in the socialist movements which eventually helped produce Europe's social-democratic consensus.

Europe's social-economic values have traditionally stigmatized moneymaking as somewhat crass. It is a view influenced by the Catholic Church's teaching against profiteering, cultivated by the landed nobility, and later unchallenged by those of socialist beliefs.

Europe's best and brightest in modern times have traditionally been steered instead toward the more prestigious and dignified professions of civil service, diplomacy, merchant banking, law, and medicine. If they went to business at all, it was to big companies, which offered status, generous perks and benefits (in lieu of lavish salaries), and job security.

Entrepreneurship has carried an additional risk of disgrace if it resulted in failure: In Europe, failure carries a stigma that is not quite the social equivalent of having spent time in a debtors' prison. The social-economic environment in Europe for small business is improving, but it still produces a dearth of aggressive entrepreneurs.

Europe continues to produce too many large "national champion" producers trapped within too small markets. This deters start-ups. Capital and human resources are concentrated in many redundant projects, thus depleting the source of engineers or other talented individuals who might otherwise strike out on their own or be employed by small innovative companies.

Without pressure from aggressive business start-ups, Europe's large, sometimes state-owned, economic entities tend to slow the pace of commercial innovation. Europe's science is good, but it doesn't get out of the labs fast enough. Europe is most notoriously weak in the commercial application of electronics to new products—precisely where small companies have proven so strong in the United States.

Strict rules about hiring and firing, high social security taxes, and the power of unions until the early 1980s to win high real-wage increases despite slow growth, have discouraged job creation by small business. Labor market rigidity, called "Eurosclerosis" in current European jargon, has created the perverse situation where companies are making large capital investments in automation machinery to replace workers at a time of terrible unemployment. Great capital investment has made European productivity rates higher than that in the United States, but a trade-off of higher productivity for double-digit unemployment is at least as serious as the U.S. disease of low investment, low productivity, and higher employment.

Europe's inflexible capital markets are also unfavorable to small business start-ups or small company financings. Money tends to flow from highly centralized, risk-abhorring banking sources to well-known, traditional clients within national borders. Yet at the same time, small businesses in Europe are more highly dependent on bank capital for financing than in America. This is because individual savings are hard to accumulate due to the prevailing low salary, high-benefit pattern of executive compensation and because, until very recently, there was almost no opportunity to raise public equity capital.

At least one small-growth company which believes it has been stunted by the poorly developed home and neighboring country equity markets is the Danish biotechnology company, Novo Industri, which created the world market for industrial enzymes in the 1960s. Only a decade and a half later was Novo well enough known that it could raise capital in London. Shortly thereafter, Novo made an offering in the United States (and instantly became one of Wall Street's darlings). Since then, however, it has fallen on hard times. It lays part of the blame on its inability to raise money early and fast enough to grow rapidly to internationally competitive size in the global pharmaceuticals business.

Europe has undertaken major efforts to remedy its competitive weaknesses. Renewed political efforts have been taken to forge the EEC into a truly common market. Billions of dollars are being invested in EEC and national R&D projects, such as Esprit and Britain's Alvey Program. European corporations have pooled resources to conduct joint research programs. Steps have been taken to advance the ECU as a common European currency to add cohesion and flexibility to European capital markets.

Largely inspired by the U.S. experience, nearly every country in Western Europe has implemented a program to stimulate small business. Prime Minister Margaret Thatcher in England and President François Mitterrand in France, in particular, have staked great political capital on their small business initiatives. To highlight the attention European leaders wish to give small business, 1983 was designated the European Year of Small and Medium Enterprises.

The vitality and role of the small business economy is not identical, of course, in each European nation. Small business is generally strong south of the Alps and less important in Northern Europe. One study of comparable small companies in various European nations found, for instance, that the same pretax bottom line outcome could yield a range of results from losses in Britain to handsome profits in Italy.

Throughout Europe, be it *travail noir* in France, *lavoro sommerso* in Italy, *schattenwirtschaft* in Germany, or the *black economy* in Britain, small business figures importantly in the underground economies which have flourished in the recent past years of economic hardship.

In West Germany, a country famous for its large, often lavishly subsidized corporations, authorities have been worried by the long-term decline of small business or *mittelständisch* (which connotes a social order rather than size). Sales and employment share of the smallest companies declined sharply between 1950 and 1970. So did the number of self-employed, from 3.3 million to 2.4 million between 1960 and 1977.[3]

The concern about the so-called new firm deficit, particularly in high-tech sectors, has grown larger in the decade to 1985, when Germany's growth rate has slowed to an average of only 1.5 percent a year. With the exception of Heinz Nixdorf, who founded Nixdorf Computer in the cellar of an electricity company in 1952, Germany has had very few high-tech entrepreneurs to apply competitive pressure to its formidable large corporations.

Part of the reason for Germany's small business start-up shortage is a cultural "security complex"—the pervasive desire to eliminate risk from all aspects of life. The security complex has helped build one of the most comprehensive social welfare systems in the world. But it has also discouraged senior executives from leaving the corporate womb to strike out on their own.

Many state, local, and corporate programs have been initiated to encourage small businessmen in the last several years. A program started by Siemens, the electrical giant with 340,000 employees, based in Germany's high-tech region around Munich, in 1983 illustrates the formidable obstacle Germany's security complex can pose: Through an in-house venture-capital group, Siemens offered to finance any potential entrepreneurs who would develop and commercialize any research it had not decided not to pursue itself. In two years, it had only one taker—which it enticed with an initial $1 million purchase order for the final product, one-third prepaid.[4]

Small business start-up is also frustrated by tangible obstacles, such as a social welfare system that can add up to 82 percent to the cost of an employee's normal salary. In some cases up to 150 applications must be filed to start a new business.

Where small business does thrive, however, it provides 80 percent of all apprenticeships under Germany's job training program. Small firms also tend to use a much higher percentage of their patents than Germany's big corporations.

Since coming to power in 1979 the Thatcher government, as part of its general effort to restimulate a free market economic environment in Great Britain, has passed over 70 measures to reverse the decline in self-employment that had been recorded during the 1970s. Much of the current concern over small business in Britain goes back to 1971 to an influential report by the Committee of Enquiry of Small Firms, known familiarly as the Bolton Report, after its chairman. The Bolton Report questioned the health of British small business—but stressed the importance of a healthy small business constituency to the general economy.

Small business' contribution to national output is lower in Britain than in most European nations. Small businesses with under 200 employees account for one-fifth Britain's national output and one-third of all jobs.[5]

Much of the Thatcher small business effort has been directed at stemming the steady rise in unemployment that has plagued her government from its inception—from 5 percent in 1979 to 13 percent in 1985. The combination of economic hardship and government incentives has helped cause self-employment to rise by 20 percent in the 1980s to 2.5 million. Some 40 percent of the self-employed have employees themselves, which has helped total employment to rise by 600,000 in the recovery between 1983 and 1985.

As in the United States, most of the new businesses were started by women, most in the general services sector. The vast majority of those starting manufacturing businesses were formerly unemployed—in one survey, only 16 percent had left a job for self-employment. Franchising, long underdeveloped in Britain, was finally expanding beyond the traditional businesses of pubs and gasoline service stations. In what has started to become a broad trend in industrialized economies, large corporations were farming an increasing amount of work out to smaller subcontractors.[6]

Britain is the bridge by which many business trends travel between the United States and Europe. It is in Britain that the first European stirrings of a spontaneous small business-led high-tech boom can be seen. The centers of high tech in Britain, which has the highest per capita number of Nobel prize winners of any nation—are clustered around Cambridge, the M4 motorway outside London, and in so-called Silicon Glen in central Scotland.

In Silicon Glen's otherwise bleak industrial landscape, some 300 electronics companies have bloomed in the past decade, accounting for $2 billion in annual sales and 42,000 employees among them. The impetus has come from the 50 U.S. companies which set up there, and from whose ranks many of the new entrepreneurs sprang. Meanwhile, in Cambridge there are about 350 more high-tech firms, 100 of which were born in the 1980s. Most are quite small. The biggest names in Cambridge are two troubled companies, Sinclair Research, founded by the prolific inventor Sir Clive Sinclair, and Acorn. Thanks to Sinclair and others, the attitude of scientists in Cambridge has changed from disdain to warming enthusiasm about marriages between academia and industry.

With many basic heavy industries in decline and massive layoffs needed to rationalize them, few European leaders have embraced small business entrepreneurship as exuberantly as France's socialist President Mitterrand. Mitterrand returned from a visit to Silicon Valley in March 1984 entirely smitten by the potential of high-tech entrepreneurship and talking about the need for lower taxes and more venture capital.

Several months later his government unveiled a program to stimulate entrepreneurship beyond the array of initiatives it had already undertaken to help *les petites et moyenne entreprises*. In September of that year, Mitterrand's prime minister, Laurent Fabius, went on television to proselytize the virtues of profitability and entrepreneurial initiative.

The spectacle of socialist boosters of free enterprise is confounding the distinctions between Right and Left which have traditionally pervaded French politics. It is also a sharp about-face for a government which had embarked on a nationalization program when it came to power in 1981. With a third of French industry under its management, the government has told the bosses of state-owned companies that they could lose their jobs if they didn't turn in improved results by year-end 1985.

Some high-tech firms have begun to appear around Lyons. Much of French small industry, however, like many small firms in Italy, are not modern enterprises but family-based craft firms whose members earn well below the national average. Many small retailers are protected by laws forbidding larger discounts to large volume buyers.

Bureaucratic procedures still hamper quick business start-ups. Despite the improved atmosphere and incentives, the number of French businesses failing each year still exceeds the number of new ones opening their doors.

Italy is the single EEC nation that has *not* undertaken major small business initiatives. It doesn't have to. Almost alone in

Europe, its aggregate small business economy is quite dynamic. Italian small business has played a strategic role in the transformation of Italy in the postwar period from an essentially poor peasant agricultural economy into one with living standards and industrial competitiveness comparable to those of other leading European nations.

Italy, a nation with one-fourth the population of the United States, has two and a half times as many manufacturing firms. The average shop, however, is much smaller, employing but one-sixth the number of employees. Only Japan, and to a lesser degree Spain and Switzerland, has a manufacturing industry characterized by so many small shops. In Italy, the small manufacturers employ three-fifths of the manufacturing work force and account for an enormous 50 percent of manufacturing output. Unparalleled in the industrialized world, they also lead Italy's prodigious export effort, accounting for almost half Italy's exports.

An additional large economic contribution by *le piccole e medie imprese* is uncounted in Italy because it takes place in the underground economy—estimated at up to 25 percent of GNP—which until recently the authorities permitted to flourish through a policy of benign neglect. It is the existence of such a large underground sector that has given the Italian economy its enormous resilience. It is the reason why Italy's 12.5 percent unemployment rate is less burdensome than it seems. It has also provided a hidden engine of growth when the rest of European growth has slowed.

Throughout the postwar period, and reaching a peak in the 1960s and early 1970s, Italian families, like those in Veneto, migrated from the hills in north and south-central Italy to the towns and villages of the plain to abandon farming and took up various artisanal activities. These evolved into small-scale family enterprises. Typically, they worked on subcontracts from larger, well-known companies. When orders arrived that were too large for the subcontractor's full-time work force to expedite, entire families and relatives, including the teenagers, worked around the clock seven days a week, often on a piecework—and cash—basis that avoided social security charges and income taxes. During the day, many hold other jobs. Throughout Italy, entire little villages produce specialized single products, such as tiles, plumbing equipment, shoes, textiles, and various machine components. This is how work is done in Prato, near Florence, the world center for furniture fabric manufacturing, for example.

In the slow growth and difficult economic period of the 1970s, Italy's large private corporations farmed out much of the production of components to this vast, small business subcontracting network. This weakened union leverage and permitted the big corporations to rationalize unprofitable operations. Today, some of those corporations, such as Fiat and Olivetti, are among the most profitable and internationally competitive in Europe. This system helped Italy to continue to grow faster than nearly all its fellow members of the EEC in the last troubled decade.

The small business subcontracting network has continued to evolve and make sectors of Italian small manufacturing the most competitive in the world. As the large corporations automated production or began to consolidate their subcontracting networks, the small subcontractors, either looking for freedom from a single large customer or in response to cutbacks, modernized their production methods. Today, these small craftsmen, some working as subcontractors and some under their own trade names, are using computer-controlled machines to produce, like Benetton, small batches of specialized goods in textiles, specialty steel, precision machine tools, luxury shoes, mopeds, industrial instrumentation, and ceramic building materials.

Financing comes from Italy's unusually large number of banks, 1,100 in all. The vast majority are small and locally based. Italian banking is not rate competitive since the big, overwhelmingly state-owned banks don't want to disturb their comfortable margins between deposit and bank loan rates. Nevertheless, these local banks have a direct vested interest in promoting their depositors' products. Many do so by visiting small towns in the United States and other countries to locate customers for their goods.

Between 1971 and 1981, the recorded number of industrial workplaces in Italy rose 50 percent to 960,000.[7] Rapid growth has taken place in other types of business as well. Many are not new businesses. They are companies that are emerging from the underground economy as the Italian economy modernizes.

Under pressure from labor leaders whose fully taxed rank and file were bearing the brunt of austerity measures to combat Italy's huge budget deficit and its high inflation, and encouraged by tax-paying big businesses, the government in 1984 initiated a crackdown on tax evasion by the self-employed. It is estimated that tax cheating denied the Italian government enough revenue to wipe out half its $60 billion state deficit. In protest of the government crackdown shopkeepers across Italy, many of whose livelihoods will indeed be at peril if they pay all taxes the government requires of them, closed their shops for a day.[8]

Most nations of the EEC, which in the past have given a disproportionately small percentage of government subsidies and assistance programs to small companies, now offer credit guarantees to small business from central and local government sources. Most offer tax exemptions. Many have initiated programs to overcome the management skills shortages of small businessmen, and some offer low-rent, short-lease workspaces to new companies. The cumulative value of these programs is in the billions of dollars.

Among the most notable are Britain's loan guarantees of 70 percent (originally 80 percent) to new and expanding businesses. Britain also provides full tax relief up to £40,000 to individuals who make equity investments in nonstock-market quoted companies, either directly or through an investment fund. Enterprise agencies, which offer new businesses a range of information services and assistance, are very popular in Britain—in the first four years of the 1980s, about 100 were created throughout the country. In some, big corporations, such as Marks & Spencer, with a social spirit and self-interest in developing the local economies in which they do business, lend experienced managers to help new businesses start life.

To help combat its unemployment problem, Britain pays £40 a week for one year to any unemployed person who undertakes self-employment to compensate him for lost unemployment benefits. Over 30,000 had taken advantage of the offer by mid-1984, far outstripping the program's initial allotted resources.

Among the more novel of the French initiatives, which include three-year tax exemptions for new firms, tax provisions to encourage leveraged management buy-outs and ESOP-like worker buy-outs, is a savings scheme intended to bring self-employment within the reach of broader sectors of society. Under the French scheme, an individual can deposit up to 200,000 francs in a new business savings account which the authorities will supplement with bank loans at soft interest rates.

One of the most popular French programs to enhance the competitiveness of existing small businesses and to stimulate France's sagging investment rate was the issuance of generous government credits to assist small businesses to purchase modern numerically controlled machine tools. France and Germany have schemes to rectify small business' great disadvantage in government procurement bidding. To encourage entrepreneurship, Germany now permits the self-employed to participate in state retirement programs.

Bernard Michaud, a beekeeper in southwest France, has an unlikely partner in his $5.5 million honey business, Lune de Miel—the $13 billion state-controlled oil company, Societé Nationale Elf Aquitaine. What is Elf doing in honey? Hint: It's *not* profits. Answer: *Jobs.*

Through the low-interest loans and technical help Elf has given him, Michaud has created 18 new jobs. Elf has made 500 other similar job creation deals with small businesses to help offset the 2,500 jobs that will be lost as one of its major gas fields runs dry. St. Gobain, the big French glass and packaging manufacturer, has assisted 150 companies in businesses ranging from vegetable packaging to telecommunications which have hired some of the 3,000 workers it has laid off.[9]

Throughout Europe, large industrial firms are helping finance and assist small companies that can absorb and retrain some of the work force it lays off as it switches to new, less labor-intensive technologies.

One of the favorite means by which leaders in Britain, Germany, the Netherlands, and Sweden have been trying to speed the commercialization of Europe's good basic science has been to create science parks or "innovation centers." Often located in renovated local factories or buildings, often near university laboratories, small incubator companies pool technical, management, and marketing expertise. The Berlin innovation center, set to open in 1990, will be located hard on the Berlin Wall in a set of nineteenth-century factories that will be renovated at a cost of $25 million. It will eventually be home to 60 small technology-oriented companies and the engineering department of the Technical University of Berlin. At the end of 1984, Britain had 13 innovation centers with 15 more planned. Germany's first innovation center opened at the end of 1983. By early 1985, seven were open and plans were in the works for 40 to 50 more.[10] Large European corporations, such as Grand Metropolitan in Surrey, England, Philips in Einhoven, the Netherlands, and Nixdorf in Berlin, Germany, are participating in the science parks with an eye both to social obligation and to spotting early exploitable innovations.

Some of these new incubator companies will ultimately be financed by venture capital, which is beginning to appear in significant amounts in Europe. A European venture-capital association was formed in 1983. In all of Europe there were 250 organizations in 18 countries supplying some amount of venture capital in 1985. The venture-capital industry is by far most developed in Britain. It accounted for two-thirds of Europe's $6 billion in venture capital in 1985, which was still one-third the U.S. venture-capital total. Holland was next with about one-sixth of all European venture capital.[11] West Germany's venture-capital pool, though small, was growing rapidly.

The European venture-capital phenomenon is directly stimulated by the U.S. boom. As recently as 1980, Britain had no venture-capital industry to speak of. One limiting problem in many European nations is that the supply of good entrepreneurial candidates is scarcer than available funding. This problem has been aggravated by traditional nationalism: Only about one-tenth of venture capital in EEC companies had its source in another member country.

As a result of the entrepreneur shortage, European venture-capital funds were investing in the United States. About one-fourth of the total raised by U.S. venture-capital limited partnerships in the mid-1980s came from Europe.

Like the U.S. boom, the growth of the European venture market is related to the growth of public stock offering opportunities by small companies. It has once again been Britain that has led the way. In 1980, the Unlisted Securities Market, an over-the-counter market for smaller companies wishing to raise equity on simplified and far less expensive terms, was launched. By 1985, the USM had 270 listings and a market capitalization of £2.9 billion. Another 42 companies with market capitalization of £600 million had graduated to a full listing on the London Stock Exchange.

Encouraged by the British experience, France launched the *Seconde Marché*. Since its inception in 1983, 100 companies have raised equity capital on this market. The Netherlands, too, launched a secondary market. In Germany, where companies are notoriously starved for equity capital, a secondary over-the-counter market was also in the works.

Enlarging equity markets is a principal goal of most of the countries of continental Europe, which are eager to wean companies away from their traditional heavy dependence on debt capital. Throughout the continent, stock markets are vastly underdeveloped in proportion to the size of the economy they support. The German stock market, the continent's largest, has a capitalization only one-twelfth that of the New York Stock Exchange, even though German GNP is about one-fifth that of America's. One formidable obstacle to the development of larger equity markets goes beyond technical difficulties: the European small businessman's own traditional resistance to share equity.

For these small business programs to succeed fully requires a transformation of the social economic environment that still frustrates entrepreneurial initiative. On this count, what Europe needs above all are a few entrepreneurial, small business cultural heros to captivate the public imagination.

To a limited extent, they are arising. Britain's colorful Sir Clive Sinclair, the inventor of the first true pocket calculator, the first working digital watch, a popular low-budget home computer, and a three-wheeled electric vehicle, is a larger-than-life figure for technical-minded young Britons. A school drop-out, Sinclair wrote for technical journals before founding his first company at twenty-two and later becoming a major catalyst of the Cambridge high-tech phenomenon. In 1983, he was knighted for his achievements. However, knighthood has become somewhat embarrassing now that Sinclair has run into highly publicized financial difficulties.[12]

For more ordinary young Britons a flamboyant role model has emerged in the bearded, shaggy-haired figure of Richard Branson. The core of Branson's Virgin empire is publishing and recording pop music (he is often seen in public with pop music stars), and also includes retailing, cable TV and radio, and Virgin Atlantic, a cut-rate London–New York airline. In 1984, Branson's company was one of Britain's fastest-growing private companies, with sales of £150 million in 1984 and pretax profits in the first half of the year of £5 million.

In France, the star business attraction is another colorful longish-haired young entrepreneur, Bernard Tapie. Growing up in a working-class suburb of Paris, the son of an appliance repairman who was a member of the Communist Party, Tapie has built a $550 million collection of nearly 50 companies since 1980. His technique has been to buy troubled companies, and then, exploiting tax and interest-rate subsidies in France's bankruptcy code, make them profitable again.

Tapie makes no bones about how he feels. "I'm here to win and get rich," he says, from his fancy offices near the Arc de Triomphe in Paris. "These old-style industrialists think it's shameful to make money." Tapie has captivated the French press, and frequently appears in public with pop stars and actresses. The socialist French government, which likes Tapie's origins and his apolitical embracing of entrepreneurship as a means to make it, is guardedly hopeful that the heavy debt leverage Tapie has utilized to finance his acquisitions doesn't prove to be his undoing. If it does, they're afraid it would be a blow to their efforts to instill France with the entrepreneurial spirit.[13]

Japan

Japan is best known for its great export companies. It is they which receive the attention when the discussion turns to Japan's extraordinary postwar growth, and today, when it enjoys a high-tech goods export/import ratio of 4 to 1 (versus 2.5 to 1 for the United States). In fact, Japan's great export companies rest upon perhaps the world's most extensive network of small manufacturing subcontractors, which should share the accolades.

Japan's small business, or *chusho kigyo* (small and medium-sized firms), economy dominates Japan's 6.3 million business workplaces. It is a small business economy that is proportionately more extensive than America's. It accounts for 50 percent of Japanese industrial output and 75 percent of total Japanese employment versus under 25 percent and 50 percent in the United States, respectively.

Japanese small firms tend to be smaller and often less modern than their U.S. counterparts. Japan has two and a half times as many manufacturing firms as the United States, but they employ one-fourth as many workers each on average. It also has two times as many retail outlets per capita as the United States and Western European countries and three times as many wholesalers.[14]

Small business is central to two of the major challenges Japan must meet if it is to be as successful a competitor in the global, information technology-based economy as it has in the past. First, Japanese modernization must reach the under-developed parts of an economy that has developed in a lopsided manner due to explosive postwar transition from a poor to a rich country. This requires a transformation—and very likely a consolidation—of hundreds of thousands of small outmoded businesses into modern enterprises. Pressure for this transformation accompanies the inexorable internationalization and liberalization of the Japanese economy.

Japan is also counting on new small businesses to help convert its extraordinary postwar success in catching up through clever application of existing technologies to competitive leadership through original breakthroughs in future ones.

To do so, it is hoping to build upon the traditional Japanese genius of imitating and improving upon the basic innovations of other cultures and produce the breakthrough innovations itself. In antiquity, Japan imported its basic language, art, and Buddhist religion from China. Likewise, in the postwar period its successful economic system was adapted from U.S. business techniques and original U.S. and European research. Between 1950 and 1981, U.S. scientists won 93 Nobel prizes for science, Europeans 68, and Japanese only 2. To give it a competitive edge in the new technologies, Japan now believes it must create small innovating entrepreneurs, of which it has produced only few to date, particularly in manufacturing, to push the Japanese innovation process expeditiously.

At the core of the Japanese economic establishment today are six giant multiindustry groups, each based around a major bank or trading company, seven giant vertically integrated industry groups, and several other large, unaffiliated companies. The six finance-centered groups—Mitsubishi, Mitsui, Sumitomo, Fuyo, Di-Ichi Kangyo, and Sanwa—derive from the *zaibatsu* or money cliques, the family-owned empires with holdings spanning the range of the economy in whom economic power came to be highly concentrated as Japan started to industrialize in the mid-nineteenth century. One of these giants, the Mitsubishi group, for example, is comprised of 45 companies whose global sales in 1983 were $140 billion. Allied with the six financial-based industrial groups are the seven large vertically integrated companies—Nippon Steel, Toshiba, Hitachi, Toyota, Nissan, Matsushita, and Tokyu—several of which were spun out as independents when the old *zaibatsu* were broken up after World War II. Finally come the large outsiders—notably Sony, Honda, and Pioneer—which managed to break into the establishment at a later date through the efforts of entrepreneurs like Akio Morita and Masuru Ibuka of Sony, and Soichiro Honda, the former Toyota Motor subcontractor who built Honda into an independent manufacturer.

These large competing companies and conglomerates have been the prime agents for carrying out Japan's plan-oriented capitalism—as well as the major recipients of Japanese government assistance. Aside from a handful of new innovative companies, such as ceramics materials firm Kyocera founded by Kazuo Inamori in the 1960s, they have been the dominant engines of Japan's remarkable growth.

These well-known giants, however, stand on a base of 830,000 small manufacturers. Some two-thirds of these are subcontractors. The relationships between subcontractor and large patron company are much closer and more extensive than in America. It is these subcontractors who imbue the Japanese economy with much of its flexibility and make feasible many of the management and manufacturing techniques so assiduously studied in the West.

The famous Just-in-Time system whereby components are delivered to the final assembly plant literally within minutes before they are needed depends on a network of reliable small subcontractors who are often grouped closely around the large patron corporation. The JIT system has enhanced the global competitiveness of the patron company by reducing its inventory costs, and by enhancing quality control through the rapid identification of defective parts.

The subcontractor network represents an efficient form of division of labor. It is the small subcontractor that absorbs the brunt of economic downturns. He allows the patron corporation maximum flexibility in maximizing in-house capacity utilization rates by being the first squeezed when orders fall.

The subcontractor also stands behind the vaunted lifetime employment guarantee that the large corporations have offered employees since early in the postwar era. Lifetime employment (which is limited to a quarter of the total Japanese work force) is possible because it is the employees of small subcontractors who are laid off in economic downturns as orders from the patron corporation shrink.

Labor mobility in the Japanese economy occurs almost exclusively in small businesses, where average pay scales start at three-fifths that of large companies and rise proportionately with size. This job mobility and the large corporations profit-related bonus compensation systems enhance wage flexibility in the Japanese labor market.

Reliance on this extensive subcontractor network helped Japan manage through the traumatic industrial restructuring that followed the quadrupling of oil prices in 1973 (Japan imports nearly all its oil). Industries such as shipbuilding, aluminum, textiles, steel, cement, and petrochemicals, sometimes with the coordinating assistance of the Ministry of International Trade and Industry, slashed capacity. Throughout industry, companies switched to new production technologies, products, and processes. The small subcontractor network helped by shifting product lines, upgrading quality, reducing costs—and by involuntarily absorbing many of the drastic rationalizations big business transferred to it.

Only a small percentage of Japanese subcontractors are truly independent. Many are dependent on a single patron firm for a quarter or more of their business, and thus are practically captives of the larger company. In many cases, the relationship is formalized in a traditional family-type arrangement. Depending whether a subcontractor is a first, second, or third grade subcontractor, the patron firm may own 5 to 8 percent of his company's equity. The patron may help him upgrade his quality by helping provide financing for the purchase of new equipment or by providing technical assistance. Although the patron corporation normally squeezes the subcontractor's profits to a bare minimum it may also help carry him when times get especially rough due to cyclic market conditions. As a result of this arrangement, the small subcontractors perpetually feign symptoms of poor profitability by driving modest cars, wearing old clothes, and behaving humbly, lest the patron company think there is further room to squeeze profits.

Most of the time they are not pretending, however. The average operating profits of large corporations, as in the United States, are higher than for small businesses. The existence of the Law for the Prevention of Delayed Payments of Subcontracting Fees is testimony to the nature of the conditions with which small subcontractors must often contend in their relationship with larger patrons.

About 20 percent of all Japanese subcontractors have reported fall-offs in business as Japanese giants in recent years have moved plants overseas or have turned to foreign sourcing of supplies. In the home appliances industry, 34 percent of subcontractors have suffered declining orders or suspensions due to overseas investments.[15]

Today, with the economic transition clouding the growth prospects of many of the traditional large Japanese corporations, many subcontractors feel uneasy about tying their destinies to a single large corporation. Many would like to find new customers. Some are experimenting privately with new products and processes. As in the United States, segmentation of increasingly affluent Japanese consumer markets is creating more niche opportunities.

Their experiments must be carried out discreetly, however. There is always the danger of provoking the wrath of the patron company and being cut off, or of having it steal the innovation itself. Matsushita is so well known for this practice that it is often referred to as *maneshita*, "to copy."

In recent years, as large corporations reduce their work forces through automation, the employment share of small manufacturing businesses—now constituting two-thirds of industrial employment—has been increasing. This has facilitated the robotization of Japan. By the start of 1985, Japan had four times as many robots in place as the United States.[16]

In the fast-growing services sector, where small business also provides over two-thirds of all jobs, its employment share is decreasing. This is because big service businesses are growing faster.

A uniquely Japanese type of small family-run service company enjoying faddish popularity in the mid-1980s was *benri-ya*, or "useful shops." For a fee, couples performed any reasonable service—such as cleaning the house or caring for the house pet—that Japan's increasingly well-off consumers might desire. With more Japanese women getting jobs, housecleaning was popular at $24 for two hours. In 1985 wake-up telephone calls cost $4; plucking gray hairs, $12. The business was relatively lucrative. Katsuyoshi Ukon, who started his *benri-ya* in 1978 (he claims to be innovator of the concept) says he cleared a net profit in 1984 of $72,000.[17]

Small business still dominates the cumbersome distribution side of the Japanese economy. Some 90 percent of those employed in the retail and wholesale trades work at small businesses. In the mid-1980s, the distribution network was still being protected against the forces of modernization by regulations. The passage of the Large-Scale Retail Store Law in 1974, for example, put an immediate halt to the rapid expansion of Japanese chain stores, which were doing as K-Mart or Sears in America in buying directly from the source and passing the savings on to consumers in the form of lower prices—prices small retailers couldn't match. This upset not only the small retailers but also the politically mighty trading companies which didn't like being bypassed as wholesale suppliers.

One effect of delaying modernization in the distribution network, as mentioned earlier, is to provide an indirect buffer against foreign imported goods, which are far more likely to be sold at chain stores following centralized and more modern buying practices. Small service firms, especially in sectors like cleaning and hairdressing, are also protected from big companies. Today, about 10,000 small firms belong to 350 price and market sharing cartels with exemptions from antimonopoly laws. The trend, however, is toward gradual liberalization: In 1966, the cartel total was 1,079.[18]

The fortunes of the majority of small businesses have been most closely linked to the development of the still comparatively underdeveloped Japanese domestic economy. Domestic growth has been slower since the second oil crisis of 1979. As a result, small business profits have suffered. Without sufficient profits small business investment in plant and equipment also suffered, and the investment gap with wealthier large businesses has widened.[19]

Japanese small business is fully integrated into, indeed helps constitute, Japan's unique social economy and its system of competition within a rigid social hierarchy and etiquette aimed at preserving group harmony. The internal rules of this social economy are often easily mistaken as purposeful deception by frustrated Western-minded free traders. But the domestic Japanese businessmen live by them just as foreigners do who trade with Japan.

Price alone, for instance, does not govern the buy and sell decision as in the West. Business friendships, which are tantamount to personal moral obligations, between buyer and seller often take precedence. A Japanese customer rarely changes gas stations because at one the price of gasoline may become a few cents cheaper. First of all, there is strong social pressure not to. But even if the motorist brooked social etiquette and changed gas stations, the two gas station owners would, privately, make reparations between themselves, probably in the form of a cash payment to the offended party. The "friendship" between customer and seller works both ways: If the customer should run into a patch of economic adversity, it would be socially incumbent upon the seller to provide his goods on credit until the rough period passed.

A similar principle governs the relationship between patron corporation and subcontractor. In that case, however, there is an additional social hierarchical dimension of familial duty, in which each party must show the other the respect due him by virtue of his position. In general, the "elder" in the relationship enjoys great power but is not supposed to exploit his position.

Western businessmen doing business in Japan often experience the internal rules of the social economy in yet another way: Those who have hired and subsequently fired Japanese representatives to conduct their affairs for them, for example, soon discover that the next Japanese representative they hire will be their last. Should he also be dismissed no reputable Japanese firm will do further business with them.

In the context of the Japanese social economy, the role of the government, often acting through MITI, is to mediate the differing economic interests of diverse groups in a manner that promotes the greater good of all groups. It does so through active dialogue and consensus building with industry, not by imposing policy leadership from above. Ideally it facilitates positive developments and blunts negative ones. It tries to do so by establishing and undertaking long-term planning and projects for which there is a consensus need but no ready mechanism on the one hand, and by promoting cooperative rationalization in making cuts in industrial capacity on the other.

MITI is highly sensitive to the potential disruptions unrestrained free-market competition can cause, and sometimes acts to minimize it in the name of maintaining orderly markets. In doing so, it often acts in the apparent best interests of existing powers and against those of upstart small enterprises.

In early 1985, an ex-boxer by the name of Taiji Sato, who runs a chain of seven gas stations called Lion Oil, tried to import inexpensive gasoline from Singapore which he intended to sell at 5 yen a liter less than the five big Japanese oil companies. Importing the gasoline was perfectly legal. But MITI decided that the long-run implications of doing so might disrupt the orderliness of the refining industry, and cause the price of kerosene to rise. Sato's banker got a call, and a MITI official made this point to him in a purely speculative, philosophical manner. Sato's banker understood this "administrative guidance." He cut off Sato's credit line, and instructed him to sell his gasoline to one of the five big refiners, which would sell it at the usual price. Sato, of course, had no choice but to comply.[20]

Collective adherence to the internal rules of the social economy and the economic management system it has produced have enabled Japan to develop more rapidly than any nation on earth. Yet there has been a growing belief in Japan that future economic competitiveness in rapidly evolving industries like microelectronics, biotechnology, new materials, and computer science requires the emergence of an innovative new generation of small business entrepreneurs who will quickly grow large themselves or pressure large corporations to achieve original innovation. Breakthroughs will provide a lead time that may make the difference between large and small commercial profits. Save for the immediate postwar years, however, Japan has produced very few such entrepreneurs.

Producing pushy entrepreneurs may also unleash a Pandora's box of problems into a Japanese social economy that is not accustomed to dealing with aggressive young businessmen— reared in postwar affluence and more influenced than any previous generation by Western individualist values—who may disregard the traditional conventions which have produced the system of economic consensus that has led to such impressive growth in the past. Nevertheless, MITI is pushing ahead to promote independent high-tech entrepreneurship.

Given the incestuous structure of Japanese industry, there are certain tangible problems for small business entrepreneurs to overcome. The Japanese capital markets are hard on small businesses, particularly in start-up situations where the owner rarely can boast prestigious connections and affiliations. There are only 150 banking institutions in Japan, of which nearly half hold assets that rank them among the largest 500 banks in the world. They also frequently hold large blocks of shares in Japan's largest companies, and aren't notably generous in supplying capital to prospective competitors. Raising money on the Tokyo stock market remains onerous for small companies. Obtaining initial customers as a new company, given the Japanese custom of friendships with great emphasis on personal backgrounds, is more difficult than in Western countries.

These problems were experienced by Shigenobu Nagamori of Nippon Densan Corp. (Nidec), one of Japan's few recent innovative start-up success stories. Nagamori, an electrical engineer, then twenty-nine, started Nidec in 1973 with a small, 3½-inch diameter motor he had designed. Working out of his home, Nagamori's initial efforts to obtain financing from the six major banks in his native Kyoto met a cold reception. Only voluntary pay cuts from his three engineering employees saved him from early bankruptcy. Nagamori's effort to find customers were no more fruitful. Everyone wanted to know Nagamori's background and affiliations, even his age. What they discovered, upon inquiry, was not very favorable by Japanese standards: Nagamori had a reputation as a top engineer, but he was also known as a lone wolf, even something of an individualist, who wasn't altogether respectful of the objectives of his superiors. He had gone into business for himself only when the financial problems of his employer, Tamashina Seiki, a machine-tool manufacturer, had threatened the future of his particular research projects. He had also taken three top engineers with him.

Unable to find an initial client for his motors in Japan, Nagamori flew to the United States. It was there he got his first customer in the Minicom Division of 3M. Today, Nidec has over 300 major corporate clients, including IBM, Digital Equipment, Olivetti—and Hitachi. It has nearly 90 percent of the world market for small motors for hard-disk drives, 20 percent for floppy disks, and nearly all laser printer motors. By 1984, sales had reached $100 million. The company had doubled its employees over the prior year to 1,150. Silicon Valley style, Nagamori has lured the best of them away from the traditionally more prestigious big companies by giving them 33 percent of the stock and convincing them that Nidec itself will one day be big. Financing is no longer a problem. The banks that once spurned him are eager lenders; Nagamori has even sold 8 percent of the equity to a venture-capital firm.[21]

In Japan there has been little boutiquing of independent small computer software companies which have proven so fruitful in America and parts of Europe. Most of the 2,000 or so software firms are really captive subcontractors of the big corporations. Due to the leverage wielded by patron companies relatively few subcontractors ever succeed in breaking free of the large corporation orbit.

Software innovation is one of Japan's major competitive vulnerabilities, as the Japanese are acutely aware. In 1985 it was purchasing about 90 percent of its fast-growing software needs for computers and telecommunications from abroad. This was critical to Japan's future competitiveness because such software will likely provide a major edge in the next phase of competition in the rapidly growing information technology industries.[22]

Just as MITI has been promoting major R&D efforts in cutting-edge technologies, such as the heralded (but so far hardly spectacular) fifth-generation computer program, it has also invested some of its surprisingly meager resources (1.6 percent of the government budget in 1983) on a package of financing incentives and local infrastructure to try to develop regional technology centers populated by small companies. In 1984, it targeted two towns on the southern island of Kyushu as technology centers. Early success was frustrated, however, by a dearth of start-up financing despite the incentives and encouragement of Japan's small venture-capital industry.

There are a total of about 50 venture-capital companies operating in Japan. Most were formed in the early 1980s. An earlier effort to stimulate venture capital was aborted by the oil crisis of 1973. Through July 1984, the largest venture-capital fund had raised $133 million.[23] Although the venture-capital movement is slowly building momentum it is plagued by a familiar pattern: Many of the over 500 high-tech venture-capital-funded start-ups are appendages of the old large corporations.[24]

Although the lion's share of government largesse goes to big business, the Japanese government has moved to direct more assistance to small business. It has recently increased programs at three government small business financial institutions, expanded subsidies to the 52 credit guarantee associations, which guarantee loans made by banks to small business, and taken measures to strengthen the small business credit insurance corporations. The central and prefectual governments also provide technical support, and sometimes managerial guidance, to help small companies upgrade their capabilities to meet the demands of the changing economy, sometimes in conjunction with subsidized long-term loans. Small business is most favored, after farmers, in the Japanese tax code.

The most ambitious undertakings to stimulate small business entrepreneurship, however, are not specifically directed at small business alone. They are infrastructural. MITI is sponsoring a five-year development project to produce a national database network for up to 10,000 computer programmers. The centralized data base will be a software library which is intended to provide information which will lead to compounding advances in programming knowledge—and ever more competitive commercial applications.

The ultimate Japanese electronics vision is a unifying system to link telephones, television, computers, facsimile machines, offices, homes, supermarkets, and banks. Japan's information network system is likely to be the last great infrastructural project of the century. When it is completed in a decade or so, it will likely be a huge boon to modern small businesses, which will have at their fingertips information and low-cost ways of reaching the market that heretofore have provided big business one of its main competitive advantages. It will also, of course, provide Japan with a powerful infrastructural building block for improved future competitiveness.

There is evidence that an entrepreneurial environment is slowly beginning to be grafted onto the internal rules of the traditional Japanese social economy. A small number of individuals are starting to leave lifetime employment, which in the Japanese context is something like a samurai abandoning his clan, for more entrepreneurial situations. Japanese computer programmers and design engineers, who are in short supply, have become job-hoppers after the Silicon Valley fashion, sometimes breaking with tradition entirely and forsaking well-established prestigious giants for promising small firms where they obtain equity interest options and can have greater impact.

It is not only in high tech that younger Japanese are breaking with tradition. Munio Nohara, for example, worked for the Mitsukoshi department store, the oldest and largest in Japan, for 13 years before becoming so frustrated with his lack of progress in scaling the corporate ladder that he struck out on his own. He had joined Mitsukoshi in 1969 after university graduation. After having scored the highest marks on the company entrance exam, his ambition to eventually become president of the company seemed a plausible one. Yet instead of working in a major section, such as women's fashions, he found himself in the relatively unimportant art department. He worked hard—sometimes over 100 hours a week. But instead of gaining a transfer, he simply became more indispensable in the art department. He finally made the decision to quit in March 1982 after an argument with his superior while all Mitsukoshi was stinging from the huge embezzlement scandal by the president. Nohara felt so despondent that he stayed up all night to compose the resignation letter, which he did with a brush and sumi-ink, in the tradition of an ancient Japanese poet.

Nohara's resignation so shocked his superior, and ultimately the new president, that he was offered an overseas job of his choice to get him to reconsider leaving Mitsukoshi. Instead, he invested all his savings, 3.9 million yen, or $16,000, in an art dealership business, which he ran from a small apartment in central Tokyo. The first year he sold 80 million yen worth of art. By 1983 he was doing well enough to open the Royal Gallery in the chic Ginza section. In 1984, sales reached 400 million yen and he had six employees.[25]

The Communist World

The industrialized capitalist economies are by no means alone in looking to small enterprise to provide fresh economic thrust. Much of the communist world is experimenting with various forms of private initiative. The goal is to bring some of the efficiency and vigor of free-market economies to complement bureaucratic socialist planning. Communist nations are not about to embark on ideologically threatening large-scale private enterprise, so most of these experiments involve small-scale industry and agriculture. In the industrialized communist world of Eastern Europe and the Soviet Union, economic planners view private initiative as a means of producing general efficiency that will help prevent them from falling far behind the rapid technological changes occurring in the capitalist world. In the less developed communist nations, notably China, experiments with private enterprise are viewed chiefly as pragmatic means of promoting development within a planned socialist context.

Economic liberalization has gone farther in Hungary than in any other Eastern bloc country. The current leadership scarcely masks its taste for more. In Hungary, privately owned stalls compete in the main market with government-owned stalls with the overt aim of applying some competitive market pressures to promote greater efficiency. There are government loans to small business. Bakers, among others, can hire up to six employees.

Sanctioned moonlighting after hours from state jobs is one of the most common private initiative experiments in the Comecon countries. In Hungarian state factories, workers can band together like private contractors and make bids to produce a specified number of items after regular work hours—on the state-owned factory machines. In Hungary, workers can sometimes double their salaries by this means.

One of Poland's responses to the Western financial sanctions directed against it for its debt troubles and political repression was an initiative to attract Western capital through direct investment in privately owned small businesses. The companies were to be export-oriented, with the first three years of operations untaxed; the foreign owners were permitted to repatriate 50 percent of their gross hard currency profits. By early 1985, Poland had 650 of these "Polonia" companies. Most were in light-manufacturing industries, such as cosmetics and clothing, although some made more sophisticated equipment. One, 350-employee Plastomed, capitalized with $150,000 by its owners in Frankfurt, was making calibrated pipettes and electronic laboratory equipment. In all, Polonia companies employed 100,000 workers and accounted for 1 percent of the GNP.

The Polish government of General Wojciech Jaruzelski in 1985 was studying a plan to increase that. The program had already been extended once before, to solicit investment beyond the 40 million Poles of the Polish diaspora who were its original targets. The government liked the program for several reasons. It was instilling a new work ethic into a state-owned system rife with absenteeism and about which a caustic street homily remarks: "Whether lying down or standing erect, a thousand zlotys you can expect." As the underground economy helps to establish the market value of goods (and is often the only source of many goods in communist countries), the Polonia companies, which set their own wage scales, were helping assign a market value to labor. At Plastomed workers were receiving about 50 percent more than they would in state jobs, though they worked a lot harder for it. Many received bonuses from the ruble and zloty earnings of the company.

Finally, the Polish government liked the Polonia companies because they often produced higher quality goods than state companies. They were thus earning precious foreign currency from sales outside the country. That has largely meant ruble sales to other Eastern bloc countries and to the Soviet Union, which has come down particularly hard on Eastern European nations to produce much higher quality goods for the inexpensive oil and other subsidies it supplies them. But in the future, companies like Plastomed hope to upgrade their quality enough to be able to export competitively to the West.[26]

Even Bulgaria, the most stalwart Soviet ally in Eastern Europe, has been experimenting with private initiative schemes. The Bulgarian Industrial Association (BIA), an investment and advisory group, was set up in 1980 to help devise ways to improve economic performance. After studying small companies in Western Europe, between 1981 and 1984 BIA sponsored nearly 200 companies, most in services and consumer goods. In the main, they were found to have outperformed their big competitors. Delighted, BIA was pushing to expand the program with inexpensive loans, liberal tax provisions, and a streamlining of red tape. BIA argued that the small companies would help fill gaps in the supply of parts and machinery left by the state companies, as well as apply competitive pressure for greater efficiency. Although the small firms would not be privately owned, they would provide a latitude of operating freedom, profit incentives, and staff bonuses. If BIA gets its way within the government, up to 10 percent of Bulgarian investment could be directed to these small-scale enterprises in the next several years.[27]

Little economic experiment goes on in the Eastern bloc, of course, unless it has the tacit approval of the Soviet Union. When Mikhail Gorbachev first came to power, Hungarian government officials, among other Eastern European leaders, were optimistic that he would be favorably disposed to their private initiative experiments. That optimism was premature. *Pravda* articles branded such private sector experiments as "revisionist."

Nevertheless, Gorbachev's Soviet Union has embarked on conservative private incentive schemes of its own as part of his drive to improve efficiency in the Soviet system in general, and to promote high-tech industries in the new five-year plan. While the worst economic results of Soviet socialism were being berated through a public exhibition of a shipment of defectively made boots with the heels attached to the toes, the Politburo was approving a program of bonuses for workers who made creative contributions in the fields of applied research, design, and technology. Experiments begun by Andropov in 1984 to give factory managers some freedom in reinvesting their "profits," to reward exemplary workers and to set prices on consumer goods were extended to new factories.

Private enterprise reforms have already been successful in Soviet agriculture. The Soviet Union has 8 million farmers who work small plots for their private gain. Together, these plots are equivalent to less than 5 percent of Soviet farmland, but they produce 25 percent of the value of agricultural output. Some collective and state farmers get between one-fourth and one-third of their income by selling food grown on these private plots in rural markets.[28]

Small private enterprise in agriculture, of course, was used by Soviet leaders in the early years after the 1917 revolution. At that time, the country was a semifeudal society. The only capitalism was limited to small industry and commerce. In an effort to leapfrog the capitalist development stage that Marx had seen as a prerequisite of evolution to a socialist society, Lenin nationalized the banks, the major factories, the railways and canals. The government tried to requisition food from the private farmers (many who had just ended tenancy on noblemen's estates) for the factory workers.

The program was a disaster. Industrial output in 1920 fell far below pre–World War I levels. To avoid economic collapse, Lenin's New Economic Policy, NEP, was implemented. NEP amounted to a partial return to a market economy, with private ownership and profit motive in retail, small industry, and the farms.

In the ensuing years there were long debates about the types and degree of bourgeois incentives that might be needed to make the economy function efficiently yet still evolve inexorably toward socialism. All the debate ended in 1927 when Stalin forcibly collectivized the farms, coerced unwilling workers to the factories and executed or put in labor camps millions who refused to cooperate.

The results, however detestably brutal the means, were inarguably successful from a strictly economic point of view. The Soviet Union was transformed rapidly into an industrial economy that between 1929 and 1961 expanded between 5.2 and 7.2 percent a year, about twice as fast as U.S. growth in the same period.[29]

Yet predictions by Nikita Khrushchev at the time that the Soviet Union would overtake the United States in per capita production by 1970 and that by 1980 Soviet socialism would have produced sufficient wealth to permit the transformation from socialism to a communist utopia have proved, in hindsight, to be embarrassing bravado.

As the economy industrialized, the centralized planning process became vastly more complicated. The bureaucracy bogged down with lethargy. Economic growth slowed sharply. Confronting capitalist competitor countries in the midst of dynamic technological transition and flagging domestic growth, Soviet planners have urgently looked for new ways to spur economic development. One way they have done so is to look back in their own history at the NEP reforms for inspiration.

In the nonaligned, decentralized worker-owned enterprise state of Yugoslavia there are over 200,000 private businesses. All of them, legally at least, have no more than five employees.

Since the death of Tito in 1980, economic problems compounded by a foreign debt crisis have forcibly subjected Yugoslavs to the market economy viewpoints of the International Monetary Fund and of its foreign bank and government creditors. Rather than provoke an economic policy backlash (as in Rumania, for example, which faced similar problems), the forcible exposure to market-economy analysis has spurred a vigorous and open debate about the utility of market-oriented reforms to combat Yugoslavia's problems. A strong constituency inside the government and out favoring the liberalization of the Yugoslav experiment has evolved. One recent center of controversy has been a book by a former judge in Zagreb, *Socialism and Private Enterprise,* which argues that Yugoslavia's private sector, if given proper incentive, could produce jobs that would help relieve the country's mounting unemployment problems as Yugoslav guest workers are sent home from a Western Europe rife with its own unemployment. Hard-line old guard communists, however, remain recalcitrant at what they see as a deviation from Tito's orthodoxy.[30]

Most of the market-oriented thinking involves small-scale initiatives, and after Yugoslav fashion, is being implemented regionally. One of the country's largest banks, the Ljubjanska Banka in Slovenia, has opened a special department to help private enterprise. In the wealthy northern regions of Slovenia and Croatia, where living standards are on par with those of Central Europe, regulations have been more loosely interpreted to permit private farmers to work other people's land under contract.

In the poorer region of Serbia, too, de facto measures have been taken to permit more small-scale private enterprise. When Dobrivoje Rajic, a metal specialist, and his wife wanted to open a metal parts factory employing 20 persons in his native village of Serbia using some of the $300,000 he had saved after a decade of working in Sweden, he at first ran afoul of the Yugoslav law limiting the number of employees in private companies to five. An unofficial deal was worked out with the local officials. Rajic and his four brothers each registered their own shops, thus making them eligible to hire a total of 25 among them. All, however, share a single plant.[31]

The most dramatic private enterprise experiments in a communist nation have been taking place in China. Eastern European nations that secretly wish for more private enterprise themselves are watching China's experiments with great hope. If demonstrably successful, they could exert strong pressure for greater liberalization reforms of the Soviet model.

The Chinese people, it has been said, are natural capitalists. Throughout Asia, they comprise a minority entrepreneurial class that is responsible for a disproportionately large portion of their nation's business activity. It is not surprising, then, that they have taken to the private enterprise economic reforms introduced by Deng Xiaoping with zeal.

Self-employment in China rose from 140,000 in 1978 to over 7.5 million in 1983, according to the government. That, however, is still less than the 8.4 million self-employed that flourished before the 1953 crackdown on private enterprise. About 2 million of today's self-employed work in urban areas, the rest of the countryside. Nearly four-fifths of the restaurants, retail shops, and service businesses that have been started since 1978 have been privately owned.[32]

Visitors following the route of Mao Tse-tung's soldiers during the historic Long March of 1934–35 find enterprising peasants everywhere. Women with sewing machines make dresses and suits while the customer waits; shoemakers spread their wares and take orders from local villagers. Especially popular among young women are red pumps with 2-inch heels. Everywhere street peddlers sell roasted chicken, nuts, apples, beer, soup, and shafhlik. At favorite rest stops, peasants have built walled, pit-style toilets for the convenience of travelers. There is no charge for their use. The peasant's reward, rather, is the human excrement to fertilize his fields. This reward is attractive enough that competitive pit toilets have cropped up side by side in the most popular rest stops. Private farming has helped bring a Green Revolution to China's agricultural and livestock sectors and provide savings enough to finance peasant entrepreneurship, from which incomes in the region of 650 yuan, or $280, are not uncommon. Families that earn 10,000 yuan, or $4,375, a year—by Chinese standards almost millionaires— now exist.[33]

One who is well on her way to that privileged status is Yang Beigui, an instinctively enterprising woman in her mid-thirties, and mother of two. She already has the only private telephone among the 50,000 people who live in Xindu County in Sichuan Province. Soon after the Peking government sanctioned private enterprise, Yang developed the idea of recycling old clothes into soles for the cotton shoe that is ubiquitous throughout China. She subcontracted the recycling work out to underemployed local peasants whose farmland had been compulsorily purchased by the government to build factories. At the start, she had 15 household subcontractors; by late 1984 she had 198. Her first order came in 1980—from a local state cotton shoe factory: It was for 10,000 yuan, and netted a slim 300 yuan profit. By 1984, she was expecting annual revenues of 250,000 yuan, or over $100,000. Based on past profit margins, that would net her a profit of close to 10,000 yuan.

Her gross profit margin in any case is limited by the Chinese government to 12 percent. On that, she must pay a 7 percent tax. The authorities imposed the profit-margin limit and the tax to prevent the explosion of wealth and cause wide disparities of income that could provoke a backlash against the new economic policies. Yang runs her business from her home in Xindu. With her profits, she and her husband, who quit his factory job of 480 yuan a year to work as her assistant, have added two more rooms to their small courtyard home, and stocked it with a washing machine, a TV, a radio, and a Japanese camera, which she purchased in Xindu for 1,000 yuan from among the hundreds of street stalls selling TV sets, food, clothes, and household wares to the sound of stereos blaring rock music.[34]

Although some in the West see incipient capitalism in China's reforms, those who know China well instead view the reforms as pragmatic efforts to cope with economic development within the planned, socialist context. The *People's Daily*, the official newspaper, wrote in 1984.:

> Great changes have taken place since [Marx'] time. We can't ask that the works of Marx and Lenin from that time solve our present-day problems. We, the successors of Marx and Lenin, have a responsibility of developing and enriching Marx' works in practice.[35]

Indeed, China's leaders have approached economic reform in a planned manner. It is building upon the Green Revolution and the past qualitative successes in improved health, education, welfare—and in being one of the world's few developing nations to control its population growth. Now, with the great improvements in productivity in rural areas having outstripped those in urban regions, the government has been cautiously devising ways to apply the efficiencies of competition to the urban industrial sector. However, disappointment with the development of its experimental international market zones is causing the government to slow liberalization plans in the area.

The Developing World

Small-scale private industrial and agricultural initiatives are resurgent in poor developing nations now that many of the large-scale capital investment projects of the past have disappointed, and foreign lenders and direct foreign investors have constricted the capital flow. Now favored are smaller-scale projects which generate lots of jobs on low investments of capital to combat world unemployment of 300 million and underemployment of one billion. Small-scale projects initiate the slow process of building domestic savings for capital formation. They help develop the kind of business culture and capitalist economic climate foreign lenders now want to see before releasing fresh funds to debtor nations. Small-scale private agriculture projects are favored to break archaic subsistence farming methods and support development of a surplus-producing exchange economy that will keep more people in the countryside rather than swelling into overpopulated cities.

Many of the countries that have succeeded in moving up the development ladder, such as Taiwan, Hong Kong, Brazil, and Spain, originally launched their growth with the help of unglamorous, low-wage, labor-intensive small-scale industries. Those industries, such as textiles, shoes, and toys, are now migrating elsewhere in the Third World to countries that are also finding them to be positive stepping-stones to economic development. Meanwhile, these more advanced developing countries are finding that small business has evolved with their economies and has helped compensate imbalances that have accompanied speedy and often lopsided economic development.

Small private enterprise was the primary building block of economic development for today's most industrialized countries. It was small business that spread business skills and values and provided the means for the initial amassing of domestic savings for investment. It was small business that then serviced the needs of big industry as it evolved and which built the distribution network to efficiently balance the production-distribution equation of economics. All along, small independent farmers provided the food which made urbanization and industrialization feasible.

This development process took place at a leisurely pace over many generations in the United States and Europe. For countries that industrialized later, such as Japan and regions of Italy, the development process happened at a compressed pace, which intensified the accompanying social, political, and economic adjustments.

In the postwar period, development in the world's poor countries has been characterized by ambitious large-scale plans that attempted to short-cut the traditional period of small-scale industrial build-up to pass directly to modern industrialization. Inspired by such leaders as Nkrumah in Ghana, Nasser in Egypt, Nehru in India, many of the nations of Africa and South America rejected direct foreign investment as "economic imperialism" and instead sought and received foreign loans to supplement meager domestic savings to carry out development projects on their own.

For the most part, it didn't work well. The large heavy-industrial projects consumed vast amounts of capital (and energy) but didn't produce nearly as many jobs as they would have if the capital had been invested in smaller-scale, less technologically advanced industries. In Indonesia, it has been estimated that a job in small-scale industry is created with $500 of investments as against up to $50,000 in large-scale capital-intensive projects.[36]

Nor did the large-scale projects train and spin off new entrepreneurs as small businesses did, and thus failed to generate domestic momentum for development.

There was too little productive investment, and debt burdens, aggravated by the sharp rise in oil prices, began to mount. By the late 1970s, investment as percentage of GNP had started to decline in many poor countries. With the world recession and the debt crisis in the early 1980s, much foreign lending has dried up. Poor countries have tried to solicit direct investment. But direct investment in recent years has been toward the industrialized countries. Asian countries, which accepted direct investment early on, still receive much of the world's direct investment in developing countries. Only one-fifth of all direct investment goes to the entire non-Asian developing world. In short, beset by deep economic problems and with limited access to foreign capital, the developing nations have had little choice but to emphasize private small-scale projects.

There have been enough positive small enterprise experiences in developing nations to allow many countries to make of this necessity a virtue. The greatest successes have been in small private agriculture. In Thailand, barefoot peasants tending tiny plots of rice paddies with the help of water buffalo in the fertile lowlands north of crowded Bangkok have planted the seeds of a steady economic transformation. Over the past 20 years, annual agricultural output gains have averaged 5 percent. Thai farmers now grow on their average seven-acre plots enough food to feed a nation of 50 million and still account for a net food trade surplus of $3.7 billion a year—nearly 60 percent of Thailand's exports. Thailand is now the world's leading supplier of rice.

Local industry has benefited from the rising income of farmers, whose demand for everything from tractors to TVs has

increased. Thailand's central plains are now filled with shop-
keepers, mechanics, and factory workers. They were virtually
nonexistent some years ago. The government's role has chiefly
been to lay infrastructural projects like irrigation and roads and
to make fertilizer use available. New land that can be developed
for farming is now running out, however, and Thailand must
move up a rung on the development ladder, perhaps to processed foods and light industry. But thanks to small-scale private agriculture, it has a solid base from which to work.[37]

Green revolutions have also taken place in India and in
China. In the mid-1970s, India spent one-quarter of its import
bill on food; today it exports grain to the Soviet Union. China,
meanwhile, exports corn to Japan and South Korea.

In a very different setting, private grain traders, despite
their generally ruthless exploitation of the desperate condition of
African villagers, are one of the few vehicles for preventing
mass starvation in the subsistence farm regions of Africa. The
World Food Program, which provides seed aid as "capital" for
rural food banks in parts of Niger and Mali, gives the villagers
some bargaining leverage when the grain traders arrive. Being
able to prove they have seed for the next year's crop encourages
the traders to provide them food on credit.

Small business is ubiquitous in the underground markets
and informal sectors of all poor nations. Smuggling rubies,
sapphires, pearls, jade, elephants, teak and, of course, heroin is
a major enterprise in Burma.

In overcrowded Cairo, Egypt, where large numbers make
their home in local cemeteries, scavengers bid for the right to
haul garbage from the city's various neighborhoods to profitably
recycle whatever can be salvaged. In the main cities of Kenya,
independent handcart owners run small fleets of handcarts that
haul farm produce arriving from the countryside to the cities'
markets, ferry retail goods between shops, and bring water
from the central depot to people's waterless houses.

Small business still normally accounts for the largest
amount of economic activity in nearly all developing nations
despite large-scale government projects, and provides the lifeline for the majority of poor populations. Small handicraft
firms of under five employees comprise three-quarters of Indonesia's manufacturing employment. Two-thirds of the labor

force of Jakarta, a city of 6.5 million, is comprised of street vendors. Most of the work is informal and independent, but in some parts of the city vendors have begun to organize into loose cooperatives. Some are encouraged by the government, which now provides low interest loans, to the frustration of local usurers.

In most of the Third World, small business employs traditional techniques of production and uses obsolete machinery. Workplaces are ill-designed for efficiency. Quality control is poor. The lack of basic standards means that mostly cheaply made goods are produced, often for local market consumption. Nevertheless, output from small businesses of this kind often provides significant economic support to poor nations' general efforts at development.

One obstacle to the spread of a popular private enterprise social-economic ethic is that foreign minority groups—Chinese in Asia and Indians in East Africa—often provide the major entrepreneurial impetus in many countries. This breeds resentment and prejudice from the often less-well-off majority. Chinese dominate private enterprise in Malaysia, although they are only a tiny fraction of the population. In Indonesia, where there are 4 million Chinese in a population of 170 million, Chinese dominate the cement, plywood, textile, auto, and cigarette businesses. But they are officially banned from owning shops outside the main cities.

In recognition of the benefits of small business, many governments have undertaken initiatives to support it. In India, which has emphasized large public-sector projects since the 1950s to work for the "social good" and to keep the private sector in check, the small business sector in the late 1970s increased its output by an average of 9.5 percent annually. Indian small business produced three-quarters of all black-and-white TVs, half of all the tape recorders, two-fifths of all Indian-produced control instruments and electronic equipment, and dominated the traditional handloom materials and handicraft industries. Since coming to power after the assassination of his mother, Indira, Rajiv Gandhi has pushed ahead with existing plans to develop the private sector. The plans had gathered momentum following a 1982 report by Parliament which sharply criticized the inefficiencies and failures of the large Indian public sector and nationalized industries, which employ 25 million. In his first budget, Rajiv Gandhi altered the tax rules to permit small businessmen earning at least a 7 percent return on assets of 2 million rupees to pay only a 50 percent income tax—reduced from 100 percent.

In the Ivory Coast, one of Africa's more free-market-oriented economies, the government now has a state program to finance up to 80 percent of a small private business venture. In Nepal, one of the poorest countries on earth, where nearly all the major companies are government-owned, King Birendra has launched a stock market and has begun privatizing state industries as the first step to developing an equity capital market. In five months, 4,000 Nepalese have purchased stock in the 11 companies listed on the blackboard in a dilapidated two-story building in Katmandu.

Finally, the World Bank in June 1984 announced that it would step up its aid projects to small business. One project in which the World Bank has long participated is Bangladesh's Grameen, or Rural Bank, Project. Between 1976 and 1984, the Grameen Project loaned $8.6 million at low interest to 63,900 usually landless peasant borrowers engaged in small-scale enterprises like crafts-making and fishnet production. Typical loans of $30 to $50 were made to each member of a group of five unrelated individuals. All group members were liable if another group member did not make repayment. In a country as poor as Bangladesh, $30 can purchase the materials to make a fishnet which can be sold profitably enough to the Japanese to stimulate reinvestment.[38]

In 1986 the World Bank, the United Nations, and the Africa Development Bank launched the Africa Project Development Facility, an organization intended to assist entrepreneurs in poverty-stricken sub-Sahara Africa in locating sources of financing from $500,000 to $5 million and offer them management and technical advice. The new organization is similar to one that has helped launch thirty-eight projects and create over 1,000 jobs in Caribbean countries since the early 1980s in diverse businesses ranging from hairpiece manufacturing in Haiti to poultry processing in Belize. The goal of the program is to bridge the financing gap facing poor nation entrepreneurs, whose capital requirements are too small to interest most foreign and development banks. This sustains the long, slow process of building up a viable private sector. The African project, although small, complements the recent $5 billion special operation of the International Monetary Fund and the World Bank to help those African nations willing to make a commitment to private enterprise.

Many of these poor nations are among the countries that hope to follow the four dragon nations of Asia—Hong Kong, Taiwan, South Korea, and Singapore—up the development ladder. In many of these countries, small business has been a critical component—and sometimes the main engine—of the fastest-growing countries in the world in the past decade.

Hong Kong, whose residents have the highest per capita income of any Far Eastern nation after Japan, is dominated by small companies of 20 employees turning out increasingly sophisticated low-wage, labor-intensive products. People work hard in Hong Kong: 10 to 12 hours a day, 6 to 7 days a week. Many of the entrepreneurs in Hong Kong have kept their assets transportable. They are ready to move away and set up shop elsewhere if the Chinese communist government tries to rein in full-blooded free-enterprise when it reclaims its rights to Hong Kong in 1997. In the meantime, the Hong Kong public sector has been growing rapidly to provide the infrastructure to facilitate the transition from the traditional textile industries to electronics.

Taiwan's average economic growth of 9 percent a year over the last two decades has been driven by small business entrepreneurs producing goods like textiles, shoes, watches, TV sets, computer component assemblies, and motorcycle parts. Some 38,000 small companies accounted for three-quarters of Taiwan's exports in the mid-1980s. Adapting quickly to new niches in the United States and other export markets, they contributed greatly to the country's $8.5 billion trade surplus in 1984. Success, however, has created a problem: Other nations, such as South Korea, archenemy China, Indonesia, India, Malaysia, and other poorer countries moving up the development ladder, have taken away its labor cost advantage and can now produce some goods at more competitive prices.

Taiwanese leaders know they must make the difficult transition to higher technology and more capital-intensive export industries. To do so they now need larger companies. The Taiwan government has never practiced macroeconomic management in the Japanese or South Korean styles. But it has provided incentives and protection for small export companies. Its solution has been to embark on a program of tax incentives to encourage local small businessmen to merge into conglomerates which can attract foreign direct investment. In the meantime, it continues to exploit an export market for some of its older industrial products in Hong Kong—where they are relabeled and sold in China.[39]

The economic success of Taiwan's erstwhile competitor, South Korea, meanwhile, brought that country an almost precisely opposite problem: how to encourage a small business economy that has been stunted by the oligopolistic market domination of its giant conglomerates, or *chaebol,* in order to stimulate competition and create a healthier economic equilibrium. In 1984, the ten largest conglomerates produced 64 percent of Korea's GNP and 70 percent of its exports. Some 88 percent of the country's manufactured goods were produced in oligopolistic or monopolistic industries in 1981. In the mid-1980s small business manufactured only one-third of Korea's industrial production and employed but half its industrial work force. The percentage has been declining for a decade.

Unlike most Asian nations, South Korea lacks a tradition of family-run firms. To encourage development, the government lavished loans and tax credits upon big companies, many of which started humbly in the postwar period, and are still owned by their founding entrepreneurs. Hyundai, for example, was started by a garage owner who repaired U.S. army trucks and then expanded during the Korean War. Daewoo was originally a textile manufacturer when it was founded 20 years ago. Until 1981, these large conglomerates met once a week in the Export Situation Room of the industry ministry to check progress against government export targets. South Korea's president presented medals to those that had met their targets on Export Day.

Those days are past. Now, the conglomerates are under fire for squeezing out small companies and hurting balanced economic development. They are accused of borrowing excessively and thus monopolizing the capital markets, and of exploiting their oligopolistic positions by charging high prices. Hyundai has begun to sell the apartments it constructs with built-in furniture, thus threatening small independent furniture manufacturers. Another conglomerate owning a major hotel has promoted a spinoff bakery operation which undercuts local small bakers' businesses.

To try to encourage the small business economy to correct the excessive concentration, the government has created federations of small businesses to be assisted by a new government agency that will promote technology transfer and cooperation between them. Banks have been instructed to direct 40 to 50 percent of all loans to small firms. At the same time, restrictions have been placed on the loans the units of each large conglomerate can make to one another. Small companies have also been given a collective monopoly of 110 simple manufacturered goods, such as toys, handbags, shoes, and towels. Big manufacturers in these industries are now required to obtain special permission to expand. The target goal is to raise small business' share of manufactured goods from 35 to 45 percent in ten years—still below small business' share in Japan or Taiwan. So far, early efforts to arrest the imbalanced industrial concentration have not been effective.[40]

Despite their profound present problems, developing countries that follow through on promoting their small business and agricultural sectors are likely to benefit in ways that nations in the early and intermediate stages of industrial development have always benefited from small business: instilling the ethoes of business enterprise into cultures where it is often quite alien, spawning indigenous entrepreneurs, building a broader base of domestic savings and skills, and in filling gaps left by earlier periods of large-scale development projects. All these are important. But they aren't enough.

Development today must occur far more rapidly than in the past. This is so because of more intense competitive pressures from other developing nations in the same technologies, and from industrialized nations with evolving new technologies that threaten to boost productivity sufficiently to cancel out the low-wage advantages of today's labor-intensive Third World industries. Meanwhile, electronic media such as TV and radio make Third World citizens more aware of their impoverished condition, and increase their impatience with slowness in over-coming it. Yet to derive the very high capital-formation rates necessary for productive investment requires a denial of imme-diate consumption gratifications. Rapid population growth, which plagues so many poor countries, often simply outstrips the progress that has been made. Frequently the irresistible influence of the dominant international economy on which they are dependent for technology, capital, essential goods, shipping, and their major markets engenders lopsided sectoral develop-ment and other conditions which may inhibit reaching a stage of economic takeoff.

Many of today's poor nations do not have a social economy that is ready for early capitalist development as the indus-trialized nations had. Finally, those countries that achieve rapid growth often end up with badly imbalanced economic develop-ment. There are abuses of precious capital controlled by the handful of wealthy businessmen fleeing the country to buy safe havens in industrialized countries. Too often, direct foreign investment ends up lining the pockets of a few already wealthy rather than being spread more productively throughout the economy.

As in the United States, small business is a complementary force facilitating change in the economies of foreign countries. Moreover, it is a highly *adaptable* force. It performs various functions in divergent types of economies—centrally planned or free market—at different stages of economic development.

Intriguingly for most of the world's nations, which rely more heavily on planned or plan-oriented economies than the free-market-oriented United States, small business may be a way to infuse an effective mix of free-market dynamism and efficiency into general economic planning. Increased economic complexity has made planning more difficult—most of all in times of technological upheaval as at present.

But what role small business plays in the future abroad—and in this country—depends very much on how small busi-ness itself will be reshaped by the technologies and economic conditions transforming the world economy.

10

The Future
of Small Business

I t is as yet too soon to foresee how well the United States
will ultimately fare against other nations in the transformation from the era of mass production industrial and nationally
oriented economies to the era of one based on rapidly evolving
information technologies and increasingly competitive global
markets. It is not too soon to say that the fourth force of the
small business economy has been a significant national resource that has augmented the competitiveness of America's
response to that transition. Competitor nations have recognized it and tried to create conditions in their own economies to
derive similar competitive advantages.

It is entirely plausible that small business will help the
economy adjust to the current transition, and then resume its
slow historic decline. The altered competitive balances of the
new economy may even accelerate its decline. In the future, its
critical mass may fall below a size that permits it to exert its
salutary functions and help the country through future rounds
of economic transition.

There will be future transitions. Very likely, they will come
with increasing speed. But will the small business economy be

sufficiently dynamic for the country to derive a competitive advantage from its small business economic asset once more?

Future Economic Uses of Small Business

It is easy to imagine how small business' responsiveness to change and its role adding economic equilibrium could be valuable in the new global economy where competitive success depends on rapid technical and commercial exploitation of innovation.

Crucially, a dynamic small business economy could help guarantee that large U.S. economic entities make the right technological choices to enhance U.S. competitiveness. In practice, technological choice is heavily affected by the existing distribution of economic and political power. Dominant corporations may not wish to endanger their present positions by promoting technologies that would eclipse their existing breadwinners. Politicians and labor unions may fight to preserve existing jobs in uncompetitive industries to advance their own self-interests. The more competitive pressure is applied on the sources of decision-making by diverse sources, the greater the likelihood that the most competitive choices will win out.

In many of the new technologies, competitive efficiency increasingly depends more on the design of a product or process than on sheer size or speed. Many contributions to design innovation can often be made with a minimum of capital. It is precisely this kind of innovation where small business' contributions have frequently been important in the past and probably can continue to be so in the future.

Paradoxically, the more interlinked the world economy becomes, and the greater the economic reach of a few huge dominant corporations, the more vulnerable all economies are to a global economic crash. Small business, as it does domestically, could, if it remains sufficiently dynamic, help absorb shocks that might otherwise make such a danger palpable.

Finally, future small business, if not the economic center, is likely to remain the core of the *national character* of U.S. business. As the operations of big corporations globalize and are staffed by a wider international range of executives around the world, they may gradually take on an internationalist perspective that transcends the interests and character of the sovereign United States. Small business, by virtue of its size, must remain more domestically focused.

The social-economic environment small business helps sustain will partly determine the U.S. future of free-market-oriented capitalism itself. As sovereign economies become increasingly interlinked, diverse international interests will have to be resolved by negotiation and international management. The large economic entities, in order to carry out business operations around the globe, will be further drawn into this management process. They will be required to consider factors that are political and not purely economic in their investment decision. In short, they are likely to become increasingly socialized, as Schumpeter foresaw. If free-market-oriented capitalism is to continue to be the guiding spirit of the economy, the vigor for it will likely have to come from smaller entrepreneurial enterprises.

Given the beneficial roles small business has served in the past and may, if sufficiently dynamic, play in the future, what are the likely prospects for future U.S. small business?

In a historically brief period, business has expanded from primarily local to national and now to increasingly global arenas. Small business was the dominant economic entity in the era of the local economy. In the era of the national economy, it became a secondary, complementary form to the large corporations which emerged in that environment. Now that the world's national economies are rapidly becoming interlinked, how will small business fare?

The answer lies in four interrelated factors: first, the evolution of long-term economic trends. Second, the ultimate impact of new technologies in altering the competitive balance between small-scale and large-scale economic entities. Third, small business' competitive problems in a global economy. Fourth, the policy actions taken by U.S. leaders to create an economic environment conducive to small business entrepreneurship.

Long-Term Trends

The current economic transition of technological and market structure change will eventually be completed like the last such transition at the end of the nineteenth century. The large corporations, joined by a new generation of large growth companies, will likely recuperate from this difficult period of restructuring and uncertainty.

As the economic environment grows more stable and the rules of the new economic game are better understood, market conditions—at least until the next economic transition—will likely again more strongly favor big business growth. The present cycle favoring small business entrepreneurship—and the present exuberance for it—will very likely again wane.

Some of the specific long-term economic trends are favorable to small business. Some are negative. Chief among the positive trends is the likely continued growth of the general services sector where small business does well. Affluence has increased the demand for personalized services. Complemented by new technologies that make small-batch production runs economical, the spread of affluence may encourage mass consumer markets to continue to segment into small, specialized markets exploitable by small companies. This is to the advantage of small business, in both the distribution and the production sectors, which thrive in market niches and on diversity.

The apparent long-term decline of efficient production unit sizes may also be helping larger small businesses in some manufacturing sectors offset historic diseconomies of production scale. The speeded-up pace with which consumer tastes and market conditions are changing—not merely a response to the economic transition, but a longer-term trend toward a faster pace of change itself—seems to favor smaller, generally more adaptive enterprises.

Foremost among the long-term negative trends are the factors behind the sustained, steady decline in small business' share of national economic output throughout the century. The trend is bleakest for the smallest companies with under 20 employees, which suffer from the rising minimum scale of competitiveness in many sectors. These smallest businesses continued to lose share throughout the late 1970s and early 1980s when many larger small businesses held their own. While the troubles of large manufacturers helped small industrial businesses retain relatively more of their share of economic output in the last decade, big business continued to make large gains against small retailers, wholesalers, and service companies.

Just as big business rose to dominate agriculture and industry, it appears well on its way, all other things being equal, to dominating the retail and service businesses as well. Big business' major competitive advantage for many years has been the economies of size benefits it has derived from organizational—management, marketing, purchasing—superiorities. Its current troubles have been largely concentrated in the mass-market industries sustaining the brunt of the economic transition. These troubles may pass as adjustment to the transition progresses.

Impact of the New Technologies

The competitive balance of these long-term trends will be affected by the impact of the new technologies. A given technology is not inherently good or bad for small business. Its effect on the competitive balance between small and large economic entities depends on how it is applied.

Today's reprogrammable computer-driven machines are making small batch production more economic and favoring ingenuity and skill over sheer size. Some experts believe they may provide small, flexible, craft-based production in some sectors with enough of a competitive edge to win the battle lost to mass-production technology a century ago.

Computer-aided-engineering and computer-aided-design can tremendously lower entry barrier costs for small firms to be competitive in devising and presenting new products to the market. Today's personal computers bring many of the advantages of the mainframe to small business. With a simple $10,000 PC system, a company can keep track of 100,000 inventory items, their costs, their sale prices, and how fast they're moving off the shelves. Computerized reporting of sales orders now permits small firms to reduce the size of the inventories they must carry, thus easing cash flow constraints. Simple spreadsheet software allows the smallest companies to run "what if" scenarios to help with business planning. Data storage on computer diskettes instead of in traditional file cabinets can sharply reduce office space requirements—and the rental costs—particularly in high-rent urban locations. Telecomputing plugs small businesses into information bases that were proprietary to big businesses in the past. It also permits them to compete more effectively from lower-cost decentralized locations.

These technology-wrought changes improve the competitiveness of small businesses. But big business is benefiting from the new technologies, too. For instance, they allow big business to do precision marketing and production for penetration of much smaller markets than in past—small business' traditional markets. Today, many new products are targeted geographically, by income or by life-style.

Application of the information technologies further enhances big business' organizational efficiency advantages. Better technology has helped account for the inroads large retailers have made in urban and in increasingly rural areas. It is now being applied to the fast-growing service industries with similar results.

Where there is standardization—and the computer is a powerful standardizing force, since to benefit from its use requires conforming to standard data systems and procedures for use—the competitive balance tilts away from smaller to larger business. Simply to organize to make full use of a computer system is an expensive and time-consuming procedure that many small businesses with their informal organizations and limited resources cannot manage. Finally, computer systems and networks themselves are creating a level of complexity of business options and strategies that only big companies have the technical virtuosity and capital to fully exploit.

Small Business in the Global Economy

It seems reasonably certain that the globalization of the U.S. economy will compound the competitive problems small business currently experiences due to its comparative organizational weakness. Globalization will draw more international competitors into a greater number of domestic markets where competition has largely been contested between domestic entities. Many of these new competitors will be large; others will compete under the self-interested protective shield of a large importer, such as a Sears, a Kodak, or a U.S. Steel. Large assemblers will shop the globe for the best deals for component supply sources, thus pitting U.S. suppliers against foreign ones and increasing the leverage of the large against the small.

More than ever before, small domestic businesses will be materially affected by the caprices of currency exchange rate markets. Unlike large businesses, they are naked, with too few resources or opportunities to hedge. Not only small businesses that depend on foreign supplies or markets are vulnerable. Purely domestic producers increasingly need to hedge against the currencies in which their foreign competitors, large and small, produce. The globalization of capital markets gives large corporations new options to shop for the most competitive financing terms in various currencies, thus increasing its already large financing advantage over smaller competitors.

As markets globalize, small business' minimal marketing and export power become glaring liabilities. With its limited resources small business is at an increasing disadvantage in matching big business' economies through the growth of global advertising. The diffusion of homogeneous popular mass media for advertising compounds its marketing vulnerability. Simultaneously, it lacks the resources to do global market studies or base sales teams in strategic locations around the world.

This disadvantage will be most acute in rapid-growth industries, particularly those with rapidly obsoleting technology or that require large sales volumes to derive economies of scale advantages. Although new technology such as CAE/CAD/CAM, and the clustering of parts suppliers as in Silicon Valley and Massachusetts' Route 128, makes it easier than in the past to enter such growth markets with a good product, the financing and marketing requirements to win competitive share on a global market are vastly higher.

Such fast-growth global industries will favor the expansion of larger distribution channels in order to obtain rapid market penetration. Small middlemen and retailers will probably continue to be squeezed out. Large distributors will pose yet another obstacle for innovative small competitors with little economic leverage who are trying to compete in these important future markets.

Finally, as governments focus on the ramifications of global competition, they will begin to undertake policies to advance their sovereign interests. These policies are likely to inadvertently trample the best interests of small business. In the mid-1980s, for example, the Reagan administration was reinterpreting enforcement rules of the antitrust laws to evaluate excessive market concentration in international, not merely domestic, terms. The Young Commission Report on Industrial Competitiveness also recommended viewing market concentration from an international perspective. The goal, to permit megamergers between large corporations to enhance their global competitiveness, may be a sound one. But from the small business perspective, the prospect of enhanced competitiveness of large corporations with more dominant domestic market share can only be chilling.

Toward a Small Business Policy

Some of these unfavorable trends can, of course, be mitigated by an intelligent policy toward small business.

The fundamental objective of any such policy should be to help level the economic playing field to give small business a better fighting chance. With the current measure of government involvement necessary to run the modern economy, no objectively ascertainable level playing field, of course, exists. Big business and small business fortunes are both powerfully affected by government—primarily, as we have seen, to the benefit of big rather than small business. There are reasonable differences of opinion about how far any government policy should go to promote small business to alter the tilt of the playing field in order to maximize the general economic welfare. The minimum concern of any policy, however, is to prevent the general competitive inferiority of the small business economy from becoming so pronounced as to render it significantly less effective in performing its current economic roles.

In any such small business policy, two groups should be kept in mind: (1) The 15 percent of companies with growth attributes, whose chief virtues are to apply competitive pressure from underneath on large economic entities and to abet the innovation process, and (2) The 85 percent nongrowth companies, whose major roles are to enhance labor market flexibility, economic diversity, and to create the critical mass necessary for the evolution from their number of the 15 percent of growth companies. Both groups are necessary for creating an entrepreneurial social economy.

The main elements of such a small business policy should be to promote the ease of entry into new businesses, and to neutralize inhibiting competitive barriers for existing small businesses. General economic growth eases these problems, since small businesses are most dynamic in such environments. But where growth does not provide the panacea, specific policies could be adopted to fill the gaps.

The most expensive gaps today are in financing. To help small companies build retained earnings needed for normal growth there is a reduced progressive tax schedule for businesses with under $100,000 income. Yet some reliable bridge-financing mechanism is also presently needed to ensure that fast-growth companies—some of whom carry the innovations that will determine future U.S. competitiveness and future U.S. living standards in the global economy—are not denied financing at a critical juncture of growth due to fickle capital market conditions. Such a mechanism could complement the evolution of the venture-capital market, and could be abolished altogether should the venture-capital market grow more stable. The financing of innovative small companies by large corporations is an encouraging development. But unless there are alternative sources of finance it could end in the limited autonomy problem of Japan's small innovative firms.

The second gap faces all new companies—raising the initial $150,000. This is the hardest financing to come by. As such, it is a major determinant of the future number of small business entrepreneurs.

This initial hurdle is greatest for the poorest and least educated, since it is hardest for them to accumulate savings on meager salaries and less likely that they have relatives in better circumstances from whom they can borrow. In this period of slow growth and economic transition there has been a growing bifurcation between rich and poor, with the result that it has become even harder for the poorer half even to contemplate building their savings for an entrepreneurial dream.

Any measure designed to overcome this initial hurdle should be viewed in the context of changes in available financing due to banking deregulation, the effect of cutbacks in SBA loan programs, and finally, from the opportunity to extend the American dream of rising through self-employment to broader segments of the population. The increased general affluence of U.S. society in the postwar period presents a great future opportunity to bring entrepreneurship within reach of larger numbers and thus strengthen the U.S. free-market economy. Spreading the distribution of wealth more evenly in a manner that doesn't endanger capital formation rates for investment would go a long way toward bringing personal seed capital within reach of potential small businessmen and could bring that opportunity to fruition.

Various programs by foreign governments suggest ways in which the initial financing gap could be tackled. One of the more imaginative programs is the French scheme to encourage prospective entrepreneurs to build savings in a special bank account, which the government supplements with soft loans (an equity scheme could be substituted). By putting the onus of savings onto the individual, it forces him to begin to think like a businessman. Perhaps such a program could be undertaken in conjunction with a form of management assistance, which first-time small businessmen so often lack.

General public infrastructure and service support—in kind, and how it is delivered—can be a very important tool in creating a favorable entrepreneurial economic environment. This is especially so if the basic services are rendered at a uniform cost for all. Small business is more dependent than big business upon good public infrastructure, such as roads, bridges, and sewers. The same is true for public services such as education, public health, and pensions.

The most important public support of all is good public education. A good education system would likely encourage entrepreneurship by teaching basic business skills, etiquette, and by instilling self-confidence. It is also essential in providing competent employees. A well-educated general work force will be especially critical for small business in the years ahead as competitive success will hinge on a skilled work force managing the new knowledge-intensive technologies. There is bound to be a shortage of skilled knowledge workers at first—and they are likely to command top compensation from big business, which can best afford to pay them. This will increase small business' competitive disadvantage. It could be a serious one if the education system continues to produce only a small percentage of students with the basic skills to manage the new technology proficiently.

Infrastructure must adapt to the new technologies. The type of great infrastructural electronic information system the Japanese are creating, for example, would be a great boon to small business (and, for that matter, to U.S. national competitiveness in general) by providing ready access to information that is hard to obtain and to customers that currently have to be reached by more laborious, and generally more expensive, means.

As Walter Wriston has observed: "To enter a business, the entrepreneur in the information age needs access to knowledge more than he or she needs large sums of money."[1]

Technical assistance, perhaps made available in conjunction with soft interest rate loans, to help small businesses upgrade their technology could be strategically vital to helping small firms cope with this period of technological upheaval and adjust to the changing economy.

The spontaneous development of local industrial incubators are favorable for small business, since they provide low-rent workplaces and a variety of services and skills in close proximity. This clustering provides economies which help offset the advantages of larger entities.

At the local level, merchants in many cities need rules that will provide greater commercial lease cost stability. At the international level, a way must be found to improve small business' ability to export competitiveness.

Small business also must have an effective voice in Washington. Lobby groups, such as the Chamber of Commerce and the National Federation of Independent Businesses, exist to protect the interests of existing small businesses. In 1985, they helped prevent the abolition of the SBA as a budget-cutting measure. There is varying opinion about the merit of the SBA's loan programs. But its advocacy programs, which provide small business a voice within the government, are widely valued. Such representation is important to make sure small business gets its share of Pentagon contracts, federal R&D dollars, and protects small business interests in antitrust law interpretations.

Finally, the SBA has been building a small business data base since 1976 that will ultimately overcome the lack of good statistical information about the small business economy. Many of the national economic aggregates, which were devised in the late 1930s and haven't been updated subsequently, also need to be overhauled to give an accurate measure of today's economy. When that is done it will be possible to reliably monitor changes in the health of U.S. small business and thus provide a more meaningful context for any policy decisions.

Probable Future

Finally, the probable future of small business will be strongly influenced by the types of new relationships it develops with the dominant core corporations of the economy. Their outlines are already visible in the new complementary relationships which big business has been forging with small business.

These are being shaped by two competing models of future economic organization. On the one hand, there is movement toward a reproduction of the national experience of several mass-production oligopolistic corporations dominating each industry on an international scale. On the other hand, there is a movement favoring smaller, computer-aided craft-type production—perhaps abetted by the clustering of various skills and service in close proximity—that can shift rapidly and flexibly between products and industries as conditions warrant.

From the present perspective, it seems likely that future industrial organization will be some combination of these two models. Those industries where technology and markets tend to be more stable and less prone to unexpected changes will likely tend toward the first model. Those marked by rapid and unpredictable change, including strong new competition from developing nations, may tend toward the second.

The future economic landscape may be shaped by large corporations deverticalizing production, so as to avoid becoming too inflexible readily to adapt to changing conditions and technologies. More reliable and attractive profits may again come from marketing and distribution, as in the earliest era of capitalism.

Increasingly, the risk/reward ratios of big business seem likely to drive it toward becoming planning, assembling, and marketing centers, with radii connecting to myriad semi-dependent smaller production plants and distribution points, as well, of course, as a smaller number of independent big ones, throughout the globe. In such a scenario, the large corporations would perform the expensive basic R&D, with government assistance where necessary. It would itself develop those products and processes that seemed like sure winners and rely on innovative small businesses to pick up, develop, and do the early commercialization of those it abandoned. Big corporations would do most of the product design and then employ a network of subcontractors to manufacture components and subassemblies. The big corporations would then assemble and market the finished product worldwide, relying on networks of distributors and retailers to penetrate the local end markets. The trend of big corporations to take minority stakes in innovative small companies, and to strategically draw closer to its suppliers, are starts in this direction.

Simultaneously, these big corporate industrial centers would likely face competition from small manufacturers using reprogrammable computerized technologies, particularly in smaller markets and on the margins between large ones. Some would be both subcontractors and brand-name producers. A few would be innovators hoping to become big-growth corporations themselves.

By clustering together as small firms do in Italy and in Silicon Valley or around Massachusetts' Route 128, these small producers could together conceivably derive some of the economies of organization size that are currently their major competitive handicaps. By banding together, they might be able to provide exporting and marketing organizations that could compete with the large corporations. Pooling knowledge of financing sources, management services, and sharing skills, they could conceivably reduce their individual financing costs, improve their individual company managements and improve productivity from more competitive devisions of labor. Cooperative purchasing could reduce cost-of-goods.

Such clusters might be informally affiliated in ways small businesses have used to offset big business' advantages in the past, such as affiliation like the independent department stores, or some franchise format. Local authorities attempting to build the future of their regions could possibly provide the organizational umbrella and the infrastructure to promote such clusters. The local industrial incubators that have sprung up in the last few years are conceivably a start in that direction.

The ability of small business to continue to be a vigorous complementary force in the future economy, of course, is qualified by evolving conditions in the economic environment. There are many ominous trends. But the demise of small business has been predicted many times in the past—always prematurely. However, today's rhapsodies of a small business renaissance are founded mainly on wishful sentiment rather than any demonstrable long-term trends.

Nevertheless, there are several reasons for believing that small business will continue to persist—even if its share of total economic output, as seems probable, continues to diminish. Small business performs some economic roles big business cannot do well or shuns. Some of these tasks are highly profitable and are the product of superior small business efficiency; most, however, yield unattractive profits that yet must be performed by some economic entity. Opportunities of both sorts will continue to arise as the economy continues to evolve in unpredictable directions.

Above all, the reason for believing small privately owned enterprise will continue to count in the foreseeable future lies in the distinct nature of small business itself: Hands-on ownership produces an economic tenacity and a type of economic activity involving rigorous self-sacrifice, and often the undertaking of unreasonable risks, that is different in kind from the business conducted by even the most efficient large corporations. In short, big business will continue to *need* small business for the foreseeable future.

Finally, despite the indisputable efficiencies of large corporations, there is something friendly and human in the dimension of small enterprise which provides an enduring appeal. People like to have it in their lives, as clients and as employers. And most importantly, for entrepreneurs themselves, the rewards and risks of small enterprise continue to be the most vital economic expression of an individual creative desire for challenging and mastering one's environment.

The INC. 100 Index
(As of May 1986)

The 1986 INC. 100 is the eighth annual ranking of the 100 fastest-growing publically held smaller companies in the United States. Companies are ranked by the percentage increase in net sales (or total revenues) over a five-year period—in this case, 1981 to 1985.

Company (rank)	Company (rank)	Company (rank)
ALC Communications (3)	ComputerCraft (60)	MBI Business Centers (70)
Action Packets (86)	Consolidated Stores (84)	Manufactured Homes (99)
Alexander Energy (34)	Consul Restaurant (87)	Medical Care Int'l (63)
Allegheny & Western Energy (19)	Convergent Technologies (39)	Medical Electronics (23)
Alta Energy (85)	DEST (67)	New York Film Works (47)
American Businessphones (6)	Datacopy (77)	ORS Automation (35)
American Healthcare Mgmt. (69)	Durakon Industries (78)	1 Potato 2 (12)
American Surgery Centers (29)	Electronic Tele-Comm. (36)	Patient Technology (41)
Amgen (58)	Endevco (16)	Personal Diagnostics (57)
Animed (80)	Energy Oil (8)	Piezo Electric Products (2)
Apollo Computer (14)	Enzo Biochem (100)	Plains Resources (88)
Applied Circuit Technology (94)	Equatorial Communications (10)	Priam (68)
Archive (26)	Expeditors Int'l of Washington (7)	Reid-Ashman (98)
Artel Communications (42)	FONAR (82)	SIS (50)
Ashton-Tate (4)	Fibronics International (28)	Saratoga Standardbreds (32)
Avant-Garde Computing (81)	First Centennial (45)	Shanley Oil (11)
Ben & Jerry's Homemade (74)	Forum Group (1)	Simmons Airlines (46)
Biomet (71)	Fuddruckers (25)	Solar Age Industries (27)
Brentwood Instruments (40)	G. D. Ritzy's (54)	StarTel (83)
Buffton (33)	Harvard Industries (72)	Sterling Software (30)
C. P. Rehab (75)	HealthAmerica (20)	Symbion (43)
Cade Industries (18)	Helm Resources (65)	Telco Systems (51)
Caremark (76)	High Plains (61)	Telebyte Technology (90)
Centocor (38)	IDEA (96)	Tender Loving Care (93)
Certified Collateral (31)	Insituform of North America (89)	Thermal Profiles (79)
Ciprico (55)	Integrated Genetics (21)	3Com (13)
Circadian (59)	Interand (92)	Time Energy Systems (37)
Comp-U-Card Int'l (48)	Iomega (5)	U. S. Intec (15)
Compression Labs (62)	Jack Henry & Associates (97)	Ungermann-Bass (66)
Computer Telephone (53)	Jacor Communications (73)	United HealthCare (49)
	Jet America Airlines (24)	V Band Systems (22)
	King World Productions (64)	VLSI Technology (9)
	LyphoMed (52)	Vitronics (44)
		Walker Telecommunications (17)
		Western-World Television (56)
		The Yankee Cos. (95)
		Ziyad (91)

The INC. 500 Index
(As of December 1985)

This listing includes the 500 fastest-growing private companies in America, as of December 1985.

A-1 Textiles (278)
ABC Supply (2)
ABO (237)
ATCOM (93)
Academic Guidance
 Services (214)
Accountants
 Microsystems (52)
Action Equipment (18)
Administrative Info.
 Systs. (253)
Advanced Computer
 Graphics (429)
Advanced Information
 Mgmt. (182)
Advanced Input Devices
 (13)
Aim Executive (187)
Akal Security (141)
Alamo Learning Systems
 (88)
Alarmtronics Security
 Systems (449)
All American Hero (15)
Allen & Assoc.
 Membership Dvel. (371)
Allenbach Industries (37)
Alliance Research (292)
Alloy Computer Products
 (138)
Aloette Cosmetics (215)
American Agrisurance
 (343)
American Cablesystems
 (259)
American Calculator &
 Computer (29)
American Leisure
 Industries (97)
American List Counsel
 (247)
American Passage
 Marketing (461)
American Plumbing
 Partsmaster (300)

American Tech. Svcs.
 Group (430)
American Television
 Systems (408)
American Trans Air (7)
Amplicon (452)
Analysis & Measurement
 Services (440)
Argosy Electronics (401)
Artesia Waters (95)
Aruvil International (170)
Associated Images (473)
Associated Packaging
 (453)
Atlantic Data Services
 (415)
BMC (254)
Baker Communications
 (186)
Baker Installations (374)
Barry Blau & Partners
 (362)
Basic Computer (70)
Bennett Funding Group
 (19)
Biesemeyer
 Manufacturing (57)
Bill Rodgers & Company
 (433)
Birch Research (67)
Blagge Enterprises (132)
Bohle (323)
Bonnecaze, McLeroy &
 Harrison (367)
Booth Organization (338)
Brad Cable Electronics
 (360)
Broderbund Software (12)
Brooks International (436)
Brougher International
 (324)
Burdeshaw Associates
 (121)
C. J. P. Development (416)
CIT Construction Inc. of

Texas (301)
CPA Services (427)
CTEC (476)
Cabinet Door (366)
Cal-Pac Roofing (493)
Calibrake (319)
California Sealing
 Devices (250)
Campmor (347)
Caprice Printing (210)
Captive-Aire Systems (65)
Carbide Technologies (175)
CardioData (158)
Carl Beavers Construction
 (315)
Centrac (304)
Central Data (392)
Central Mass. Health
 Care (9)
Central Petroleum
 Transport (445)
Century Marketing (130)
Champion Awards (147)
Checks To-Go (312)
Cheyenne Services (438)
Chrishawn Associates
 (271)
Citibag (265)
Claremont Financial
 Services (117)
Clark Manufacturing (83)
Coal Products (41)
Coated Papers (444)
ComDesign (60)
Comanche Contractors
 (266)
Comark (491)
Comfab (337)
CommTek (21)
Commonnwealth Equity
 Services (78)
Commonwealth Mortgage
 (223)
Communications
 Consultants (55)

Spectrum Computers (124)

SpeeDee Oil Change & Tune-Up (84)

Star & Crescent Herbs (272)

Star Software Systems (51)

Star Video Entertainment (152)

Starmark (298)

Staubach (91)

Stop 'N Shop (310)

Stravina (139)

Summa Four (230)

Sunbelt Distributors (287)

Sunbelt Express (159)

Super 8 Motels (81)

Support Systems Intl. (CA) (479)

Support Systems Intl. (SC) (68)

Swintec (318)

Systems Mgmt. American (273)

Systems Research & Applications (228)

Systems of the Future (102)

T. H. Hill Associates (221)

TABS Associates (220)

TRC Temporary Services (26)

TVX Broadcast Group (336)

Tech Data (192)

Techne Electronics (251)

Technicomp Publishing (229)

Technology Constructors (236)

Tek-Aids Industries (447)

Telco Research (498)

Tele America (422)

Teleconnect (28)

Teletronic Services (466)

Temporary Solutions (189)

Tessco (327)

Testa Communications (239)

Texas Drug Reps (451)

Thacker Jewelry (368)

Tiresias (406)

Tool King (492)

Toucan Business Forms (280)

TravelCenter (369)

Turner Brothers Construction (47)

U. S. Robotics (137)

UAI Technology (386)

US Signs (196)

Ugly Duckling Rent-A-Car System (176)

Underwriters Financial of Florida (480)

Unified Mortgage (58)

United Personal Computer (36)

V. I. P. Structures (382)

VR Business Brokers (127)

Vanguard Groups International (123)

Vanguard Plastics (377)

Vanguard Technologies (99)

Varitel Video (61)

Viar (328)

Video Products

Distributors (8)

Video Service of America (325)

Viking Electric (85)

Virginia Textiles (288)

Vista Technology (56)

Vocational Training Center (455)

Wabash Computer Systems (202)

Waterbeds Plus (462)

Watkins Manufacturing (150)

Weathervane Window (201)

Wegener Communications (177)

Weingart (307)

Weldon Electronics (191)

West Insulation Systems (399)

Western Extrusions (126)

Western Medical Specialties (342)

Western Pacific Data Systems (257)

Whitebirch (219)

William M. Hansen Associates (424)

Williams Generics (403)

Winters Electric (197)

Woodsmith Publishing (106)

World Leasing (222)

Xscribe (17)

Yantis (261)

ZBS Industries (384)

ZZYZZX Technologies (291)

Zenger-Miller (169)

Zycor (183)

Notes

1

1. Figures are derived from the Central Intelligence Agency, *The World Fact Book* (Washington, D.C.: U.S. Government Printing Office, 1984).

2. Cited in "Managing America's Business," *The Economist*, December 22, 1984.

3. John K. Galbraith, *The New Industrial State* (Boston: Houghton Mifflin, 1971), p. 32. Galbraith does not predict small business' demise but its increasing subservience to large corporations.

4. Robert L. Heilbroner and Aaron Singer, *The Economic Transformation of America* (New York: Harcourt Brace Jovanovich, 1984), p. 344.

5. Report of the President's Commission on Industrial Competitiveness, *Global Competition: The New Reality* (Washington, D.C.: U.S. Government Printing Office, January 1985), vol. 1, p. 9.

6. Lester C. Thurow, "A Time to Dismantle the World Economy," *The Economist*, November 9, 1985.

7. *Global Competition*, p. 20.

8. William Baldwin, "A Nation of Spendthrifts," *Forbes*, January 28, 1985.

9. See Michael S. Piore and Charles F. Sabel, *The Second Industrial Divide* (New York: Basic Books, 1975), for a fascinating and full account of these two competing technologies throughout history and particularly in the context of the current economic transition.

10. "Managing America's Business."

11. Bernard Weinraub, "President Urging an Economic Shift," *New York Times*, March 29, 1985.

12. Cited in Arthur Levitt, Jr., "In Praise of Small Business," *New York Times Magazine*, December 6, 1981.

2

1. The story of Wilson Harrell is adapted from Joseph P. Kahn, "Portrait of a Compulsive Entrepreneur," *Inc.*, April 1985; and Thomas Friedman and Paul

Solman, *Life and Death on the Corporate Battlefield* (New York: Simon & Schuster, 1982).

2. Alfred Chandler, *The Visible Hand* (Cambridge: Harvard University Press, Belknap Press, 1977), p. 3.

3. Cited in Joseph D. Phillips, *Little Business in the American Economy* (Westport, Conn.: Greenwood Press, 1958), p. 14, from "Small Business Problems of the Tire and Rubber Manufacturers and Retailers" (Senate Small Business Committee, 77th Cong., 1st sess., 1941), Print No. 3, p. 62.

4. Phillips, *Little Business*, which deals chiefly with firms that have under three employees in particular, stresses this point.

5. *The State of Small Business: A Report of the President, 1983* (Washington D.C.: U.S. Government Printing Office, 1983), p. 67.

6. *The State of Small Business: A Report of the President, March 1984* (Washington, D.C.: U.S. Government Printing Office, 1984), chap. 1.

7. National Federation of Independent Business Research and Education Foundation, "Small Business in America," San Mateo, California, n.d.

8. Figures derived from U.S. Department of Commerce, *Statistical Abstracts of the United States, 1984* (Washington D.C.: U.S. Government Printing Office, 1984), pp. 532, 540.

9. U.S. Department of Commerce, *Statistical Abstracts of the United States, 1985* (Washington, D.C.: U.S. Government Printing Office, 1985), p. 516.

10. *State of Small Business*, March 1984, p. 74.

11. Figures are derived from Federal Trade Commission and W. T. Grimm data on mergers and acquisitions based on companies with less than $10 million in assets, cited in Council of Economic Advisers, *Economic Report of the President, February 1985* (Washington, D.C.: U.S. Government Printing Office, 1985), p. 193.

12. Estimates of the size of the U.S. underground economy vary from 2 percent to 25 percent of GNP. These are based on middle-range estimates from "The Underground Economy's Hidden Force," *Business Week*, April 5, 1982.

13. There are no statistics on noncorporate births. Nevertheless, net noncorporate income-tax returns in the 1970s increased by an average of about 375,000 a year. Given the estimated failure rates for small business, it is reasonable to assume that roughly 1.5 million start-ups would be necessary to produce this annual net increase. Net noncorporate business growth is derived from *Statistical Abstracts of the United States, 1984*, p. 532.

14. This rough estimate is calculated on the assumption that the actual 450,000 corporate start-ups invest on average of $75,000 each, and the 1.5 million noncorporate start-ups invest on average $25,000. Thomas Gray, chief economist for the Small Business Administration, says that approximative research by his department based on different calculations also suggests that the $70 billion estimate is probably in the right ballpark. (Thomas Gray, in an interview with author, January 6, 1985.)

15. *State of Small Business*, March 1984.

16. "Small Is Beautiful Now in Manufacturing," *Business Week*, October 22, 1984.

17. *State of Small Business, March 1984*, p. 433.

18. Meg Whittemore, "The Great Franchise Boom," *Nation's Business*, September 1984.

19. *State of Small Business, March 1984*, pp. 181–212.

20. John K. Galbraith, *The New Industrial State* (Boston: Houghton Mifflin, 1971), pp. 9, 10.

21. Fernand Braudel, *Afterthoughts on Material Civilization and Capitalism* (Baltimore and London: The Johns Hopkins University Press, 1977), pp. 12, 114.

22. Braudel, *Civilization and Capitalism: The Perspective of the World* (New York: Harper & Row, 1979), vol. 3, pp. 630–31.

23. Robert L. Heilbroner, *The Making of Economic Society* (Englewood Cliffs, N.J.: Prentice-Hall, 1980), p. 124.

24. Joseph A. Schumpeter, *Capitalism, Socialism and Democracy* (New York: Harper & Row, 1942).

25. P. 156.

26. P. 134.

27. P. 106.

28. Cited in Robert L. Heilbroner and Aaron Singer, *The Economic Transformation of America* (New York: Harcourt Brace Jovanovich, 1984), p. 182.

28. Cited in Thomas Cochran, *Basic History of American Business* (New York: D. Van Nostrand, 1968).

3

1. Interview with author, April 10, 1985.

2. For an excellent account of global economic development, and what it means to this country, see Robert B. Reich and Ira C. Magaziner, *Minding America's Business* (New York: Harcourt Brace Jovanovich, 1982). Reich's article "Toward a New Public Philosophy" in *Atlantic*, May 1985, also contains interesting commentary.

3. Interview with author, March 12, 1985.

4. Max Geldens, "Towards Fuller Employment," *The Economist*, July 28, 1985.

5. "High Tech: Dream or Nightmare?" *CBS News Special Report*, Broadcast September 4, 1984.

6. Dwight B. Davis, "Automation USA," *High Technology*, May 1985.

7. "Is Manufacturing Un-American?" *The Economist*, June 15, 1985.

8. For a fine account of the breakdown of the labor-business alliance and its political consequences, see Thomas Byrne Edsall, *The New Politics of Inequality* (New York: W. W. Norton, 1984).

9. John Holusha, "GM's Innovations at Saturn," *New York Times*, January 14, 1985.

10. Cited in Peter F. Drucker, *Innovation and Entrepreneurship* (New York: Harper & Row, 1985), p. 9.

11. *The State of Small Business: A Report of the President, 1985* (Washington, D.C.: U.S. Government Printing Office, 1985), pp. 78, 79. Most of the job-creation figures in the following section are derived from *State of Small Business 1983, 1984,* and *1985.*

12. Estimated from payroll figures from the Bureau of Census, *Enterprise Statistics*, 1977, and payroll data by establishment size, 1982, for the industry sectors not included in the enterprise data. The estimated figure is probably conservative.

13. William Serrin, "Jobs Increase in Number, but Trends Said to Be Leaving Many Behind," *New York Times*, October 15, 1984.

14. David Mills, "Industrial Fluctuations, Firm Size and Employment," Office of Advocacy, Small Business Administration, Final Report: SBA-7152-AER-83, August 12, 1982.

15. *State of Small Business, 1985*, pp. 78, 79.

16. Ibid., p. 32; *State of Small Business, 1984*, pp. 42–50.

17. The data base each team used was the Dun & Bradstreet file for making credit ratings. To render the data meaningful for the purposes of the study, each team had to make assumptions about errors and omissions. About half the companies in the D&B data base with more than a single plant site didn't report employment for each site. Thus, if the company was credited only for the employment it did report, it would introduce a bias by making the company appear smaller than it was. This is what the MIT team did. The Brookings group, on the other hand, made assumptions that credited big companies with a greater share of the employment gains. For a more complete discussion of this issue see *State of Small Business, 1983*. Tom Richman, "What America Needs Is a Few Good Failures," *Inc.*, September 1983, also treats the problem and the row it caused in Washington.

18. Most of the data in this section is drawn from *State of Small Business, 1984*, chap. 4.

19. "The Displaced Ones," *The Economist*, December 8, 1964.

20. Robert B. Reich, *The Next American Frontier* (New York: Penguin Books, 1984), p. 142.

21. Bruce Posner, "Towards a More Perfect Union," *Inc.*, January 1984.

22. See Eli Ginzburg, "The Role of Small Business in the Process of Skill Acquisition," in Stuart W. Bruchey, ed., *Small Business in American Life* (New York: Columbia University Press, 1980).

23. Michael S. Piore and Charles F. Sabel, *Second Industrial Divide* (New York: Basic Books, 1975).

24. Ibid.

25. Lucien Rhodes, "Sole Success," *Inc.*, February 1982.

26. James Fallows, "America's Changing Economic Landscape," *Atlantic*, March 1985. Fallows' stimulating article focuses on many of the employment-related aspects of the current transition. In particular, it adds a cogent perspective on the "declining middle" controversy and stresses the importance of occupational and geographic mobility in adjusting to the process of ongoing economic change.

27. James Brooke, "For the Brass City, an Era Has Ended," *New York Times*, March 6, 1985.

28. Thomas J. Lueck, "Connecticut Growth Makes Its Economy One of Best in U.S.", *New York Times*, September 18, 1984.

29. William E. Schmidt, "Growing Job Problem: Finding People to Work," *New York Times*, October 28, 1984.

30. Martin Tolchin, "Foreigners' Political Roles in U.S. Grow by Investing," *New York Times*, December 30, 1985.

31. Joel Kotkin, "The Case for Manufacturing in America," *Inc.*, March 1985.

4

1. Bro Uttal, "Free-for-All in Computer-Aided-Engineering," *Fortune*, June 11, 1984; Jon Levine, "Why the Giants Can't Catch Silicon Valley's 'Little Three'," *Business Week*, March 25, 1985; Andrew Pollack, "A Computer Maker Stumbles," *New York Times*, February 27, 1986.

2. Robert L. Heilbroner and Aaron Singer, *The Economic Transformation of America* (New York: Harcourt Brace Jovanovich, 1984), p. 110.

3. Christopher Lorenz, "A Vicious Race to Get Ahead: New Product Development," *Financial Times*, September 19, 1984.

4. For a stimulating vision of what the future of business may look like, see Norman MacRae, "Into Intrapreneurial Britain," *The Economist*, February 16, 1985.

5. Stephen Kindel, "The Workshop Economy," *Forbes*, April 30, 1984.

6. Report of the President's Commission on Industrial Competitiveness, *Global Competition; The New Reality* (Washington, D.C.: U.S. Government Printing Office, January 1985), vol. 1, p. 16.

7. "America's High-Tech Crisis," *Business Week*, March 11, 1985.

8. *Global Competition*, p. 20.

9. Interview with author, December 20, 1985.

10. The Bayh-Dole Act of 1980 permits small business and universities to have title to inventions made under government sponsorship. The Stevenson-Wydler Technology Innovation Act of 1980, supported by the Presidential Commission Report of 1983 chaired by David Packard of Hewlett-Packard, made technology transfer to industry an official mission. See Herb Brody, "National Labs, at Your Service," *High Technology*, July 1985.

11. David E. Sanger, "Joint Research: Barriers Fall," *New York Times*, April 23, 1985.

12. Daniel J. Boorstin, *The Americans* (New York: Vintage Books, 1974), p. 380.

13. Peter Drucker, "The Discipline of Innovation," *Harvard Business Review*, May-June 1985.

14. Alfred Chandler, *The Visible Hand* (Cambridge: Harvard University Press, Belknap Press, 1977), p. 306.

15. From Harold C. Livesay, *American Made*, cited in Heilbroner and Singer, *Economic Transformation of America*, p. 148.

16. Willis R. Whitney, cited in Boorstin, *The Americans*, pp. 541–42.

17. Thomas Friedman and Paul Solman, *Life and Death on the Corporate Battlefield* (New York: Simon & Schuster, 1982).

18. Joseph A. Schumpeter, *Capitalism, Socialism and Democracy* (New York: Harper & Row, 1942), p. 132.

19. Interview with author, March 12, 1985.

20. Robert B. Reich, *The Next American Frontier* (New York: Penguin Books, 1984), p. 175.

21. George Gilder, *The Spirit of Enterprise* (New York: Simon & Schuster, 1984); and Arthur Levitt, Jr., "In Praise of Small Business," *New York Times Magazine,* December 6, 1981.

22. Arthur K. Watson, "Address to the Eighth International Congress of Accountants," New York, September 24, 1962. Cited in Clifford M. Baumback and Joseph R. Mancuso, *Entrepreneurship and Venture Management* (Englewood Cliffs, N.J.: Prentice-Hall, 1975), p. 70.

23. Cited in "The New Entrepreneurs," *The Economist,* December 24, 1984.

24. Gellman Research Associates, "The Relationship Between Industrial Concentration, Firm Size and Technological Innovation," May 1982, cited in *The State of Small Business: A Report of the President, 1983* (Washington, D.C.: U.S. Government Printing Office, 1983), p. 123.

25. William F. Mueller; John Culbertson; and Brian Peckham, "Market Structure and Technological Performance in the Food and Manufacturing Industries" (Madison, Wisc.: Research Division, College of Agricultural and Life Sciences. University of Wisconsin, Madison, February 1982), cited in *State of Small Business, 1983,* pp. 122-26.

26. "The Primrose Path," *The Economist,* April 27, 1985; "An Anti-Depressant for America's Drug Industry," *The Economist,* January 12, 1985; and "The Medicine Men Spend More to Discover Less," *The Economist,* May 16, 1985.

27. Steven Solomon, "The Great Tunafish War," *Forbes,* April 3, 1978.

28. Karl H. Vesper, *Entrepreneurship and National Policy* (Chicago: Heller Institute for Small Business Policy Papers, 1983), p. 9.

29. Clyde H. Farnsworth, "Happy Birthday, Xerox 914," *New York Times,* August 9, 1985.

30. Peter Drucker estimates that an industry's structure changes when the growth rate is 40 percent over ten years. See "The Discipline of Innovation," *Harvard Business Review,* May-June 1985.

31. For a list of some of the companies and their products, see "High-Tech Help for the Disabled," *Venture,* February 1985.

32. "Supercomputers Come Out into the World," *The Economist,* August 11, 1984.

33. "Shedding Light on Computer Links," *High Technology,* May 1985.

34. Barry Gross, "Out of the Test Tube, and Onto the Frying Pan," *Washington Post,* February 18, 1985; also Vesper, *Entrepreneurship and National Policy.*

35. See, for example, Gilder's *Spirit of Enterprise,* where he argues that creative men with access to money are the key to growth.

36. "High-Tech Ventures Ripe for Mergers," *Washington Post,* October 31, 1984.

37. "Exxon: A Drive to Disaster in the Office," *Business Week,* June 3, 1985.

38. Bruce Posner, "Strategic Alliances," *Inc.,* June 1985.

39. Laurie P. Cohen, "Raytheon Is Among Companies Regretting High-Tech Mergers," *Wall Street Journal,* September 10, 1984.

40. Lynn Asinof, "Small Firms Turn to Big Business for Capital, Markets, Technical Aid," *Wall Street Journal,* November 5, 1985.

41. Beth McGoldrick, "The Plight of High-Tech CFOs," *Institutional Investor,* January 1985.

42. William M. Alpert, "A $230 Million Turkey," *Barron's,* August 27, 1984.

43. "3 Executives get 25 Years in Worker's Death," *New York Times,* July 2, 1985.

44. Tom Peters, "Why Smaller Staffs Do Better," *New York Times,* April 21, 1985.

45. For more on the trend, see Bruce Posner, "In Search of Equity," *Inc.,* April 1985.

46. Harold Geneen, "Why Intrapreneurship Doesn't Work," *Venture,* January 1985, adapted from the chapter, "Entrepreneurial Spirit" of his book, with Alvin Moscow, *Managing* (Garden City, N.Y.: Doubleday and Company, 1984).

47. "Small Is Beautiful Now in Manufacturing," *Business Week,* October 22, 1984.

48. Joseph Fitchett, "Venture Capital: Europe Hopes to Cash In," *International Herald, Tribune,* February 8–9, 1986.

49. Interview with author, December 20, 1985.

5

1. John F. Persinos, "Working the Line," *Inc.,* December 1984; "Buy-It-Yourself Railroads," *Newsweek,* April 22, 1985.

2. "The Revival of Productivity," *Business Week,* February 13, 1984.

3. "Parts for GM Unit," *New York Times,* May 5, 1985.

4. Interview with author, December 1984.

5. Joel Kotkin, "The Case for Manufacturing in America," *Inc.,* March 1985.

6. Dero A. Saunders, "In the Passing Lane," *Forbes,* September 10, 1984.

7. "Computer Dealers That Are Selling Top Brands Gain Big Edge in Market," *Wall Street Journal,* August 23, 1984.

8. "The Big Guns Aimed at Small Retailers," *Business Week,* July 1, 1985.

9. Robert B. Reich and Ira C. Magaziner, *Minding America's Business* (New York: Harcourt Brace Jovanovich, 1982), make an especially lucid presentation of the shortcomings of common productivity measures.

10. Eli Ginzburg, "The Role of Small Business in the Process of Skill Acquisition," in Stuart W. Bruchey, ed., *Small Business in American Life* (New York: Columbia University Press, 1980).

11. "Small Is Beautiful Now in Manufacturing," *Business Week,* October 22, 1984.

12. Robert L. Heilbroner, *The Making of Economic Society* (Englewood Cliffs, N.J.: Prentice-Hall, 1980), pp. 170–79.

13. "The $7 Billion Gray Market: Where It Stops Nobody Knows," *Business Week,* April 15, 1985.

14. "Gray Market Expands to Industrial Goods," *Inc.,* July 1985.

15. "The Supreme Court Backs Cut-Rate Distributors, *Inc.,* August 1984.

16. Damon Darlin, "Small Business, Big Influence," *Wall Street Journal,* May 20, 1985.

17. Heilbroner, *Making of Economic Society,* pp. 120–23.

18. Steven Solomon, "Maxiprofits in Minimills," *Forbes,* December 11, 1978; Mark K. Metzger, "F. Kenneth Iverson of Nucor: Man of Steel," *Inc.* April 1984.

19. *The State of Small Business: A Report of the President, 1984* (Washington, D.C.: U.S. Government Printing Office, 1984), pp. 196, 222–23.

20. Robert Reinhold, "The Great Oil Era Ends in Texas," *New York Times,* September 16, 1984.

21. Tom Richman, "Not Everyone Can Move to Southern California, You Know," *Inc.,* May 1983.

22. "Splitting Up," *Business Week,* July 1, 1985.

23. *The State of Small Business: A Report of the President, 1985* (Washington, D.C.: U.S. Government Printing Office, 1985), p. 164.

24. "Trucks: Overseen or Overlooked?" *New York Times,* August 13, 1985.

25. "Taking Public Services Private," *Nation's Business,* August 1985.

26. Manny Ellenis, "Rolling Out the Red Carpet," *Nation's Business,* August 1985.

27. Kevin Farrell, "The States Enter the Venture Capital Game," *New York Times,* January 27, 1985.

28. Steven Greenhouse, "The Industrial Belt Searches for Ways to Retool Its Image," *New York Times,* August 18, 1985.

29. "Low Rankings, High Ambitions," *The Economist,* September 14, 1985.

30. Flora Lewis, "Texas Looks Ahead," *New York Times,* April 5, 1985.

31. Thomas J. Lueck, "Colleges Help to 'Incubate' New Industry," *New York Times,* December 3, 1984.

32. Steven Greenhouse, "An Ore Carrier's Troubled Odyssey," *New York Times,* July 14, 1985.

33. "Incubate and Flourish," *The Economist,* November 30, 1985.

34. John Herbers, "Local Incentives Draw Industry to Poorer Zones," *New York Times,* July 28, 1985.

35. Joann S. Lublin, "States Expand Enterprise Zones Despite Lack of Federal Incentives," *Wall Street Journal,* July 30, 1984.

36. Herbers, "Local Incentives."

37. Sandra Salmans, "Bronx Gets Piece of Silicon Valley," *New York Times,* April 29, 1985.

6

1. Interview with author, April, 16, 1985.

2. For more on the "safety valve" myth and its influence on American cultural beliefs and historical impact, see the classic, Henry Nash Smith, *The Virgin Land* (New York: Vintage Books, 1957).

3. Cited in Rowland Berthoff, "Independence and Enterprise: Small Business in the American Dream," in Stuart W. Bruchey, ed., *Small Business in American Life* (New York: Columbia University Press, 1980), p. 38; from the *Congressional Record,* 74th Cong., 2d sess., 1936, 80, pt. 7: 8131 (May 27, 1936; John A. Martin).

4. Cited in David E. Gumpert, "The Future of Small Business May Be Brighter than Portrayed," *Harvard Business Review,* July-August 1979, from the 1978 Report of the Subcommittee on Antitrust, Consumers and Employment, of the Committee on Small Business, House of Representatives, 95th Cong., 2nd sess.

5. Clyde and Sally Griffen, "Small Business and Occupational Mobility in Mid-Nineteenth Century Poughkeepsie," in Bruchey, *Small Business in American Life*.

6. Ginzburg, "Role of Small Business," in Bruchey, *Small Business in American Life*, p. 372.

7. U.S. Senate, Committee on Education and Labor, *Report on the Relations Between Labor and Capital (1885)*, 1:473, cited in Robert L. Heilbroner and Aaron Singer, *The Economic Transformation of America* (New York: Harcourt Brace Jovanovich, 1984) p. 226.

8. Ibid, pp. 165, 149.

9. Eli Chinoy, *Automobile Workers and the American Dream* (Garden City, N.Y.: Doubleday and Company, 1955).

10. Cited in "Managing America's Business," *The Economist*, December 22, 1984.

11. Katya Goncharoff, "Courses on Entrepreneurship," *New York Times*, August 27, 1985.

12. Karl Vesper, *Entrepreneurship and National Policy* (Chicago: Heller Institute, 1983).

13. *The Gallagher Report, Volume XXXIII, No. 30*, Second Supplement (New York: July 29, 1985).

14. *Wall Street Journal*, May 20, 1985.

15. Self-employment data comes from Joseph D. Phillips, *Little Business in the American Economy* (Westport, Conn.: Greenwood Press, 1958), p. 4, which draws upon Spurgeon Bell's *Productivity, Wages and National Income* for data between 1880 and 1930, and Commerce Department, *The Survey of Current Business (1953)* and *Business Statistics* for data between 1940 and 1950. Current data comes from *The State of Small Business: A Report of the President, 1985* (Washington, D.C.: U.S. Government Printing Office, 1985).

16. Sabin Russell, "Being Your Own Boss in America," *Venture*, May 1984.

17. "Taking Work Home," *Le Monde*, excerpted in "The Work Revolution," *World Press Review*, January 1985.

18. Russell, "Being Your Own Boss."

19. "Unsinkable Family Businesses," *Fortune*, February 18, 1985.

20. *The State of Small Business: A Report of the President, 1984* (Washington, D.C.: U.S. Government Printing Office, 1984), pp. 347, 350, 364.

21. Philip S. Gutis, "A One-Woman Act No More," *New York Times*, August 18, 1985.

22. Interview with Thomas Gray, chief economist SBA, January 6, 1986.

23. *State of Small Business, 1984*, pp. 49, 102–103.

24. "There's Life After Smokestack Jobs," *U.S. News & World Report*, August 20, 1984.

25. See Orvis F. Collins, and David G. Moore with Darab Unwalla, "The Enterprising Man and the Business Executive" cited in Clifford M. Baumback and Joseph R. Mancuso, *Entrepreneurship and Venture Management* (Englewood Cliffs, N.J.: Prentice-Hall, 1975). The studies surveyed and analyzed by the authors include W. Lloyd Warner and James C. Abegglen, *Occupational Mobility in American Business and Industry* (Minneapolis: University of Minnesota Press, 1955), which looked at over 8,000 business leaders; Mabel Newcomer, "The Little

Businessman: A Study of Business Proprietors in Poughkeepsie, New York," *Business History Review,* Harvard Graduate School of Business Administration, vol. 35, no. 4 (Winter 1961); and a study of Michigan small business manufacturing entrepreneurs conducted by the authors.

26. "WSJ/Gallup Survey," *Wall Street Journal,* May 20, 1985. Some of the data recorded by Gallup is as follows:

	Fortune Executives %	Small Businessmen %	Entrepreneurs %
College degrees	94	47	76
Ethnic origins (*not* Anglo-Saxon or Northern European)	15	17	41
Religion:			
Protestant	65	65	44
Roman Catholic	21	17	16
Jewish	7	8	19
No preference	6	8	16
Fired from a job	9	10	31
Vacations—more than two weeks year	52	36	28
Local civic organization member	71	65	43
Drives U.S.-made car	74	85	45

27. Cited in Baumback and Mancuso, *Entrepreneurship and Venture Management.*

28. Edward Banfield, *The Unheavenly City* (Boston: Little, Brown, 1968, 1970), argues that underlying the problem of poverty is a chronic present-oriented social value system that is unwilling or unable to defer concrete present gratifications for a less concrete future reward. Future-orientedness, he argues, is essential to upward mobility. From a strictly economic point of view, this logic is compelling as savings are a prerequisite of investment, which leads to the generation of wealth. From the point of view of a small businessman, it is even more compelling, since, as most entrepreneurs can attest, small businesses in their early stages require great self-sacrifice and stamina on the often irrationally optimistic faith in future profits.

29. "From Saigon to San Diego," *The Economist,* April 27, 1985.

30. Miriam Rozen, "New Networks of Immigrant Entrepreneurs," *New York Times,* September 30, 1984; Martin Gottlieb, "For South Asian Immigrants, Newsstands Fulfill a Dream," *New York Times,* March 3, 1985.

31. *The State of Small Business, 1984,* pp. 371, 379.

32. For more on family businesses, see Steven Proleesch's three-part series "The Family Business," *New York Times,* June 10-12, 1986.

33. Merri Rosenberg, "Franchising an Ad Agency," *Venture,* May 1984.

34. "Coast Foundry Offers History as Well as Cast Iron," *New York Times,* May 6, 1985.

35. Vesper, *Entrepreneurship and National Policy* (Chicago: Heller Institute, 1983).

7

1. "Grumman: One D...d Thing After Another," *Forbes*, February 5, 1979; Alexander L. Taylor III, "Making a Mint Overnight," *Time*, January 23, 1984; "Chrysler Accord Seen on Gulfstream," *New York Times*, June 19, 1985.

2. Taylor, "Making a Mint Overnight."

3. "The Forbes Four Hundred," *Forbes*, October 28, 1985.

4. Robert L. Heilbroner, *The Making of Economic Society* (Englewood Cliffs, N.J.: Prentice-Hall, 1980).

5. Richard Behar, "The Rising Tide," *Forbes*, January 14, 1985.

6. Figures derived from *Statistical Abstract of the United States, 1985* (Washington, D.C.: Government Printing Office, 1985), pp. 516–17.

7. Ibid., p. 518.

8. Sanford L. Jacobs, "Hide and Sneak," *Wall Street Journal*, May 20, 1985.

9. Standard failure data is imprecise and determined inferentially from other statistical measurements.

10. *The State of Small Business: A Report of the President, 1983* (Washington, D.C.: U. S. Government Printing Office, 1983), pp. xv-xvi, 70–71.

11. "Incubate and Flourish," *The Economist*, November 30, 1985.

12. Roger Neal, "Color It Profitable," *Forbes*, January 28, 1985.

13. "Sweet 'n Low Buffeted by Rival Aspartame," *New York Times*, May 27, 1985.

14. Vesper, *Entrepreneurship and National Policy* (Chicago: Heller Institute, 1983).

15. Robert Reinhold, "Starting Up in Silicon Valley: Long Hours, Forsaken Lives," *New York Times*, February 6, 1984.

16. Robert L. Heilbroner and Aaron Singer, *The Economic Transformation of America* (New York: Harcourt Brace Jovanovich, 1984), p. 194.

17. "A Texas Yankee's Software Sensation," *Business Week*, May 27, 1985.

18. Ralph Whitehead, Jr., "Name Your Price," *Inc.*, December 1984.

19. Andrew Feinberg, "Inside the Entrepreneur," *Venture*, May 1984.

20. "The Entrepreneurs: Loners and Workaholics," *Wall Street Journal*, May 20, 1985.

21. Feinberg, "Inside the Entrepreneur."

22. "The Wildcatter Becomes an Endangered Species," *Business Week*, July 1, 1985.

23. *The State of Small Business: A Report of the President, 1984* (Washington, D.C.: U.S. Government Printing Office, 1984), p. 191. On a historical value basis, large corporate net worth increased at a 9.7 percent annual compound rate versus 5.7 percent for small business; business receipts of large corporations grew at a 13.8 percent compounded average annual rate versus 9.5 percent for small ones.

24. Ibid., p. 209.

25. Ibid., pp. 202–204.

26. Ibid., chapters 1, 2.

27. Thomas C. Cochran, *200 Years of American Business* (New York: Dell Publishing, Delta Books, 1978), p. 26.

28. Cited in Arthur Levitt, Jr., "In Praise of Small Business," *New York Times Magazine,* December 6, 1981.

8

1. Robert D. Hershey, Jr. "The Pain of a Farm Banker," *New York Times,* July 10, 1985; "Old MacDonald Sold His Farm," *The Economist,* December 1, 1984.

2. "Mom-and-Pop Videotape Shops Are Fading Out," *Business Week,* September 2, 1985.

3. Geoffrey Smith and Paul B. Brown, "Emerging Growth Stocks—Why So Many Peak So Early," *Forbes,* January 28, 1985.

4. Cited in "Peaks and Valleys: Interview with Don Valentine," *Inc.,* May 1985.

5. Eric N. Berg, "Millions in Kaypro Parts May Be Gone," *New York Times,* September 13, 1984.

6. Gary Slutsker, "Cashing In," *Forbes,* May 20, 1985.

7. Smith and Brown, "Emerging Growth Stocks."

8. *The State of Small Business: A Report of the President, 1985* (Washington, D.C.: U.S. Government Printing Office, 1985), chap. 5.

9. "A Bad Aftertaste for Searle's Aspartame Suppliers," *Business Week,* July 15, 1985; "Cell Products Says Loss of Contract Could Put Firm Out of Business," *Wall Street Journal,* September 24, 1984.

10. Jacob M. Schlesinger, "Sanyo Sales Strategy Illustrates Problems of Little Distributors," *Wall Street Journal,* September 10, 1984.

11. "Hyponex's Nationwide Push," *New York Times,* May 27, 1985.

12. Stanley C. Hollander, "The Effects of Industrialization on Small Retailing in the United States in the Twentieth Century," in Stuart W. Bruchey, ed., *Small Business in American Life* (New York: Columbia University Press, 1980).

13. David Diamond, "The Dark Side of Franchising," *New York Times,* January 12, 1986.

14. Anthony Ramirez, "A New Industry Is Fixing to Fix Your Personal Computer," *Fortune,* March 18, 1985.

15. Nicholas Lemann, "Change in the Banks," *Atlantic,* August 1985.

16. *Statistical Abstract of the United States, 1985* (Washington, D.C.: U.S. Government Printing Office, 1985), p. 516.

17. Richard Sylla, "Small Business Banking in the United States, 1780–1920," in Bruchey, *Small Business in American Life.*

18. Henry Kaufman, "Reshaping the Financial System," *New York Times,* July 14, 1985, adapted from a June 1985 statement before a subcommittee of the House Committee on Energy and Commerce.

19. Interview with author, May 1978.

20. John K. Galbraith, *Economics and the Public Purpose* (New York: Signet, New American Library, 1973), pp. 45–46.

21. David O. Whitten, *The Emergence of Giant Enterprise 1860–1914* (Westport, Conn.: Greenwood Press, 1983).

22. George Gilder, *The Spirit of Enterprise* (New York: Simon & Schuster, 1984).

23. *State of Small Business, 1985.*

24. "An Idea That's Working: Federal Funds for High-Tech Start-Ups," *Business Week,* October 22, 1984.

25. Lawrence M. Friedman, "Law and Small Business in the United States: One Hundred Years of Struggle and Accommodation," in Bruchey, *Small Business in American Life.*

26. Hollander, "Effects of Industrialization," in Bruchey, *Small Business in American Life.*

27. Harold G. Vatter, "The Position of Small Business in the Structure of American Manufacturing, 1870-1970" in Bruchey, *Small Business in American Life.* Vatter points out that between December 1939 and December 1944 the share of manufacturing employment by small businesses with under 100 employees fell from 25.9 percent to 18.9 percent.

28. Report of the President's Commission on Industrial Competitiveness, *Global Competition: The New Reality* (Washington, D.C.: U.S. Government Printing Office, January 1985), vol. 1.

29. One of the most prominent export initiatives, the 1918 Webb-Pomerene Act, freed export association cartels from certain antitrust strictures. But the law benefited only a handful of large corporations in industries where there were few producers and the United States dominated world trade.

9

1. Jane Sasseen, "A Nation of Workshops," *Forbes,* April 30, 1984; "Out of the Shadows," *The Economist,* March 30, 1985; Anne Marshall Zwack, "The Gold in the Rainbow," *Capital International,* Autumn 1985.

2. Guy de Jonquieres, "Can Europe Catch Up?" *Financial Times,* excerpted in *World Press Review,* August 1985.

3. Chris Hill, "Germany," in D. J. Storey, ed., *The Small Firm—An International Survey* (New York: St. Martin's Press; London and Canberra: Croom Helm, 1983). Statistical definitions of foreign small business vary from country to country, and are thus not directly comparable to the United States or to each other.

4. Heidi Fiske, "Europe, Inc.," *Inc.,* September 1985.

5. "Money for Most," *The Economist,* October 26, 1985.

6. "Lots of Loners," *The Economist,* March 23, 1985.

7. James Buxton, "Backyard Image Out of Date," *Financial Times,* June 12, 1984.

8. "Pastassessment," *The Economist,* July 14, 1984; and "Don't Pay, Won't Pay," *The Economist,* November 24, 1984.

9. "French Business Joins a War on Unemployment," *Business Week,* November 5, 1984.

10. "Planting Science Parks in Britain," *The Economist,* March 16, 1985.

11. "Europe's Venturers: A Solitary Breed," *The Economist,* September 28, 1985.

12. James M. Perry, "Britain's Sir Clive Sinclair Keeps Bouncing Back with New Inventions, but His Firm Is in Trouble," *Wall Street Journal,* June 6, 1985.

13. "The *Enfant Terrible* Shaking Up French Business," *Business Week,* November 26, 1984.

14. Jurek Martin, "Key Role Played by Family Enterprise," *Financial Times*, June 12, 1984.

15. Ministry of International Trade and Industry, *White Paper on Small and Medium Enterprises in Japan, 1983* (Tokyo, 1983).

16. Kenneth Fleet, "A Robot Era," *The Times*, excerpted in *World Press Review*, January 1985.

17. "Have Granny, Will Travel," *The Economist*, April 6, 1985.

18. "Land of the Setting Sun," *The Economist*, June 30, 1984.

19. MITI, *White Paper*.

20. Murray Sayle, "Japan Victorious," *New York Review of Books*, March 28, 1985. Sayle argues that the Japanese social economy, which can only be penetrated by foreign businessmen willing to spend years painstakingly building business connections after the Japanese custom, gives Japan a built-in competitive advantage over the United States, where social-economic practices award business primarily according to price. To insist that Japan "open" its markets to free trade in the Western sense is really nothing less than an impossible demand to renounce Japanese culture. He suggests that a negotiated consensus on trade (much as the Japanese do among themselves with MITI's mediation) would yield far more satisfactory results.

21. Joel Kotkin and Yoriko Kishimoto, "Rising Sons," *Inc.*, April 1984; Joel Kotkin and George Gendron, "Trading Places," *Inc.*, July 1985.

22. "Japan's Soft Point," *The Economist*, August 10, 1985.

23. Teresa Ma, "The Battle to Keep Competitive Edge," *Financial Times*, December 18, 1984.

24. Jonathan Tucker, "Japan's Technology Agenda," *High Technology*, August 1985.

25. Nobuko Hara, "Why Traditional Loyalties Are Changing," *Financial Times*, February 18, 1985.

26. Michael T. Kaufman, "New Ventures Provide Profit Lesson in Poland," *New York Times*, April 22, 1985.

27. "Let a Thousand Flowers Bloom," *The Economist*, October 20, 1984.

28. "The New Kulaks," *The Economist*, January 12, 1985.

29. Robert L. Heilbroner, *The Making of Economic Society* (Englewood Cliffs, N.J.; Prentice-Hall, 1980).

30. Steven Solomon, "Is Yugoslavia Really Out of the Woods?" *Institutional Investor*, April 1985.

31. Ivan I. Stefanovic, "Sidestepping Socialism in Yugoslavia," *Venture*, September 1984.

32. Christopher S. Wren, "Free Enterprise in China: The Unbroken Shackles," *New York Times*, September 15, 1984.

33. Harrison E. Salisbury, "In Mao's Footsteps," *The Gazette* (Montreal), December 29, 1984, from *New York Times*.

34. Alain Cass, "Recycling Rags to Private Riches in China," *Financial Times*, September 25, 1984.

35. Amanda Bennett, "China's Leaders Reject Part of Marxism and Defend Recent Economic Changes," *Wall Street Journal*, December 10, 1984.

36. D. J. Storey, "Newly and Less Developed Areas," in Storey, *The Small Firm*.

37. "Solving the Third World's Growth Crisis," *Business Week*, August 12, 1985.

38. Sabin Russell, "Now, It's the World's Turn," *Venture*, September 1984.

39. "Taiwan Sharpens Its Dragon Teeth, *The Economist*, June 22, 1985.

40. Susan Chira, "Korea's Unpopular Giants, *New York Times*, January 5, 1985; Small Is Suddenly More Beautiful," *The Economist*, January 28, 1984.

10

1. Walter B. Wriston, *Risk and Other Four-Letter Words* (New York: Harper & Row, 1986), p. 125.

Index